MONOPOLY IN AMERICA

BARRY E. HAWK

JURIS

Questions About This Publication

For assistance with shipments, billing or other customer service matters, please email us at: subscriptions@jurispub.com

For editorial assistance, please email us at: editorial@jurispub.com

To obtain a copy of this book, please visit: http://www.jurispub.com/Bookstore/

To learn more about Juris Publishing Inc, please visit: www.jurispub.com

Printed in the United States of America

ISBN 978-1-57823-559-9

Juris Publishing, Inc.
www.jurispub.com

ACKNOWLEDGMENTS

I am deeply grateful to Hannah Ashbrook, Jacob Bortner-Hart, Leah Ennis, Cristina Langford, Gail McDonald, Odeya de la Mure, Summer Perez and Michael Regan for their research assistance. I would also like to thank Juan Fernandez and Herbert Mayner at the Fordham Law library for their help in securing historical sources. Last, I am delighted to acknowledge the guidance of James Keyte whose comprehensive knowledge of antitrust law and his exceptional editing skills have greatly improved the style and substance of *Monopoly in America*.

Barry Hawk
Tuxedo Park
July 2022

SUMMARY TABLE OF CONTENTS

Acknowledgments iii
Summary Table of Contents v
Table of Contents vii

Chapter One

INTRODUCTION 1

Chapter Two

COLONIAL AMERICA 17

Chapter Three

REVOLUTION AND FOUNDING OF THE UNITED STATES–1763 TO 1800 79

Chapter Four

ANTEBELLUM AMERICA 113

Chapter Five

MODERN ERA–1870 TO TODAY 143

BIBLIOGRAPHY 191

TABLE OF AUTHORITIES 205

INDEX 211

TABLE OF CONTENTS

Acknowledgements iii
Summary Table of Contents v
Table of Contents vii

Chapter One

INTRODUCTION

I. Colonial America (1600 to 1763) 4
II. Revolution and Founding (1763 to 1800) 6
III. Antebellum Era (1800 to 1861) 8
IV. Antitrust Laws (1870 to today) 9

Chapter Two

COLONIAL AMERICA

I. Introduction 17
II. Colonial Law 18
III. Colonial Opposition to Government Grants of Monopoly or Exclusive Trading Privileges 20
  A. English Antimonopoly Revolution 21
  B. Antimonopoly Tradition in the Colonies 24
    1. Settlement trading companies and their monopoly privileges 26
    2. English trading monopolies and mercantilism 34
    3. Colonial grants of monopoly privileges 37
    4. Inventions (patents) and author works (copyrights) 50
      a. Patents 50
      b. Copyrights 52
IV. "Monopolization" Practices 53
  A. Engrossing 55
  B. Forestalling and Closed Markets 58
    1. Closed markets 58
    2. Forestalling 63
  C. Pricing Practices 66
    1. Just prices 66

2. Price controls (fixing official prices) 70
3. Price fixing (cartels and guilds) 74

Chapter Three

REVOLUTION AND FOUNDING OF THE UNITED STATES – 1763 TO 1800

I. English Trading Monopolies and the Revolution – Boston Tea Party 80
II. Engrossing, Forestalling and Price Controls at Our Nation's Birth 85
III. State (and Local) Monopoly Grants and State Constitutions .. 95
IV. Federal Constitution 97
A. No Ban on Monopoly 97
B. Patents and Copyrights 102
1. Patents 103
2. Copyrights 108

Chapter Four

ANTEBELLUM AMERICA

I. Banks and Corporations 116
II. Engrossing, Forestalling and Private Monopoly 125
A. Forestalling and Engrossing 125
B. Private Firm Monopoly 127
III. Government Grants of Monopoly Privileges 129
A. State Constitutional Limits on State (and Local) Monopoly Grants 130
B. State Legislatures and Monopoly Grants 134
1. Corporations as monopolies 134
2. State monopoly grants 135
C. Federal Constitutional Limits on State (and Local) Monopoly Grants 137
1. Commerce clause and federal supremacy clause 137
2. Impairment of contracts clause 139

Chapter Five

MODERN ERA – 1870 TO TODAY

I. Government Monopoly Grants 144
A. The *Slaughter-House Cases* 144
B. Natural Monopoly and the Theory of Public Utilities 149
C. Federal Constitutional Constraints on Monopoly 152
D. State Constitutional Constraints on Monopoly 155
E. Federal Grants of Monopoly Privileges 159
II. Forestalling and Engrossing Laws 159
III. The Early Antitrust Movement 162
IV. Private Monopoly Under the Federal Antitrust Laws 170
A. Cyclical Enforcement 170
1. Trustbusting (1890 to 1920) 171
2. Hibernation (1920 to 1937) 171
3. Expansion (1937 to 1970) 172
4. Retrenchment (late 1970s to 2020) 174
B. Reasons for the Cycle of Enforcement 175
1. Political support 176
2. Popular support 176
3. Facts/economic conditions and assumptions 178
4. Developments in economic theory 179
5. Legal process concerns about litigation costs, administrability and certainty of legal rules, court (and jury) capacities and false positives 183
6. Consumer welfare to the exclusion of historical political and social concerns about monopolies 184
C. The Fundamental Conundrum Concerning Private Monopoly 186

BIBLIOGRAPHY 191

TABLE OF AUTHORITIES 205

INDEX 211

Chapter One

INTRODUCTION

American history did not begin in 1890 and American attitudes toward monopoly did not begin with the Sherman Act. Colonial and antebellum Americans did not need instruction from Louis Brandeis to oppose monopolies and they did not need instruction from Joseph Schumpeter to exclude some monopolies from general censure. Americans have always hated monopoly—both public and private. At the same time, Americans have accepted—sometimes begrudgingly—government grants to incentivize production and innovation. And private monopolies resulting exclusively from skill, foresight and industry have been viewed as welcome entrepreneurial success.

From the first settlements in Virginia and Massachusetts, Americans have expressed a deep aversion to monopoly. Of course, monopoly—and fervent opponents of monopoly—are hardly unique to America. Monopolies have been around for millennia and indeed have been condemned for millennia by religious figures, philosophers, political leaders and the general populace.[1] Muhammed declared: "[w]hosoever monopolizes is a wrongdoer."[2] Charlemagne denounced as monopolists "those who by tricks, surprises, and other unjust means amass goods with the aim of a shameful gain."[3] During the *ancien régime* in France, cries of "monopoly" were made against hoarding and speculation by unknown resellers during periods of grain shortages and price volatility. The abbé de Véri wrote that under the stress of shortage, everyone's "first thought is to believe in monopoly."[4] The same thought was echoed in colonial America. Not to be outdone by Charlemagne's passionate eloquence, a handbill signed "Vengeance" was circulated throughout Boston in 1779 urging citizens to "rid the community of those monopolizers and extortioners, who, like canker worms, are gnawing upon your vitals."[5] In colloquial terms, this might be called the "conspiracy

---

[1] See Barry Hawk, Antitrust and Competition Laws 17–25 (2020).

[2] Muslim Ibn al-Hajjaj, Sahih Muslim 965 (Abdul Hamid Siddiqui 2011).

[3] See 1 Steven L. Kaplan, Bread, Politics and Political Economy in the Reign of Louis XV 57 (1976).

[4] Id. at 60.

[5] See Franklin D. Jones, Historical Development of the Law of Business Competition, 36 Yale L. J. 43, 54 (1927).

theory" of monopoly. The most representative figure of a monopoly opponent was a street protester or rioter—often a mother—demanding action against sellers and hoarders of bread and other household necessities.

There is another sense in which the term "monopoly" has been used in England, the American colonies and later the United States. "Monopoly" describes royal or government grants of exclusive privileges. This was the most common use of the term "monopoly" in America before the Civil War. Elizabeth I granted a monopoly or exclusive right to produce and sell playing cards. American colonial authorities granted monopolies to trade in tobacco and beaver fur. The federal government in the early 19th century chartered a single central bank. During the colonial and revolutionary periods, the most representative figure of a monopoly opponent was a trader claiming that he was excluded from doing business. During the antebellum period, the most representative figure of a monopoly opponent was a farmer who condemned banks because they benefited the wealthy.

Long before all this, Aristotle offered a more precise definition of monopoly: a single seller of goods.[6] Modern economists have refined Aristotle's concept with a focus on market power to raise price or reduce output. Modern antitrust law limits "monopoly" to firms holding a significant degree of market power. There is nothing like this in the "conspiracy theory" of monopoly, which covers an ill-defined group of practices like engrossing and forestalling without any inquiry into market power. Since the Civil War, private firm "single seller" monopolies or firms enjoying significant market power in an economic sense have replaced government grants of monopoly as the targets of censure. The most representative figure of a modern monopoly opponent is a competitor of a successful firm—supported by an army of antitrust lawyers and economists.

In sum, there are three kinds of monopoly from an historical perspective: 1) "monopolistic" practices perceived as raising prices, 2) government grants of monopoly or exclusive privileges and 3) private firm monopoly in the modern economic sense. All three types are found in American history, although the importance of each varies considerably over time. From colonial times to the Civil War, monopoly in America was monopoly in the first two senses—

---

[6] See Aristotle, Politics i, 11 and Ethics v, 5.

"monopolizing" practices like forestalling and government grants of monopoly privileges. Complaints about "monopolizing" practices probably reached their peak of intensity during the wartime inflation of the Revolutionary period in the 18th century when food rioters demanded action against "monopolizers" who charged excessive prices. Even more consistently, government grants of monopoly privileges were vigorously opposed from the first settlements until the latter part of the 19th century. For example, colonial opposition to the English trading companies contributed to American independence—the Declaration of Independence included English trading monopolies among George III's "injuries and usurpation." A later example of successful opposition to government grants of monopoly privileges was Andrew Jackson's war against the Second Bank of the United States—albeit with the unintended consequence of delaying effective central banking in the United States until the 20th century.

After the Civil War, monopoly in the third or modern sense of a dominant firm enjoying significant market power came to prevail over the earlier notions. This has meant that private firms (largely unblessed by government privileges) like Standard Oil—and now Big Tech firms—have replaced the 17th century colonial fur trading monopolies, the 18th century English trading companies and the antebellum Second Bank of the United States as the favorite targets of monopoly opponents. How did this come about? The rise of the large industrial and commercial firms after the Civil War generated considerable opposition that ultimately resulted in enactment of state and federal antitrust laws. Monopoly (now cast actively, as "monopolization") became an important element in this broader antitrust world—a world quite different from the prior three centuries of concerns about engrossing, forestalling and government grants of exclusive trading privileges. The prior episodic application of forestalling and engrossing laws has been institutionalized into the modern law enforcement industry of public officials, lawyers and economists. There was nothing comparable to this antitrust industry before 1890. The legal standards have been greatly clarified—amorphous complaints about "monopolizers" have morphed into more precise legal theories like the rules to determine predatory pricing. Economic analysis now prevails over political and social concerns about monopoly. Popular attention to monopoly has declined, which should not be surprising given that antitrust law has become steeped in highly technical economic analysis. Concepts like leveraging or raising rivals' costs hardly resonate with the modern counterpart of the colonial mother on the street demanding action against excessive prices.

But the antitrust world may be changing once again. In the last few years, federal and state authorities have dramatically increased enforcement efforts against both the business practices of dominant firms and mergers involving dominant firms, particularly in sectors like digital platforms and markets with networks effects. Some of the concerns motivating this increase in enforcement activity go back as far as colonial America (albeit voiced in different terms), notably denial of the opportunity to compete and undue political influence. Other values are either new—such as privacy rights—or rest on modern economic concepts like network effects.

Judges and lawyers have been known on occasion to use history in ways that would disturb professional historians. An isolated sentence from the writings of an historical figure is quoted to support an argument or legal position. This is often done with no little to no broader historical context. The opposing party (or the judge) then either simply avoids the historical reference or cites another historical source to support an opposing argument or legal position—again often without its broader context. Many uses of history might be generously viewed as creative lawyering to support a legal position in litigation rather than an accurate capturing of the complexities of the past. The Revolutionary and Founding period provides examples. The period is frequently invoked for many purposes, such as support for political programs and legislative agendas, as well as legal interpretation of constitutional provisions. Scholars have castigated the propensity of judges and lawyers to selectively cite isolated statements of Thomas Jefferson and other Founders to support legal positions. Mindful of those sentiments, I press on.

The history of the antimonopoly tradition and its expression in modern antitrust law also are interesting on their own. I hope the reader will agree with me. The remainder of this chapter offers a tour d'horizon of the American experience with the notion of monopoly, which is elaborated more fully in the following four chapters.

I. COLONIAL AMERICA (1600 TO 1763)

America was born as a business venture with parent investors in England and the Netherlands; monopoly was godfather. The early settlements in Virginia and Massachusetts, as well as the Dutch settlement in New Netherland, started primarily as business ventures in the form of trading companies. Antimonopoly sentiment during the early colonial period was directed primarily toward the initial settlement charter monopolies, English trading companies and grants of exclusive rights or monopoly privileges by colonial authorities. "Monopolists" were placed with "Papists" and "bad magistrates" in the forbidden category of persons excluded from the proposed colony in Virginia. Several generations later, William Penn initially planned to receive a monopoly of the Indian trade[7] as part of the "proper maintenance" of his new colony, but he changed his mind when merchants would not accept his monopoly privileges.

Colonials objected strenuously to the English mercantilist policy that gave England a monopoly of colonial output. The American colonies acted not so much as team players in the English system, but more as independent actors. They smuggled goods in contravention of the monopoly restrictions and encouraged the manufacture of competing goods as a form of import substitution.

Colonials also objected to monopoly grants of colonial authorities. The saga of the New York "Bolting Acts" is one example of rural opposition to what was perceived as a monopoly grant favoring urban merchants. In 1680, Governor Andros granted a group of New York City merchants a monopoly of making, bolting and packing flour for export from the province. The monopoly so benefited Manhattan that flour barrels and windmill sails remain on the New York City official city seal today. New York City enjoyed the monopoly privilege for about fifteen years, after which vigorous rural opposition led to its repeal.

In the Massachusetts Bay Colony, we find a Puritan mix of morality and law condemning "monopolistic" pricing. After conviction by the secular authorities for "excessive pricing," church elders in 1639 severely admonished Robert Keayne for selling goods at excessive prices "to the Dishonor of God's name, the Offence of the General Court, and the Publique scandall of the Country." However, moral convictions did not always prevail over monopoly profits. The Pilgrims and Puritans, both of whom voiced strong moral and political condemnation of monopoly, received opposing government grants of monopoly privileges concerning beaver furs

[7] During the colonial period and in most of American history, contemporaries called the indigenous tribes "Indians," unlike the present term "native Americans." This history uses the contemporary term "Indians."

which ended only after armed conflict. Puritans complained that Pilgrim efforts to protect their monopoly "have brought us all, and the gospel under a common approach, of cutting one another's throats for beaver."

Opposition to monopoly was not limited to the English colonies. Dutch New Netherland also opposed trading monopolies, although it was the Company authorities in Amsterdam that embraced a policy of free trade, while the New Amsterdam authorities (supported by colonial interests) often proposed monopoly privileges.

Colonials, like their ancestors in England and Europe, also enacted measures against engrossing (cornering the market) and forestalling (buying goods before they get to market), particularly to protect local closed markets and to prevent direct purchases and bulk buying from ships carrying imported goods. Despite the threat of imprisonment, pillory and forfeiture of goods, however, colonial forestalling and engrossing laws probably were less successful than intended.

Yet, not all forms of monopoly grants were opposed. From the beginning of the settlements, products or processes resulting from invention received privileges as an exception to a general principle disfavoring monopoly. The first patent for a term of fourteen years was granted in 1646 by the Massachusetts Bay Colony for improved sawmills and scythes. And colonial authorities granted monopoly or exclusive trading privileges to incentivize local production of a broad variety of goods and commodities.

II. REVOLUTION AND FOUNDING (1763 TO 1800)

At the beginning of the Revolutionary War, complaints about the English trading monopolies intensified and contributed to the movement for independence. In 1775, violence broke out in Boston and many other cities protesting the tea monopoly of the East India Company. In 1776, representatives from the thirteen colonies signed the Declaration of Independence. English trading monopolies were listed among George III's "injuries and usurpation" — "cutting off our Trade with all parts of the world."

During the war, we find popular seizures of the goods of "monopolizers" with forced sales at reasonable prices. Food riots are commonly found. In July 1777 in Boston, about a hundred women put the merchant Thomas Boylston in a cart, seized the keys to his warehouse and confiscated coffee that he had refused to sell. In 1779 in Philadelphia, crowds of armed men forced shopkeepers to lower prices of foodstuffs, escorted a merchant, butcher and speculator accused of raising prices to the city jail, and then seized a merchant suspected of exporting flour and forced him to sell the flour to them at prices they were willing to pay. A mass meeting created citizen committees to investigate flour engrossing and to set price ceilings. Ultimately, the local militia were called in to restore order in the City of Brotherly Love.

The American revolutionaries added a political element to protests against "monopolizers"—support for independence from England. A patriot did not charge excessive prices. The link between patriotism and prices can be seen in the "leagues and covenants" organized to boycott English goods beginning in 1764.

Wartime inflation triggered further demands for action against the "monopolizers." Toward the end of 1778, an Army officer urged the Pennsylvania civil authorities to take measures to protect the poor "as Grain is so dear and the Monopolizers and Forestallers is to blame, for I look upon them to be worse than the Savages or any Enemy that's against us." General Washington himself complained: "Speculation, peculation, engrossing, forestalling with all their concomitants, evidence the decay of public virtue." Others in the Congress shared Washington's sentiments. In November, a Committee of Congress advised the Supreme Executive Council of Pennsylvania: "the dangerous practices of Engrossers have increased .... This seething of the Kid in its Mother's milk calls for the most exemplary punishment." Other Founders chimed in. James Madison declaimed that "[t]he spirit of monopoly" had created "an artificial scarcity of commodities wanted for public use, the consequence of which has been an increase of their price." Even fervent Federalists like Alexander Hamilton decried the price raising effects of "monopoly."

Price controls were often tried and usually failed, but for many reasons other than the administrative and enforcement difficulties, notably, rural opposition. Price controls in the colonies also became associated with violence and extra-legal action. After the end of the war, states began to repeal even longstanding price control measures like bread assizes.

After the Declaration of Independence, two states (Maryland and North Carolina) elevated opposition to monopoly to the constitutional level by including antimonopoly provisions in their state constitutions. The majority of states did not follow these two examples, probably out of recognition that some monopolies were justified as promoting a public interest—e.g., short-term privileges to encourage local production and manufacture. Similarly, the federal constitution did not include a ban on monopoly, while the intellectual property clause concerning patents and copyrights was viewed as a legitimate exception to the antimonopoly principle.

III. ANTEBELLUM ERA (1800 TO 1861)

During the antebellum era, the agrarian nation of the 18th century was becoming the industrial-mercantile nation Hamilton had envisioned. U.S. territory and its natural resources more than doubled and now extended across the continent. Significant improvements in transportation and communications fueled an economic expansion. All the while, the antimonopoly tradition continued. For example, around 1826 the legislature of Alabama declared: "The sponge of monopoly has absorbed nearly the whole wealth of the nation." Banks replaced the English trading monopolies like the East India Company as the chief targets of antimonopoly action. The earlier colonial (sometimes violent) opposition of the debtor community of farmers and small businesses to urban creditor banks and merchants was reinforced when western expansion strengthened the political influence of the debtors.

Andrew Jackson's crusade against the Second Bank of the United States was the antebellum period's most controversial example of successful antimonopolist action. In Jackson's view, the Bank threatened the people's liberty because it concentrated enormous power in private hands and used that power to influence legislation, as well as favoring the rich over humble citizens like farmers, mechanics and laborers. The refusal to recharter the Bank was a costly victory, however. The failure to provide a replacement for the Bank condemned the United States to unsound currency and credit institutions for almost a century. There is an important lesson here: demands for action against monopoly can have harmful unintended consequences if plans are not made in advance as what to do after the monopoly is eliminated. Unfortunately, it is often easier to complain about a monopoly than fashion a replacement for it.

Antimonopoly sentiment against the banks was not confined to the West and South. In the late 1830s, a group of dissident Democrats in New York formed the Equal Rights Party known as the Loco-

Focos. The Loco-Focos condemned all monopoly, but focused particular attention on the banks. In a way, the Loco-Focos might be regarded as militant predecessors of today's Progressive Democrats and neo-Brandeisians.

The antimonopoly tradition remained vigorous and effective in the antebellum years. Many states—particularly the new western states—amended their constitutions to restrict the power of state and local authorities to grant monopolies. Legislatures and courts in states without a constitutional provision—like Pennsylvania and New York—endorsed the antimonopoly principle and constrained grants of monopoly privileges.

Who were the principal opponents of monopoly before the Civil War? Although farmers and the urban poor were more often against monopoly than urban merchants and manufacturers, one also finds in the vast historical record many examples where farmers, merchants and others favored monopoly when it was in their economic self-interest to do so. Sectional differences also could be important, particularly when the new United States expanded beyond the Appalachians. Again, speaking generally, opposition to monopoly often was stronger in the West and South.

IV. ANTITRUST LAWS (1870 TO TODAY)

After the Civil War, large firms replaced government grants of monopoly as the principal target of antimonopolists. Some of the most prominent firms took the legal form of the trust which explains why the antimonopolist tradition was embedded in the "antitrust movement" and then the "antitrust laws." This had the enormous effect of cabining the antimonopoly tradition in a law enforcement model that ultimately would be restricted to economics concerns that narrowed (if not discarded) broader social and political concerns that had previously animated the tradition.

The antitrust movement in the U.S. we understand today began with complaints primarily by farmers in the South and West about the railroads. Farmers were then joined by small businesses and artisans who broadened the targets to include large industrial firms. Like the earlier antimonopoly movements against the English trading companies and colonial monopoly grants, freedom to trade (or exclusion of actual and potential competitors in modern terms) was an important concern, along with undue political power, higher prices, loss of local jobs and wealth inequalities. The variety of concerns and the number of member constituencies gave considerable strength to the antitrust movement.

The initial legislative response to the antitrust movement came from the states when they enacted antitrust laws. Then in 1890, the federal government responded with passage of the Sherman Act. The Congress—comprised of both vocal opponents of the trusts and more discrete sympathizers—first decided that something had to be done (albeit for very different reasons) to meet the popular demand for action against the trusts and large firms. Congress then did what it has often done: enact an ambiguously worded statute and pass the buck to the courts to deal with its interpretation.

The American antitrust movement was markedly different from the response of European states to the large new firms of the industrial world. The Europeans lacked a vigorous antimonopoly tradition that in the United States went back several centuries to the initial founding of the Virginia and Massachusetts colonies—a popular tradition that not only was expressed in learned treatises and political pamphlets, but also implemented in statutes and state constitutions. The American tradition was motivated in part by the greater American distrust of power—both public and private power. This distrust complemented other monopoly concerns about exclusion from trade and higher prices. The American distrust of public power declined significantly with the New Deal and later acceptance of extensive government intervention into the economy. This has had the perhaps unintended consequence of diverting antimonopoly attention away from government to private firms.

Today, concerns about government monopoly grants appear anemic when compared with the prior three centuries of outrage voiced by colonists and antebellum Americans. Private firms, including most of Big Tech, raise the hackles of critics of monopoly—not recipients of government monopoly privileges. Why? There are several reasons.

First, natural monopoly and public utility theories have provided economic and legal rationales for many monopolies that previously had been challenged as unlawful. Federal and state regulation has moderated antimonopoly complaints in many industries characterized as "natural monopolies." Monopoly concerns continue to exist, however. The economic concept of natural monopoly has not eliminated the historical concern that government monopoly grants run the risk of political corruption.

Second, popular and political acceptance of economic regulation—supported by judicial deference to legislative purpose and a broad recognition of the state's police power with respect to health, safety and public order—have trumped earlier American opposition to government grants of monopoly privileges. Federal and state constitutions and statutes impose few effective constraints on state and local grants of monopoly privileges when compared with the colonial and antebellum periods. For example, neither the federal commerce clause nor the federal supremacy clause has fulfilled their antebellum potential as antimonopoly instruments. The federal antitrust laws have been interpreted as not prohibiting a state or local government from adopting a policy to displace competition with a public or private monopoly where there is "active supervision" by the authorities. This carve out of antimonopoly prohibitions rests on considerations of "federalism and state sovereignty" which ironically—or perversely to some observers—has attenuated federal protections against state and local grants of monopoly privileges.

Third, the decline in concern about government monopoly grants since the Civil War reflects shifts in the constituencies and general political views of many traditional supporters of vigorous antimonopoly action. After all, it was the Democrat Andrew Jackson who fought the federally chartered Second Bank of the United States in the 1830s. But Democrats for the last century have prioritized the benefits of federal (and state) economic intervention over the (potential) harms of government grants of monopoly. The focus on private firm monopoly is consistent with this prioritization.

Like the antitrust laws generally, enforcement of the monopolization provisions of the Sherman Act has seen periods of intense activity and periods of less activity. After a slow start, the Sherman Act was used successfully to challenge and break up many poster children of the 19th century antitrust movement like Standard Oil and American Tobacco. In 1920, monopoly-busting ended when the Supreme Court rejected the government's request to break up U.S. Steel for unlawful monopolization.[8] Antitrust law challenges of monopoly, and the antimonopoly tradition, went into hibernation during the good times of the Roaring Twenties and the bad times of the early Depression. Cooperation and not competition was the aim of U.S. economic policy during Franklin Roosevelt's first term. In 1937,

[8] United States v. U.S. Steel Corp., 251 U.S. 417 (1920).

the pragmatic president reversed that policy. The reversal reflected the view that the Depression and slow economic recovery resulted from domination of industry by a small number of large firms. This initiated an era of aggressive antitrust challenges to monopoly which lasted until the 1970s. After the successful challenge to Alcoa's aluminum monopoly,[9] government actions against monopolies increased following World War II. There was one highly successful use of section 2 against monopoly in a case that was started in 1969—the *AT&T* litigation. The break-up of AT&T[10] is viewed by many observers as generating decades of consumer benefits with new entrants and numerous opportunities for new competition.

Beginning in the late 1970's, antitrust law retrenched. Government challenges to monopoly were sparse between 1980 and 2020, certainly when compared with the trustbusting and post-war expansionary periods. The important exception was the successful government action against Microsoft in the 1990s. The complaint alleged that Microsoft engaged in practices—notably self-preferencing and coercive tying—in order to prevent or deter rivals from gaining a foothold in the market for operating platforms which Microsoft dominated.[11]

But the retrenchment era is over, at least from the perspective of the White House and antitrust agencies. Both the Justice Department and the FTC, as well as state antitrust authorities, have recently resurrected aggressive enforcement—notably investigations and monopolization actions against a number of firms, particularly in digital platform and other high-tech markets. A new era has begun.

There are several explanations for the cyclical history of antitrust law and monopoly since 1890: political support, popular demand for action, facts (economic conditions), economic theory, legal process concerns and the predominance of consumer welfare analysis.

---

[9] United States v. Aluminum Co. of Am., 148 F.2d 416 (2d Cir. 1945).

[10] United States v. AT&T Co., [1970-1979 Transfer Binder] Trade Reg. Rep. (CCH) 45,074 (D.D.C. filed Nov. 20, 1974) (complaint alleging monopolization, attempted monopolization, and conspiracy to monopolize), settled by consent decree, 1982-2 Trade Cas. (CCH) 64,900 (D.D.C. 1982).

[11] United States v. Microsoft Corp., 253 F.3d 34, 64 (D.C. Cir. 2001) (en banc) (per curiam); Government's Complaint, United States v. Microsoft Corp., 87 F. Supp. 2d30 (D.D.C. 2000) (Nos. 98-1232, 98-1233).

Executive support and congressional funding were critical in both the trustbusting era and the expansionary era that began in 1937. This suggests that the recent renewal of aggressive enforcement by the federal agencies will continue until there is a change in the executive and legislative support for it. Elections count as much as "antitrust schools." Of course, aggressive enforcement by the agencies must obtain acceptance in the courts.

Popular support was an important motivator during the trustbusting era. But since the end of World War II, popular attention to monopoly—either for or against—has considerably weakened. This suggests that aggressive antitrust enforcement against monopoly does not necessarily depend on popular support.

Changes in the facts/economic conditions and assumptions are important in understanding the enforcement cycles. The best example is comparison of the post-war expansionary period and the retrenchment period. By 1945, U.S. firms were relatively free from foreign competition, given the still existing trade barriers to entry and the economic weakness of potential foreign competitors. A reasonable assumption was that any market power enjoyed by U.S. firms could be expected to persist and there was reduced risk that aggressive enforcement might chill innovation or other procompetitive behavior. By the end of the 1970s, however, introduction of foreign competitors into U.S. markets counseled relaxation of that assumption.

This suggests that the recent increase in enforcement activity should not be surprising to those familiar with history (or life in general): the facts changed and new issues have arisen that generate responses and demands for action. That is, economic conditions have changed since 1980 when we had not yet entered the digital world. The current monopolization actions against the digital platform and other tech firms will test the prior retrenchment era assumption that monopoly, once attained, will eventually go away in a Schumpeterian cycle of innovation.

Developments in economic theory were significant factors in shifting from expansion to retrenchment. In the 1950s, economic theory supported aggressive antimonopoly enforcement, notably structuralist theories holding that market structure leads to poorer market performance. The "new learning" in the early 1970's challenged both the underlying economic assumptions of the structuralists and eroded theoretical and empirical support for de-concentration.[12] Since 1980, economic theory has continued to develop with dynamic theories of harm like raising rivals' costs and strategic behavior in markets with network effects.

What are the implications for the future? One key question is whether challengers of monopoly can persuade courts to accept strategic theories of harm. The answer may well depend on the courts' legal process concerns.

Legal process concerns about costs, administrability of legal rules, false positives and the capability of jurors and judges to understand complex facts and economic theories have made the litigation wars of modern antitrust more costly and difficult to win.

What are the implications for the future? Critics of monopoly must directly and persuasively address courts' legal process concerns if they are to be successful.

For the last half century, **consumer welfare analysis** has dominated antitrust law—arguably to the exclusion of political and social concerns that generated the state antitrust laws and then the Sherman Act in the first place. Yet, to be sure, modern economics has increased analytical rigor and enabled courts to create specific legal rules for different kinds of practices that for centuries had been lumped together or conflated under the rubric "monopolistic" practices.

Hence, today, parties challenging monopolies must either frame their arguments in economic terms or show how social and political concerns can be integrated into an economics-based antitrust analysis.[13]

This book examines the American antimonopoly tradition from its inception in the early 1600s to the present debate about the effectiveness of antitrust laws to deal with today's monopolies. The modern antitrust law pivot away from government monopoly grants to private firm monopoly raises questions that remained largely in the background before the antitrust movement of the 19th century: how do we apply laws dealing with private monopoly so as not to stifle entrepreneurial drive, incentives and innovation? should the law condemn all private monopolies or only those without justification? How will the yin (opportunity to compete) and yang (entrepreneurial spirit and success) be reconciled by courts and authorities in deciding whether a successful firm has violated the

---

[12] See Hawk, supra note 1, at 121.

[13] See id. at 169–74.

law—a reconciliation often hidden by opinions couched in the minutiae of economic and legal analysis. This book is intended to provide an often-overlooked context in answering those questions.

Chapter Two

COLONIAL AMERICA

I. INTRODUCTION

The early English settlers brought with them a deep aversion to monopoly. By the time of the Revolutionary War, the now American colonists had nurtured that aversion into a robust antimonopoly tradition. Of course, as mentioned earlier, Americans were hardly the first in history to condemn monopoly. Intellectuals, philosophers and religious figures have condemned monopolies for millennia.[1] One can also find in the same millennia an occasional law or legal principle intended to combat monopoly, like those in Rome and later in Europe. But the American antimonopoly tradition was to surpass earlier attempts to prevent and constrain public and private monopoly.

There were two strands to the colonial antimonopoly tradition. The older strand was directed at an ill-defined group of "monopolistic" practices that included forestalling, engrossing and price speculation. These practices were condemned under laws in England, France and many other societies for centuries. Legal prohibitions reflected popular condemnation of "monopolizers" who were viewed as responsible for price hikes and excessive prices. American colonists echoed these popular condemnations of "monopolizers." A 1979 Boston handbill signed "Vengeance" urged citizens to "rid the community of those monopolizers and extortioners, who, like canker worms, are gnawing upon your vitals."[2] This older strand of the colonial antimonopoly tradition is discussed in section IV below.

The second strand of the colonial antimonopoly tradition was directed at government grants of monopoly privileges. Although younger in its lineage, the second strand has played a more important role in American history. The depth and vigor of this colonial (and English) objection to government grants of monopoly privileges are probably unique in history. While not always successful in preventing monopolies, it was probably more successful than earlier attempts in other societies to constrain state or elite monopoly grants.

---

[1] See Barry E. Hawk, Antitrust and Competition Laws 17-27 (2020).

[2] See Franklin D. Jones, Historical Development of the Law of Business Competition, 36 Yale L. J. 43, 54 (1927).

The colonial settlements began at a time when England was not only refining political ideas about monopoly, but also creating legal principles that succeeded in limiting the Crown's grants of monopoly privileges. The American colonists ultimately went further than their English parents by establishing the principle that popular legislatures were limited by the antimonopoly principle, unlike the Parliament after the Glorious Revolution in 1688. This will all be discussed in section III. In the next section, we put the antimonopoly tradition into its legal context.

II. COLONIAL LAW

Before American independence, the sources of law in the colonies—including laws that reflected antimonopoly sentiments—were not as clear as they were following independence with the creation of state and then federal law. Three points relevant to monopoly should be noted.

First, evidence of the colonial opposition to monopoly as expressed in legal rules and principles goes well beyond English "common law" or colonial court decisions. American colonial law was a blend of charters, royal orders, English common law, English statutes, colonial legislation and colonial court decisions. Colonial law was not simply a local replication of English common law or even a faithful copy of Parliamentary legislation.[3] For example, in the early 18th century four colonies (Maryland, North Carolina, Pennsylvania and South Carolina) claimed the benefits of the common law, but only limited categories of English statutes.[4]

Moreover, the "common law" as understood in the American colonies was not necessarily the common law developed in the central courts of London. Many colonists had greater familiarity with other English court decisions that often differed from the London courts.[5] As to Parliamentary laws, the English Attorney General Richard West acknowledged the legal complexities in 1720: "all statutes in

---

[3] Reports of American cases did not become easily accessible until after independence. Even now, only scattered collections of colonial cases have been published. Many colonial statutes survive only in the form of rare editions. See Lawrence Friedman, A History of American Law 33 (1973).

[4] Morton Horwitz, The Transformation of American Law: 1780–1860 6 (1979).

[5] See Julius Goebel, Jr., King's Law and Local Custom in Seventeenth-Century New England, 31 Columbia L. Rev. 416 (1931).

affirmance of the common law, passed in England antecedent to the settlement of a colony, are in force in that colony, unless there is some private act to the contrary; though no statutes, made since those settlements, are thus in force unless the colonists are particularly mentioned."[6] Hence, neither English court decisions about monopoly nor Parliamentary acts constitute the only sources of colonial legal rules regarding monopoly—although they certainly influenced colonial legal principles.[7] Settlers in colonial America who came from England considered themselves English subjects and claimed all the rights of Englishmen; this was more important than any specifics of English "common law" or its application in the colonies.

Second, opposition to monopoly was dispersed throughout the colonies. Laws in the various colonies could be quite different given their geographical separation, starting dates and government structures.[8] Yet, differences were moderated to some extent by codification, and colonial law was more codified than English law of the period. For example, the Massachusetts Laws and Liberties of 1648 was the product of more than a decade of efforts to reduce to writing the laws of the Massachusetts Bay Colony.[9] Codes also spread among colonies more easily than court decisions.[10] The Massachusetts Code was widely emulated in Connecticut,[11] New York, Pennsylvania and Delaware.

Third, colonial laws were subject to review by the English Board of Trade or Privy Council to ensure that they were "not repugnant" to English law and policy.[12] The test imposed no particular laws on the colonies, not even the common law; instead, its ambiguity gave wide discretion to both the colonists and the mother country to

---

[6] Horwitz, supra note 4, at 6.

[7] See, e.g., Friedman, supra note 3, at 33–35.

[8] Friedman, supra note 3, at 34–35.

[9] See George Haskins, Codification of the Law in Colonial Massachusetts: A Study in Comparative Law, 30 Ind. L. J. 1, 3–4 (1954).

[10] See Friedman, supra note 3, at 92–93.

[11] Of the 78 provisions in Robert Ludlow's Connecticut code of 1650, twenty-two were copied almost verbatim from the Massachusetts code and thirty-six were adopted with certain deletions or amendments.

[12] See Elmer Beecher Russell, The Review of American Colonial Legislation by the King in Council 15-16 (1915). England retained a second (and not always effective) check on colonial authorities and legislatures: instructions to colonial governors to veto anticipated legislation of objectionable character.

decide the legal rule in a specific situation.[13] Only about five percent of the four hundred colonial pieces of legislation submitted were disallowed.[14]

Colonial laws concerning trade, however, were closely reviewed by the Board of Trade or Privy Council, especially those measures intended to encourage local manufacturing. These were often disallowed as repugnant to English policy. Unsurprisingly, these reviews of colonial legislation were resented by the colonials as protecting monopoly privileges. Indeed, the Continental Congress listed English review of colonial laws as the basis of eight counts in its indictment of grievances against the Crown. As just one example, the Board of Trade/Privy Council rejected an exemption from poll taxes because it would encourage the growth of towns, which in turn might lead to the development of local manufacturing (especially of woolens) and reduction of English exports.[15] Other examples are seen below.

Let us now turn to the younger and more fundamental strand in the colonial antimonopoly tradition—opposition to government grants of monopoly privileges. This strand continued to exercise considerable legal and political influence up to the Civil War after which it declined in importance compared with the modern antitrust focus on private monopoly.

III. COLONIAL OPPOSITION TO GOVERNMENT GRANTS OF MONOPOLY OR EXCLUSIVE TRADING PRIVILEGES

The colonial settlements began in a period when England was not only refining (and strengthening) antimonopoly political theory but also creating legal principles that succeeded in constraining royal grants of monopoly privilege. This itself was probably unique in history. The millennia-old condemnations of monopoly by religious and secular critics had rarely translated into meaningful checks on monopolies. In the past, there were no consistently effective legal constraints on rulers and elites who exercised their political power to obtain monopoly profits to wage war, live better and subsidize supporters. In the late 16th century, however, the English began to create legal checks on royal grants of monopoly privileges. But the

---

[13] Id. at 139–40.

[14] See Oliver Morton Dickerson, American Colonial Government 1696–1765 227 (1912); Russell, supra note 12, at 221. The most common disallowances concerned bills of credit, currency and descent of property. Id. at 237–38.

[15] Id. at 240–41.

American colonists went even further than their English parents by securing the principle that legislatures also were limited by the antimonopoly principle. They did so by embedding a more robust antimonopoly principle in constitutions, statutes and legal principles.

We must remember that colonials used the term "monopoly" simply to denote the grant of exclusive trading privileges to one or more persons. This is far different from the modern sense of monopoly which limits "monopoly" to firms holding a significant degree of market power—as discussed in Chapter Five. Here we use the term "monopoly" in the colonial sense when discussing colonial opposition to monopoly. To modern antitrust lawyers and economists, many of the colonial "monopolies" would not be considered "monopolies"—at least without further facts showing power to raise price (or output) in a defined market.

A. English Antimonopoly Revolution

Importantly for the American colonies, there was considerable political and legal attention in England paid to monopolies at the time of the first settlements in Virginia and Massachusetts. Royal grants of monopoly (or patent[16]) rights came under serious attack towards the end of the Tudor period in the late 16th and early 17th centuries. On the legal front, the English courts' development of a common law principle disfavoring monopolies began with the guilds. In 1599 in *Davenant v. Hurdis*, Edward Coke successfully challenged guild restrictions, arguing that monopolies were implicitly prohibited by Magna Carta and statutes of Edward III.[17] This was successful creative lawyering in its use of English history.[18] Whether

---

[16] The term "patent" was commonly used to denote any royal or legislative grant of monopoly privileges, whether or not it involved an invention. Only later in the 18th century did the term "patent" (short for letters patent) begin to have the modern meaning, that is, a grant of exclusive privileges by the state over the commercial exploitation of an invention for a limited time. See Edward Walterscheid, To Promote the Progress of Science, 2 J. Intel. Propr. L. 1, 10 (1994), citing Christine Macleod, Inventing the Industrial Revolution: The English Patent System, 1660-1800, at 40 (1988).

[17] Davenant v. Hurdis, 72 Eng. Rep. 769, 778 (K.B. 1599).

[18] The provision most relevant to monopoly was Chapter 41 of Magna Carta which guaranteed safe conduct and trading liberties for foreign merchants:

> "All merchants shall have safe and secure exit from England, and entry to England, with the right to tarry there and to move about as

or not Coke exaggerated the relevance of Magna Carta, the common law rule he announced became part of the accepted law.[19]

Guilds would soon be successfully challenged in other European polities, but the English common lawyers went further, successfully challenging royal grants of monopolies. In the late 16th century, Elizabeth I granted an unprecedented number of monopolies to servants and courtiers. Hostility from merchants, artisans and consumers followed.[20] In 1602, common law courts began to invalidate royal grants of monopoly. In *Darcy v. Allen*,[21] the court rested its invalidation of the grant of a playing card monopoly on constitutional objections to royal authority, freedom of the individual to engage in a trade and concern about high prices.[22]

Parliament then entered the antimonopoly fray. In 1623, the House of Commons complained to James I about monopoly grants, including those relating to gold thread, apothecaries and housing construction.[23] After an unsatisfactory response from the king, Parliament enacted the Statute of Monopolies of 1624, which condemned arbitrary granting of monopolies by the Crown.[24] Despite the 1624 Statute, however, royal grants continued to be issued and considerable litigation ensued. Indeed, only a few years after Darcy's monopoly of playing cards was declared invalid, the

---

> well by land as by water, for buying and selling by the ancient and right customs, quit from all evil tolls, except (in time of war) such merchants as are of the land at war with us. And if such are found in our land at the beginning of the war, they shall be detained, without injury to their bodies or goods, until information be received by us, or by our chief justiciar, how the merchants of our land found in the land at war with us are treated; and if our men are safe there, the others shall be safe in our land."

W.S. McKechnie, Magna Carta 399 (2d ed. 1914).

[19] See Donald O. Wagner, Coke and the Rise of Economic Liberalism, 6 Econ. Hist. Rev. 30 (1935). See generally William Searle Holdsworth, History of English Law 343-62 (1924).

[20] Christopher Hill, The Century of Revolution 89 (1982).

[21] Darcy v. Allen, 77 Eng. Rep. 1260 (Q.B. 1602).

[22] See Hawk, supra note 1, at 24.

[23] Harold G. Fox, Monopolies and Patents: A Study of the History and Future of the Patent Monopoly 113 (1947).

[24] As noted above, by the end of the 17th century the royal letter-patent with respect to inventions had been converted into a modern version of the patent. See William Letwin, The English Common Law Concerning Monopoly, 21 U. Chi. L. Rev. 355, 359 (1954).

same monopoly was given to the Company of Card Makers—under authority of the 1624 Statute.[25] Nonetheless, the case law and the 1624 Statute continued to provide rich sources of legal support for colonial opposition to monopoly.

The English antimonopoly legal principle was narrower in scope than the colonial and, later, United States conception. The 1624 Statute itself exempted monopoly privileges granted by towns and cities.[26] Moreover, the common law antimonopoly principle announced in *Darcy* was limited to royal (government) grants of monopoly, not purely private monopolies.[27] This is clearly seen in in the definition of monopoly of Edward Coke himself.[28] By contrast, the American antimonopoly tradition eventually extended to purely private monopoly. And even with respect to government grants, the American tradition was more rigorous than the English rule: the former constrained legislatures and elected bodies, and not only executive authorities (as seen later in the chapter).

In one critical respect, the English and American principles were similar: both excepted some monopoly grants from the general prohibition. Under the 1624 Statute, not all monopoly grants were unlawful[29]—only grants that resulted from abuse of procedures[30] or

---

[25] Fox, supra note 23, at 128 n.21.

[26] 21 Jac. 1, c. 3. § 9. Section 9 provided that the Act did not apply to any cities or towns, or any of their privileges, "or unto any corporations, companies, or fellowships of any trade, occupation, or mystery, or to any companies or societies of merchants within this Realm, erected for the maintenance, enlargement, or ordering of any trade of merchandise . . . "

[27] English common law did prohibit "engrossing" or cornering of the market by private parties. Engrossing in colonial America is discussed later in the chapter.

[28] Coke wrote: "an institution or allowance by the King, by his grant, commission, or otherwise, to any person or persons, bodies politic or corporate, of or for the sole buying, selling, making, working, or using anything; whereby any person or persons, bodies politic or corporate, are sought to be restrained of any freedom or liberty that they had before, or hindered in their lawful trade." See Fox, supra note 23, at 8–9.

[29] Later actions in the Parliament support this view. In 1640, it was moved in the House of Commons that "every Projector Monopolizer in all respects might bee disabled to sett in this howse." When the motion was put to the House, however, it was resolved upon the question "That the word 'unlawful' should be joined to the word 'Monopolist'." See Fox, supra note 23, at 141. [Footnotes omitted]

[30] Abuse of procedures in the granting or operation of the monopoly was a significant cause of concern, in addition to perceived effects on freedom to

that served no public purpose (as determined under a shifting reasonableness standard). In modern terms, there was no per se monopoly rule. Indeed, many royal grants of monopoly were upheld even after the 1624 Statute. For example, the Court of Exchequer in 1655 upheld the validity of a soap monopoly as a reasonable regulation of trade (in modern parlance), noting and rejecting popular condemnations of "monopoly" as "too hasty in their censure."[31] This presages U.S. decisions that uphold state laws granting monopoly privileges where they are legitimate exercises of state police powers.[32] The court's criticism of popular expressions of monopoly is another example of a common theme throughout history: judges are far more cautious in condemning "monopoly" than people in the street (or the academic in the classroom).

Let us turn to the antimonopoly principle in the colonies where the colonists often took a more aggressive position toward monopolies than their English forebearers.[33]

B. Antimonopoly Tradition in the Colonies

In 1641, the Massachusetts Bay Colony, after extensive public consultation with the magistrates and elders in each town,[34] condemned monopoly in strong language: "No monopolies shall be granted or allowed amongst us, but of such new Inventions as yet are profitable to ye Countrie, & that for a short time."[35] As we shall see below, the Massachusetts declaration was not at all atypical. From our country's origin (and even before the Statute of

---

trade. See Fox, supra note 23, at 174 ("During the debate on monopolies in 1601 it is clear that the attack was not so much on the monopolies themselves as on the methods used by the agents or substitutes of those who were the actual patentees."). In the Long Parliament in 1641, when Sir John Culpeper raged against the "monopolies and polers of the people," it was not the existence of monopolies he was quarrelling with so much as the fact that "they have marked and sealed us from head to foot." Id.

[31] Hayes et al v. Harding, (1656), Hardres 53, quoted in Fox, supra note 23, at 184.

[32] See Chapter Five.

[33] See Hans B. Thorelli, The Federal Antitrust Policy 37 (1954).

[34] See Paul Samuel Reinsch, The English Common Law in the Early American Colonies, in 1 Select Essays in Anglo-American Legal History 367, 373 (1907) ("a more careful process of legislation is perhaps nowhere recorded").

[35] Bruce W. Bugbee, Genesis of American Patent and Copyright Law 61 (1967).

Monopolies of 1624), monopoly privileges granted to the initial settlement trading companies were challenged.

There are several explanations for the more robust antimonopoly tradition in the colonies than in England. First, there was self-selection of the emigrants who chose to leave their homes and start a new life in the colonies. These were the pioneers whose spirit of individualism and risk-taking was antithetical to the idea of monopoly and exclusive trading.[36] They had far greater opportunities for advancement in the comparatively vast and open lands of the colonies and were congenitally inclined against monopoly to a greater extent than their peers left behind in the towns and rural areas of England and other European polities. Second, the colonists were at the receiving end of the English trading monopolies, discussed below, and viewed themselves more harmed than helped by monopoly. For example, English merchants often supported trading monopolies, while colonial merchants opposed them. Third, there was a muscular religious or moral element to the colonial disdain of monopoly, at least in the early settlements in New England.

These three explanations certainly fit the English colonies, unlike the situation in the French settlements where monopoly grants faced less opposition. For example, when the United States purchased the Louisiana Territory from France in 1803, monopolies previously granted by the French kings had to be expressly abrogated.[37] The Dutch colony of New Netherland presents yet again a different picture. For the roughly half-century before its absorption into the English realm in 1664, the Dutch Company authorities in the home country resisted monopolies in favor of free trade, often rejecting colonial proposals for trade restrictions and monopoly privileges. After New Amsterdam became New York, however, the aversion to monopoly in the English colonies also became the norm in the former Dutch colony.

Let us turn to how the English and Dutch colonies dealt with three kinds of government grants of monopoly privileges: settlement trading companies; reciprocal monopolies in England and the colonies (mercantilism); and colonial grants of monopoly privileges.

---

[36] See Thorelli, supra note 33, at 568.

[37] In 1712, Louis XIV granted a 15-year monopoly of trade and commerce to Anthony Crozart, but it was surrendered in less than two years. A similar grant was made in 1717 (and surrendered in 1730) to a trading company controlled by John Law.

1. *Settlement trading companies and their monopoly privileges*

"[A] trading company grew into a colony, and the colony into a state." James Bryce, The American Commonwealth (1889)

America was born as a business venture with parent investors in England; monopoly was godfather. The early settlements in Virginia and Massachusetts,[38] as well as the Dutch settlement in New Netherland, started primarily as business ventures in the form of trading companies. But then over the course of several decades, an increasing number of permanent settlers took a larger role in the political and business life of the colonies. The American settlements looked more like the western Mediterranean colonies of the Greek city states than the later European colonies in Africa and Asia.

The early English and Dutch colonies in the Americas were organized and operated by trading companies modelled on the joint stock companies, like the East India Company, that were granted monopoly rights to trade between Europe and east Asia.[39] Indeed, the North American companies were funded to a certain extent from fortunes earned in the East Asian trade. These colonial companies included, among others, the Virginia Company, the New Plymouth Company, the Massachusetts Bay Company[40] and the Dutch West India Company (VOC).

These joint stock companies evolved to meet the needs of the new global sea trade.[41] They closely mirrored a modern corporation with a company charter and bylaws concerning the rights and duties of managers and shareholders.[42] The European/Asian maritime trade required deep water ships and permanent trading posts—which often entailed bribes and payoffs to local chieftains and officials—as well as a long turn-around time for voyages.[43]

---

[38] Of course, there also was an important religious element to the Pilgrim and Puritan settlements in New England.

[39] John J. McCusker and Russell R. Menard, The Economy of British America, 1607–1789 342 (1985).

[40] See Gary M. Walton and James F. Shepherd, The Economic Rise of Early America 35–36 (1979).

[41] See Barry Hawk, Law and Commerce in Pre-Industrial Societies 238–41 (2015).

[42] Ron Harris, The Formation of the East India Company as a Cooperation-Enhancing Institution, SSRN eLibrary Draft 2, 5 (Dec. 2005).

[43] See, e.g., id. at 21–22.

The joint stock company allowed investors to enjoy the potentially large profits of a company involved in monopolized trade.[44] In modern parlance, exclusive monopoly rights safeguarded against free riding by later entrants.[45] At the same time, the vertically integrated joint stock company was better positioned to exercise market power and sustain monopoly prices.[46] Tradable shares allowed investors to participate in a highly profitable monopoly, while not necessarily requiring them to commit to a long-term investment. Providing joint stock companies and their shareholders with monopoly rights was likely more politically acceptable if a larger number of people could benefit from the monopoly.[47] Hence, the joint stock company satisfied the wealth-maximizing goals of both merchants and those seeking to gain from the enormous profit potential of the trading companies.

In a similar sense, some of the early colonial American settlement were joint ventures with the English government. Private investors contributed capital and organized the settlements. In return, the English Crown awarded exclusive trading privileges and land grants, while reserving the right to enjoy whatever advantages might accrue from the concession, including the requirement that the products of newly discovered and occupied lands should be sent only to England and its other colonies.[48]

The first English colonial investments were financial disasters, in part because investors in North America initially sought gold and a sea route to China and India. Trading monopolies were granted by the English Crown and the Dutch Estates General as investment incentives. Ultimately, however, neither gold nor a "Northwest Passage" was found, and these early ventures failed as businesses. After a time, the English trading companies (and their monopoly privileges) were replaced with royal governors and locally-elected

---

44 See S.R.H. Jones and Simon P. Ville, Efficient Transactors or Rent-Seeking Monopolists? The Rationale for Early Chartered Trading Companies, 56 J. Econ. Hist. 898, 910 (1996).

45 Walton and Shepherd, supra note 40, at 35–36.

46 Jones and Ville, supra note 44, at 911.

47 Some scholars suggest that capital needs, risk, and agency and information concerns do not sufficiently explain why merchants would want to include passive investors and provide them with tradable shares while those investors contributed no human capital. See id. at 909–10.

48 Charles M. Andrews, The Colonial Period of American History: England's Commercial and Colonial Policy 15 (1938).

or appointed officials. Control of the English colonies passed to the home country and the colonists themselves.[49] The Dutch colony met a somewhat different fate. Organized in 1621, the Dutch West India Company (VOC) was bankrupt by the 1640's. In 1645, the VOC authorities in Amsterdam took over management of the colony through their agent director in New Amsterdam.[50]

Let us look more closely at the travails of the first Virginia settlements, which nicely illustrate the history of trading company monopolies in early colonial America. The 1609 Company charter granted a seven-year monopoly on trade in all commodities of the colony.[51] After seven years, no profits were realized; investors received only land for their money as forests were cleared. In 1616, a continued lack of profits and funding forced the Company to relax its monopoly privileges by permitting anyone—whether or not connected with the Company—to import cattle, grain and munitions into Virginia if the Company failed to meet the needs of the settlers. Ship captains and passengers were now permitted to trade directly with settlers, thus significantly reducing Company revenues as relaxation of the trading monopoly also reduced prices. Then, in 1619—less than ten years after the first settlers had arrived—the trading monopoly was completely ended when all persons were explicitly permitted to trade with the colonists.[52]

This did not end all monopolies in Virginia. In 1622, following an Indian massacre of settlers and ensuing financial difficulties, Company agents in London successfully petitioned for a monopoly of all Virginia tobacco imported into England. But after opposition from the Virginia plantation owners, as well as some in Parliament and royal advisors who preferred free trade, the Privy Council rescinded the contract establishing a Company tobacco monopoly.[53] The Council in Virginia then wrote to Lord Mandeville, expressing

---

[49] Chester Whitney Wright, Economic History of the United States 60 (2nd ed. 1949).

[50] See Harold C. Syrett, Private Enterprise in New Amsterdam, 11 William & Mary Q. 536, 537 (1954).

[51] 2 Philip Alexander Bruce, Economic History of Virginia in the Seventeenth Century 268–88 (1896).

[52] Id. at 285.

[53] 1 Acts Privy Council, Colonial, I, §§ 98, 100; Discourse of the Old Company, 1 The Virginia Magazine of History and Biography 287, 293–294 (1894). See also 1 Joseph Dorfman, The Economic Mind in American Civilization 21 (1946); Andrews, supra note 48, at 159–64.

its satisfaction at the annulment of the contract, and emphasizing that the Company's contracts had been made "wholly without their consent and privity" and were intended for private gain rather than the profit of the Crown or the welfare of the colony.[54]

The final chapter of the Virginia trading company was written later in the 1620s when the Virginia assembly and authorities formally terminated not only the monopoly privileges, but also the Company itself (at least with respect to activities in Virginia). Renewal of the charter was rejected, because it would have meant that the "freedom of our trade with England under the King's regulations" would again be monopolized under the guise of "managing" the trade.[55] Thus, antimomopoly sentiment in England—as well as in the colonies—was politically effective in terminating a government granted monopoly.

Another example of successful colonial opposition to trading company monopolies concerns fishing in New England waters. Objection by one colony (Virginia) killed a fishing monopoly originally included in the 1619 charter for the Council for New England organized by Ferdinando Gorges.[56] The Virginia Company had sailed in New England waters under its charter, which entitled both Massachusetts and Virginia anglers to fish in each other's area. After the Virginia Company complained to the Privy Council and the House of Commons, the fishing monopoly was rescinded. Again, colonial opposition—combined with English support—ended another monopoly of a critical industry. The English support should not be underestimated.

Economic and financial conditions certainly contributed to failure of these early trading company monopolies. But failure also came at a period in England when monopoly privileges in general, as well as monopoly privileges included in the initial proposals for the American colonies, were criticized and hotly debated. For

---

[54] Calendar State Papers Colonial, America and West Indies: Volume I: 1574–1660, 111, https://www.british-history.ac.uk/cal-state-papers/colonial/america-west-indies/vol1/pp108-112. As late as 1628, the planters continued to refer to "these pernicious contracts, which so often for these six years have been continually intruded and made on their tobacco without their knowledge or privity." Andrews, supra note 48, at 159–64, citing Virginia Magazine, VII, 264.

[55] 1 Dorfman, supra note 53, at 8.

[56] The New England Council differed considerably from other early colonial companies. Unlike a trading company the New England Council had no governor, quarter courts or joint stock subscriptions.

example, the prospectus of the first Virginia settlement charter was condemned in England in the following terms:

> "The often renewed complaints against Companyes heretofore hath happened by reason of the Monopolizings of trade into a few men's hands, and though the ice of this busines hath been broken by the purses, cares, and adventures of a few, yet we seclude no subject from the future benefit of our present care, charge and hazard of person and adventures."[57]

Of course, company officials defended the proposed trading privileges. In 1601, John Wheeler, governor of the Merchant Adventurers, denied that the company was a monopoly.[58] Wheeler argued that trade must not be managed in a "dispersed, loose and straggling manner," lest English goods be sold at low prices and foreign goods in England at high prices.[59] The political debate in England about trading companies and their monopoly privileges was thus framed in terms of "monopoly" versus "free trade." In fact, in the Parliament of 1621-22, critics of the trading companies were called Free-traders; defenders of the trading companies were called Protectionists or Monopolists.[60]

The idea of monopoly trading privileges for new settlements did not die easily. Much later in the 17th century, William Penn initially contemplated that his company would have a trading monopoly. Penn's company had a capital stock of £10,000 and 10,000 acres of land ready to support fur trading and manufacturing, among other activities. But potential investors objected to any monopoly privileges promised in the company prospectus.[61] The

---

[57] Alexander Brown, The Genesis of the United States 463–65 (1890) concerning the clxi Circular Letter of the Virginia Council (1610).

[58] 1 Dorfman, supra note 53, at 7.

[59] Wheeler argued further that the company did not constitute a monopoly because of its large and dispersed membership with any investor free to buy a share. He also argued that the company's policy of determining how much each member should ship was not unlawful price fixing, but an antimonopolistic measure that prevented wealthy members from harming poorer members.

[60] Brown, supra note 57, at 1016–17.

[61] The prospectus appeared to include a company trading monopoly: "It is no small convenience and ease to . . . planters (happily unacquainted in trade) that they may have some part of their estates improving in a united way and care,

plan was abandoned.[62] Penn also contemplated that he should receive a monopoly of the Indian trade as part of the "proper maintenance" of the colony. This also was abandoned because of anticipated investor resistance. Penn's agent, James Logan, wrote him that merchants also would not countenance monopoly.[63] A more sympathetic view of William Penn's motives is offered by Franklin Jones: "William Penn ... was offered £6000 for a monopoly of trade, but he refused to sell the privilege because he wanted 'to do things equally between all parties.'"[64] In any event, William Penn—for either altruistic or selfish reasons—ultimately embraced the view that monopolies were against "the Law of the Land."[65]

The Dutch colony in New Amsterdam and the Hudson Valley had a history quite different from the English settlements in Virginia and Massachusetts—even though they, too, began as trading company operations. Flushed with profits from the trade in East Asia, Dutch merchants and other investors turned their attention to America.[66] In 1614, the Estates General passed an ordinance granting exclusive trading privileges for a certain period to the New Netherland Company to discover "new passages, havens, lands, or places."[67] The New Netherland Company itself was created out of a failed cartel.[68] In 1611-12, a private firm had begun to purchase beaver furs from the Indians around the mouth of the Hudson River. This was a profitable venture until a second competitor appeared and reduced profits for all. After cartel-like negotiations between the two

---

whilst they thereby may with less distraction, and more freedom . . . apply themselves to their particular plantations, for here a few hands do the work of the whole." See 1 Dorfman, supra note 53, at 87.

[62] See id.

[63] Id.

[64] Franklin D. Jones, Historical Development of the Law of Business Competition, 36 Yale L.J. 42, 46 (1926)., quoting Bolles, Pennsylvania: Province & State (1899) 113.

[65] In The Excellent Priviledge of Liberty & Property Being the Birth-Right of the Free-Born Subjects of England, Penn wrote: "Generally all Monopolies are against the great charter because they are against the Liberty and Freedom of the Subject, and against the Law of the Land." William Penn, The Excellent Priviledge of Liberty and Property Being the Birthright of the Free-born Subjects of England (1687), excerpts reprinted in A.E. Dick Howard, The Road from Runnymede: Magna Carta and Constitutionalism in America 413–25 (1968).

[66] See John Brodhead, History of the State of New York 23 (1853).

[67] Id. at 60.

[68] Jonathan I. Israel, Dutch Primacy in World Trade, 1585–1740 109 (1989).

competitors failed, a third company—the New Netherland Company—was chartered by the States General in 1614. Four years later, the charter expired and the companies' monopoly privileges were absorbed by the Dutch West India Company (VOC).

Initially, Dutch trading companies were given no political powers (unlike their counterparts in Massachusetts and Virginia). But, in 1629 the VOC was given a 24-year trading monopoly along with considerable political powers such as making alliances, building forts, appointing and discharging governors and administering justice.[69] In a sense, the Dutch created an armed commercial monopoly intended to implement agricultural colonization of New Netherland, with New Amsterdam designated the exclusive trading point for export of local goods and imports to the settlers. To incentivize settlers to go to the new territory, they were deeded as much land as they might be able "properly to improve."[70]

Testable estates (transfer by will) were granted to Dutch "patroons" who succeeded in establishing a settlement outside of Manhattan with at least 50 adults.[71] Within each estate, the patroon had exclusive privileges to hunt, fish, fowl and grind grain. At first glance, the "feudal" aspect of the New Netherland settlements may seem at odds with the "modern" values of the 16th and 17th century Dutch, who probably more than any other group in Europe had left the "feudalism" of the medieval period (with the exception of city states on the Italian peninsula). The explanation is that land was scarce in Holland; the newly wealthy Dutch merchants and investors—who were greatly profiting from the East Asia trade—had little opportunity to buy land in Holland to improve their social status and otherwise enjoy themselves. The opportunity lay rather in the "boundless estates" spread along "the magnificent rivers of New

---

[69] Brodhead, supra note 66, at 135; Mariana Griswold Van Rensselaer, History of the City of New York in the Seventeenth Century 91 (1909).

[70] Brodhead, supra note 66, at 194. Patroons also had "free liberty of hunting and fowling." Exploration was encouraged: ["Whoever should] discover any shores, bays, or other fit places for erecting fisheries, or the making of salt ponds," was promised an absolute and exclusive property right in discoveries.

[71] 1 Van Rensselaer, supra note 69, at 91. Patroons did not multiply and flourish as the VOC expected. Only one patroonship succeeded and survived—the Van Rensselaers. Id. at 93. Servants and other workers were bound to remain in service to the patroon for 10 years.

Netherland: [t]he lord of the Amsterdam counting-house might now become the lord of the New Netherland manor."[72]

While patroons were prohibited from manufacturing cloth or other goods, they were free to trade along the Atlantic coast from Newfoundland to Florida, so long as cargoes were brought to New Amsterdam.[73] Patroons also were free to trade within New Netherland, except for furs whose trade had been reserved for the VOC. The monopoly of the Indian fur trade failed, however, when individual traders secured the best fur trade and patronage of the Indians.[74]

A last note on the Dutch colony. It significantly differed from its English cousins in one important respect: it was the Company authorities in Amsterdam that embraced a policy of free trade, while the New Amsterdam authorities (supported by colonial interests) often proposed trade restraints and monopoly privileges, as discussed later in the chapter.

Our discussion so far has focused on initial trading company monopoly privileges, particularly in the early years of the Virginia settlement where the founding trading company's activities were formally ended after several decades. The Massachusetts colonies of Plymouth and Massachusetts Bay present a more complex picture of trading company privileges that survived several decades longer than in Virginia; monopolies in the fur and Indian trades are examples. These monopolies—although originally granted in company charters—are examined in section 3 below, together with grants of monopoly privileges by royal and colonial authorities who became the ultimate decisionmakers in colonial trade matters.

In sum, the system of joint stock companies holding a monopoly of the trade of a colony, so common among the European nations of this period, lasted only a few generations in the case of the English and Dutch colonies in America. They ended because of economic conditions and opposition from English and colonial critics. But monopolies did not disappear with the joint stock companies.

---

[72] Brodhead, supra note 66, at 199.

[73] 1 Van Rensselaer, supra note 69, at 92.

[74] William B. Weeden, Economic and Social History of New England 1620–1789 179 (1891), citing O'Callaghan, New Neth. 340, 456 (1846).

2. *English trading monopolies and mercantilism*

A more comprehensive system of English control of colonial trade followed in the aftermath of joint stock company monopolies. The policy was intended to give England a monopoly of colonial output and, conversely, the colonists a monopoly to meet English demand.[75] Although the policy manifested with the first American settlements, it was strengthened in the last half of the 17th century with passage of the Navigation Acts.

The English trading system often is described as mercantilist. Rather than a coherent or consistent theory, mercantilism was more a shared perception among those who controlled northern and western Europe from the 16th to the 18th centuries that foreign trade should serve the interests of government in a symbiotic relationship.[76] Yet, in practice, mercantilism varied over time and country, as different measures often benefited private rather than public interests.[77] Certain common objectives, however, can be seen: 1) increase home country power and wealth; 2) create a large mercantile marine; 3) develop domestic industry and provide full employment by keeping rival foreign goods out of the home market and securing as wide a market as possible for domestic goods in foreign countries; and 4) facilitate home production to avoid dependence on foreign sources of supply, particularly in time of war.[78]

The English authorities used a variety of means (commands, recommendations and money) to pressure the colonists to produce staples and agricultural goods, like tobacco, and then ship them exclusively to England for consumption or reexport from England in order to improve the English balance of trade.[79] This was a cardinal mercantilist principle[80] that continued to be followed well after the initial settlements. For example, authorities in England in 1670-1674

---

[75] Andrews, supra note 48, at 15.

[76] McCusker and Menard, supra note 39, at 46.

[77] Chester Wright, supra note 49, at 49.

[78] Id. at 49-50.

[79] One scholar concludes, however, that nothing of real importance ever came of these demands. See Andrews, supra note 48, at 13, citing Records of the Virginia Company, I, 266-267; II, 36; Records of the Massachusetts Bay Company, I, 388, 403; Calendar State papers, Colonial, 1660-1668; §84; Andrews, British Committees, pp. 119-120, 124, 125, 128, 129.

[80] Id. at 11-13.

demanded cultivation in America of a wide variety of products for export to the mother country.

The protection of English home markets was reinforced by discouragement—and even prohibitions—of colonial manufacture of goods that could compete with those manufactured in England or other colonies. As we will see below, the restriction on colonial manufacturing had implications for colonial grants of monopoly, which sometimes accompanied subsidies and other encouragements of colonial manufacturing. English merchants with monopoly privileges objected to colonial monopoly grants aimed at incentivizing colonial trade. The English system also was intended to ensure that the colonists purchased imported goods only through English merchants who were granted exclusive trading privileges.

To be fair, the restrictions benefited not only English interests, but also colonial ones. For example, the restrictions on non-English vessels protected early colonial shipping from Dutch competition and presented New Englanders with a significant opportunity to make profits building ships. Indeed, by 1775 a third of British-owned shipping was said to be of colonial build.[81] Yet, even with the comparative advantages in colonial shipbuilding, there would have been only a very limited market for New England ships absent the trade restrictions of the Navigation Acts; As Daniel Vickers concludes: "Although the Navigation Acts were designed to benefit Britain alone, colonies that had successfully replicated the socioeconomic structure of the mother country, and built some mercantile muscle of their own, reaped many of the same rewards."[82]

Implementation of English mercantilist policies in the first half of the 17th century was often unsuccessful. For example, despite royal commands, Virginia planters continued for many years to send their tobacco to the Netherlands, in both English and Dutch ships that went directly from the colony to Dutch ports.[83] Later in the 17th century (from 1651 to 1673), conflicts with the Dutch—and the initial failures to restrict the American colonies to their appointed role in the trading system—prompted the authorities in London to enact a

---

[81] Id. at 89.

[82] Daniel Vickers, The Northern Colonies: Economy and Society, 1600-1775, in 1 Cambridge Economic History of the United States 245 (Stanley L. Engerman and Robert E. Gallman eds. 1996).

[83] Andrews, supra note 48, at 17. See also 1 Bruce, supra note 51, at 346 and 363.

series of measures further restricting colonial imports and exports—the much resented Navigation Acts. These measures, among others, provided that: 1) colonial goods had to be carried directly to England in English ships;[84] 2) foreign merchants were excluded from dealing directly in the commerce of the English colonies; they could engage in colonial trade only through merchants resident in England; and 3) certain "enumerated" commodities produced in the colonies could be exported only to England or other English colonies.[85]

Despite the Navigation Acts, implementation of the English mercantilist system was never complete with respect to the American colonies. Enforcement of the Navigation Acts weakened as the center of gravity of colonial administration shifted from England to America.[86] The consensus among historians is that the Navigation Acts and associated trade restrictions did not entirely achieve their objectives. Colonials employed several strategies to avoid or moderate the restrictive influence of the Navigation Acts. They imported goods from the Continent either directly or through the non-English possessions in the West Indies. They shipped products directly to the Continent. And the successors or heirs of Virginia planters, who defeated a trading company monopoly for tobacco in the 1620s, continued to defy English trade restrictions by shipping their tobacco directly to the Netherlands in both English and Dutch ships.[87] Last, colonists commonly disobeyed official strictures—all a century before the Boston Tea Party. They smuggled goods to and from the French West Indies islands.[88] To be sure, smuggling probably was motivated more by a desire for profits than by an ideological opposition to monopoly, which is true more generally: American

[84] These were defined as vessels that were English-built and owned, commanded by an English captain and manned by a crew three-quarters of whom were English sailors; "English" was further defined as "only his Majesty's subjects of England, Ireland, and the Plantations."

[85] "Enumerated" goods included sugar, tobacco, cotton, indigo, ginger and various dyewoods. Walton and Shepherd, supra note 40, at 66–68.

[86] Dickerson, supra note 14, at 173–74. The Board of Trade initially sent directions to colonial governors, councils and chief law officers. Over time, however, colonial assemblies usurped the chief functions of governors and councils and made law officers dependent on colonial legislatures for their salaries and expenses. Id.

[87] Andrews, supra note 48, at 17. See also 1 Bruce, supra note 51, at 346 and 363.

[88] See Wright, supra note 49, at 125.

colonists often condemned monopoly when it was in their economic interest to do so. It is doubtful that popular colonial objections to monopoly were invariably expressions of purely moral or intellectual indignation, as economic self-interest and opposition to monopoly often went hand in hand.

In sum, from the beginning in the early 17th century, the American colonies acted not so much as team players in the English mercantilist system, but more as independent actors who refused to follow the monopoly rules. Not only did they fail generally to produce goods only for England, but colonial authorities also encouraged the manufacture of competing goods as a form of import substitution and a source of needed revenue. This is discussed in the next section.

3. *Colonial grants of monopoly privileges*

Colonial authorities lacked the modern financial and administrative resources to ensure provision of all essential goods and services needed by the settlers. For example, local taxation powers and issuance of bonds were generally unavailable. Thus, for community needs colony-wide authorities often turned to private actors—many of whom were connected to government personnel through social and economic ties. The modern distinction between the public and private worlds was not as clearly drawn in the 17th and 18th centuries. Colonial authorities incentivized individual entrepreneurs, partnerships and even locally chartered joint-stock companies to establish everything from river ferries to iron manufacturing—often through monopoly grants. Local grain mills and blacksmith shops also were common recipients of monopoly privileges.[89]

Like the federal government, states and localities today, colonial authorities issued licenses and franchises to private parties for infrastructure projects like roads, bridges, ferries and inns.[90] And also like today, they granted what the European Union would call "state aids" or subsidies to encourage production of agricultural products,

[89] McCusker and Menard, supra note 39, at 342.

[90] McCusker and Menard distinguish between "public" and "mixed" (public and private) enterprises. The distinction should not obscure the fact, however, that (attempts to create) monopolies, even for a short term, frequently if not ordinarily, were motivated by both public interests and the private interests of the monopoly holders.

manufacture of goods and extraction of resources. Importantly for our purposes, these licenses and state aids often were accompanied by an ancillary grant of monopoly or exclusive trading privileges, typically for a defined time period.[91] These privileges were intended to incentivize private investment and are discussed below.

This approach applied to all or most of the colonies, with one exception: the Dutch colony in New Netherland. After the Dutch West India Company (VOC) relinquished its own fur trading monopoly in 1639, the VOC authorities in the home country embraced free trade principles and rejected monopolies proposed by the colonial authorities. The Dutch authorities in the Netherlands appear more consistent in their condemnation of monopoly (during the short period of their term in New Netherland) than the English colonies. For example, the VOC authorities in Amsterdam refused to grant monopolies for potash, bricks and salt works, announcing a strong general condemnation of monopolies:

> "The grants we not only entirely disapprove, but require that you will not give one single grant more hereafter, as it is in our opinion a very pernicious management, principally so in a new and budding State, whose population and welfare can not be promoted but through general benefits and privileges, in which every one who might be inclined to settle in such a country, either as a merchant or a mechanic, may participate."[92]

Price controls on bread, beer, wine and other provisions were likewise rejected, because they unduly hampered the individual in his pursuit of profit.[93]

What drove this Dutch opposition to monopoly? The quotation above suggests the answer: the principal objective was to attract more settlers to the colony, which meant ensuring the widest possible latitude in economic affairs.[94] This pragmatic reason contrasts with any deep-seated Dutch principles about individual

---

[91] See Oscar and Mary Handlin, Commonwealth - A Study of the Role of Government in the American Economy: Massachusetts, 1774-1861 78 (1947).

[92] Joel Munsell, The Annals of Albany Volume IV 88 (1850), quoting Albany Records Volume IV 99. See also 1 Dorfman, supra note 53, at 76. See also 1 Van Rensselaer, supra note 69, at 437.

[93] Harold C. Syrett, supra note 50, at 543.

[94] See id. at 543-50.

rights, an abstract theory of economic freedom or a Dutch Magna Carta. As Harold Syrett summarized: "the Company ... looked on the New World as the proverbial land of opportunity for individuals with the requisite amount of initiative."[95] Monopoly ran counter to the articulated goals of opportunity and initiative.

Like the English, settlers in New Netherland claimed the privileges and rights of their home country. But, ironically, unlike the English settlers, the Dutch claimed monopoly privileges as freeborn Dutch citizens! For example, New Netherland bakers cited the home country Dutch practice of restrictions on entry and price controls, among other economic regulations.[96] In a sense, the colonial bakers wanted a guild-like system that accredited bakers working on a planned schedule and selling bread at prices negotiated with the authorities. But the Dutch bakers had to wait until they were part of the English colony of New York before they attained that objective—thanks to their enhanced political position when leading Dutch bakers rose through the ranks of municipal service to attain high office.[97]

Let us look at a selective summary of colonial monopoly grants and policy in three areas: i) infrastructure, staple goods and extraction of resources, ii) import substitution and iii) inventions and author works. The summary is intended to provide a flavor of colonial monopoly grants, opposition to them and their successes and failures.

i. Infrastructure

We begin with those colonial monopoly grants that are probably the least controversial today—monopoly grants in connection with the building and operation of infrastructure projects like roads, bridges and ferries. These were common in colonial times. Public ferries were established in Virginia as early as 1640 with a concession for life to Henry Hawley to operate a ferry at the mouth

---

[95] See id. at 549.

[96] See Simon Middleton, How It Came that the Bakers Bake No Bread: A Struggle for Trade Privileges in Seventeenth-Century New Amsterdam, 58 William and Mary Q. 347, 361 (2001).

[97] Id. at 372. In 1801, New York bakers demanded an end to the regulation of baking and the freedom to charge whatever the market would bear for their bread. Id. at 350.

of the Southampton River, on condition that he charge only a penny for each passenger.[98]

Many if not most of these projects concerned public services that were considered legitimate monopolies under English law as a "common right" or a "prerogative of the King." Rates, service obligations and other terms of trade for these types of services were generally regulated by the authorities. Today, many of these colonial grants would be considered legitimate public utilities or public services.[99] As discussed later in Chapter Four, however, monopoly and exclusive rights concerning infrastructure like ferries and bridges generated important constitutional issues in the 19th century.

ii. Staples and extraction of resources

Grants of monopoly and exclusive trading privileges—often with a fixed term—were given to encourage local supply of foodstuffs, household items and other goods viewed as important to the settlers. These included, among others, salt, flour, corn, sugar, paper and stoneware.[100] For example, in the 1720s New York granted a monopoly for its first sugar refinery.[101]

What was considered an appropriate subject for government encouragement might strike some modern observers as rather catholic in reach. However, there were observable demand and supply dynamics. For example, **beer** was considered a sufficient necessity to support a monopoly grant. In 1652, George Fletcher in Virginia obtained a monopoly for brewing in wooden vessels for a period of fourteen years. In 1750, an exclusive right to manufacture **sperm whale candles** for fourteen years was granted in Massachusetts.[102] In the same year, Massachusetts granted a monopoly to a **canvas** manufacturer.[103] Monopoly (or monopsony) grants were given to buyers of **Indian corn** in order to counter the sellers' "unreasonable prices." In 1638, facing a scarcity of corn and fearing that "if every man have liberty to truck with the Indians" the Indians would charge

---

[98] 1 Bruce, supra note 51 at 421, citing General Court Entries, Robinson Transcripts, p. 14.

[99] For further discussion, see Chapter Five.

[100] Stuart Bruchey, The Roots of American Economic Growth, 1607-1861: An Essay in Social Causation 70-71 (1965).

[101] McCusker and Menard, supra note 39, at 343.

[102] Weeden, supra note 74, at 654-55.

[103] Id. at 495.

"unreasonable prices," Massachusetts authorities gave William Pynchon a monopoly of the corn trade along the Connecticut River. In return, he was obliged to resell the corn at a fixed maximum price. The scheme ultimately failed, which illustrates an important point: it was not always the colonists who opposed monopoly; London often said no for its own reasons. For example, the Board of Trade resisted attempts to monopolize the Indian trade,[104] and in 1729 a series of ten colonial acts concerning trade with the Indians was disallowed.[105]

Let us turn to some of the most economically important goods, which as we shall see provided a greater rationale for affording monopoly privileges: salt, flour mills, and coal and iron. We will then look at two industries whose legal monopoly privileges not only generated considerable opposition, but also ultimately failed to sustain monopolies in the face of economic conditions: fishing and furs.

Salt production was a frequent subject of monopoly grants, not unlike other places and periods of history like imperial China.[106] In 1609, investors in the new colony in Massachusetts received a monopoly of salt manufacturing.[107] Later, the General Court of Massachusetts Bay Colony granted S. Winslow a ten year monopoly to mine and manufacture salt.[108] John Winthrop later was granted a monopoly for twenty-one years for making salt by a process of his own.[109] The Virginia Assembly in 1662 encouraged Colonel Edmund Scarborough to produce salt with an embargo on imported salt, in addition to payments and other incentives.[110] In 1691, Connecticut, in face of a salt shortage attributed to war in Europe, offered a ten year monopoly of salt manufacture (except for small amounts made at home for family use).[111]

Flour production was favored with monopoly grants, often leading to significant political conflict. The saga of the New York "Bolting Acts" is a prime example of rural opposition to what was perceived as monopoly grants favoring urban merchants. In 1680, Governor Andros granted a group of New York City merchants a

---

[104] Dickerson, supra note 14, at 241.

[105] George II, 2 Privy Council Register, 97–106 (1729).

[106] See Hawk, supra note 1, at 25.

[107] Bernard Bailyn, The New England Merchants in the Seventeenth Century 19 (1955).

[108] Weeden, supra note 74, at 171.

[109] Id. at 198.

[110] Bugbee, supra note 35, at 58–59.

[111] Id. at 69.

monopoly of making, bolting and packing flour for export from the province (the "Bolting Acts"). The Bolting Acts so benefited Manhattan through its millers, bakers, coopers, merchants and shipowners that flour barrels and windmill sails remain on the official city seal today.[112] The city enjoyed the monopoly for fourteen years,[113] but it was finally repealed after vigorous rural opposition.[114] New York City merchants in turn protested the repeal, decrying its harm to tax-paying city residents who depended on the bolting trade protected by the monopoly. According to the city merchants, the livelihood of two thirds of the city—which paid from 20 to 30% of provincial taxes—was sacrificed for some thirty bolters in rural districts—all in the name of "libertisme of Trade."[115] The city merchants complained further that repeal of the monopoly had reduced the quality of New York flour, thus enabling Pennsylvania flour to supplant it in West Indian markets. In 1700, the New York City Corporation passed a retaliatory ordinance levying an "Imposition" on all flour and "harde bread" brought into the city; New York farmers reacted by refusing to pay taxes to the royal governor until he secured the city ordinance's repeal. As Carl Bridenbaugh concludes, the "incident has considerable significance as an indication of the widespread mercantilist views of New York merchants, and of growing bad feeling between country and town."[116] Indeed, it was a 17th century version of modern tensions between upstate New York and New York City. It also shows that the self-interest of one class (in this case, merchants) could trump the general colonial aversion to monopoly.

Two other groups benefiting from colonial monopoly or exclusive trading privileges were operators of **flour mills and sawmills**.[117] Indeed, they were among the most numerous recipients of monopoly grants. As early as 1621, Governor Yeardley in Virginia built the first windmill in America.[118] By 1645, there were a sufficient number of windmills in Virginia to require official price regulation

---

[112] See 2 Van Rensselaer, supra note 69, at 214–15.

[113] Carl Bridenbaugh, Cities in the Wilderness - The First Century of Urban Life in America 1625-1742 36 (2013).

[114] Id. at 183.

[115] "Since the repeal of the act] The People Desert . . . [and] the Buildings ... fall to Decay." Quoted in Bridenbaugh, id.

[116] Id. at 20.

[117] See Weeden, supra note 74, at 63.

[118] 2 Bruce, supra note 51, at 487–88.

following complaints that local monopolies were charging the planters excessive milling fees. A new law then limited the prices that millers could charge for grinding.[119] Two more examples are from Boston and South Carolina. In 1643, Boston offered the exclusive right of grinding corn for the public to the builders of a tide mill. In 1712, South Carolina promised an eight-year monopoly for the first sawmill built in the province, and a five-year monopoly for the first grain mill.[120]

Monopolies or exclusive trading privileges for **coal and iron** products and processes were often granted. In Massachusetts in 1637, a monopoly was granted to Abraham Shaw for "one half the coles or yronstone on any common ground."[121] In 1641, a monopoly of iron smelting was granted for two years.[122] A monopoly for making bar iron was granted by the General Court on the condition that it be sold under £20 per ton.[123] In 1645, the General Court granted a twenty one year monopoly of all ironmaking, with the limitation that the holders had the right to export only such quantities of their products as exceeded what the "inhabitants shall have neede, and use of, for their service, to be bought and paid for by the said inhabitants."[124] This ironmaking venture nevertheless failed after only seven years—material costs were high, equipment had to be transported 3,000 miles from England and labor costs were prohibitive (for example, skilled ironworkers were nonexistent in Massachusetts and difficult to find even in England). In 1652, the company went bankrupt. This is another example of monopoly failure (despite government privileges) in the face of challenging conditions for supplying colonial needs.

One more example concerns an attempted monopolization of ship masts under the grant of a ten-year monopoly of all naval stores production in both the Massachusetts Bay and Plymouth colonies.[125] The scheme never materialized because the necessary monopolies on both sides of the Atlantic could not be maintained. In England,

---

[119] Subsequently, millers were required to keep scales and weights on hand to ensure accurate measurements in order to avoid evasion.

[120] Victor S. Clark, History of Manufactures in the United States 50–51 (1929).

[121] Weeden, supra note 74, at 173.

[122] Id.

[123] Id. at 178.

[124] Bailyn, supra note 107, at 64–67.

[125] Id. at 133–34.

rivalries among governmental and business groups were too intense and the system of awarding contracts too transparent to allow long-term monopolies. In New England, the mechanisms necessary to enforce a monopoly were not yet effective, as political influence was lacking and the timber trade in New Hampshire was still competitive and loosely organized.

As mentioned above, the initial investment hopes for North American ventures centered on gold deposits and a northern passage to China and India and the trade in silks, spices and other goods that this would bring. These were never found; investors turned to fishing and fur as alternative sources of profits. Both received monopoly privileges that not only generated considerable opposition, but also ultimately failed in the face of economic conditions and successful competition from traders.

Fishing was viewed as the most important and profitable resource in New England. Even before the first settlements, John Smith visited New England and in a widely read pamphlet described how the proper management of New England's fisheries could become the basis of a thriving colonial economy.[126] In 1619, the charter for the New England Company organized by Ferdinando Gorges[127] included a fishing monopoly granted by the Privy Council in the form of an injunction that all the king's subjects not "visit, frequent, trade or adventure to traffick into or from the said territories, lands, rivers, and places aforesaid" without written consent.[128]

As discussed earlier, the Virginia Company previously had fished in New England waters under its charter that included reciprocal rights for it and the New England Company. The Virginia Company submitted a complaint about the New England Company monopoly to the Privy Council, which in turn sent it to a House of Commons committee chaired by the anti-monopolist Edward Coke. This fueled a broader Parliamentary debate about royal privileges and monopolies[129] which culminated in the 1624 Statute of

---

[126] Id. at 5–7.

[127] The New England Council differed considerably from other early colonial companies. Unlike a trading company, the New England Council had no governor, deputy governor or quarter courts.

[128] Andrews, supra note 48, at 324–25.

[129] Herbert Osgood, The American Colonies in the Seventeenth Century 3 (1904).

Monopolies discussed earlier. But the New England fishing dispute continued for another fifteen years. Finally, monopoly opponents in Parliament prevailed in 1639 when the charter for the Massachusetts Bay colony was amended to provide for open trade for the New England fishing industry.[130]

The New England **fur trade**, like fishing, also was expected to yield high returns on investment and generate needed revenue for settlers.[131] Yet the fur trade is another example of monopoly grants that were sought and received, but also ultimately failed in practice—as the Pilgrims at Plymouth found to their dismay. Around 1627, eight prominent Pilgrim leaders received a six-year monopoly of the Plymouth Colony's fur trade in exchange for assumption of the Pilgrims' debt to English merchants.[132] For the first several years, the Plymouth fur trade flourished, despite complaints against the monopoly by competitors in the Puritan Massachusetts Bay Colony to the north. The Puritans and other competitors continued to trade with the Indians, despite the Pilgrim's monopoly grant, leading to bloodshed among the devout trading factions. Puritans complained that Pilgrim efforts to protect their monopoly "have brought us all, and the gospel under a common approach, of cutting one another's throats for beaver."[133] Despite the martial attempts to enforce the legal monopoly, the Pilgrim fur trade collapsed by the end of the 1630s; it was never revived.

Opposition to monopoly grants for fur trading ultimately prevailed; two examples reveal the forces at work. Sir Richard Saltonstall and others petitioned for a monopoly of trading posts at points farther north than those already established. And in the previous year, the Massachusetts Bay Company had entertained a proposition from the Commissioners of the United Colonies to form a stock company privileged with monopoly of the Indian trade for ten years. In the face of vigorous opposition (and practical realities of competition), both efforts came to nothing. Other attempts to monopolize fur trading also failed. In the 1640s, fur trading was still

---

130 See Andrews, supra note 48 at 324–25: a clause was especially inserted saving to all the king's subjects the "liberty of fishing as well in the sea as in the creeks of the said province and the priviledge of salting and drying of their fish and drying of their nets upon the shore."

131 1 Weeden, supra note 74, at 129–30.

132 Bailyn, supra note 107, at 23–24.

133 Quoted in 1 Dorfman, supra note 53, at 32–33.

important in Massachusetts, but it was reported that too much competition had forced fur traders to turn to husbandry.[134]

Another example of failed monopoly grants for fur trading is found in New Netherland.[135] The Dutch in the 17th century reputedly were the foremost merchants of the time, but their carefully organized fur monopoly at Renssalierwyck failed when traders outside Dutch jurisdiction secured the patronage of the Indians.[136] For example, in 1650 the New Netherland authorities complained to the commissioners of the New England Confederation that William Pynchon was endangering trade by paying the Indians excessive prices for furs; the New England commissioners replied that trade should be open.[137]

Protests against fur monopolies came not only from actual or potential competitors. Monopoly grants could also impose additional taxes and restraints on the monopoly grantee itself. In Connecticut,[138] opposition came from the recipient, William Pynchon, a wealthy landowner in England and New England and an official of the Connecticut colony. In 1638, the Connecticut authorities "gave" him the monopoly of the fur trade in his area. As he already enjoyed effective control of the fur trade from his strategic settlement at Springfield, Pynchon saw little reason for a state-authorized monopoly, especially when it entailed payment of a tax—although he coyly cited God's aversion to monopoly as the reason for his objection: "the public goode and the liberty of free men to make a monopoly of trade . . . I hope the Lord in his mercy will keep me from coveting any unlawful gaines; or [consent to] any man's hinderance where God doth not hinder them." Here we see the not uncommon blend of self-interest (lower taxes) and invocation of high principle (no monopolies).

iii. The challenges of colonial import substitution

Colonial measures to encourage production, including grants of monopoly privileges, went well beyond satisfaction of local demand for foodstuffs and extraction of resources like iron ore. Throughout the early colonial period and then accelerating during the 18th

---

134 1 Weeden, supra note 74, at 147.

135 Id. at 179.

136 See O'Callaghan, New Neth., pp. 340, 456.

137 1 Dorfman, supra note 53, at 50. [Footnote omitted]

138 Id. at 49.

century, colonial assemblies and other authorities encouraged local manufacture of an increasingly broad range of goods, notably textiles. In modern terms, these colonial monopoly grants reflected a policy of import substitution, that is, having the colonies make rather than import goods. Of course, a colonial policy of import substitution flew in the face of the English mercantilist system discussed above: the colonies were to make and sell (and then only to England) goods that England (or its other colonies) did not provide on its own.

We next examine three aspects of colonial import substitution and monopoly: i) colonial measures to encourage domestic production (with emphasis on monopoly privileges as incentives); ii) English opposition; and iii) the success (or failure) of import substitution in light of the English resistance and economic conditions.

i. Colonial measures like state aids to encourage domestic manufacturing and production

Despite English disapproval, colonial authorities gave direct assistance to local artisans and entrepreneurs in the form of subsidies, loans, land grants, premiums to meet quality standards[139] as well as other forms of state aid, including the provision of raw materials.[140] Monopoly privileges sometimes accompanied these state aid schemes. For example, in 1724 a monopoly for ten years was granted to a weaver in Connecticut. Massachusetts granted a monopoly in 1726 to a producer of "good even thread, well drove, of good bright color, being wrought wholly of good strong water-rotted hemp."[141]

---

[139] Premiums were awarded to raise the standard of manufactures by rewarding goods of exceptional or improved quality. For example, Maryland in 1682 began to offer premiums on the best manufactured pieces of linen. For a short time, similar premiums were offered to encourage manufacture of woolens. A less successful effort is found later in 1759 when Virginia set up a public corporation to encourage arts and manufactures by means of premiums. Clark, supra note 120, at 38. Funding was to be furnished through private subscriptions. The corporation was empowered to grant prizes for new discoveries or the introduction of new industries. An amendment later provided that specified premiums should be offered for wine and silk made in Virginia. The law was not a success, probably because the trustees were not able to raise sufficient subscriptions.

[140] See id. at 31--33.

[141] 2 Weeden, supra note 74, at 495-6.

The most common colonial subsidies were for manufacture of textiles, particularly linen and to a lesser extent woolen articles. Bounties were offered to encourage domestic spinning and weaving to replace imports of cloth. In 1640, Massachusetts gave a bounty on cloth made in the colony from native wool. In 1662, Virginia gave a bounty of five pounds of tobacco for every yard of woolen cloth made in the province and later raised the bounty to six pounds for every yard of woolen or mixed fabric of home manufacture.[142] During most of the period from 1671 to 1776, Maryland offered bounties for raising hemp and flax.[143] State aids, like today, were not always successful. For example, Pennsylvania repealed its bounties on hemp production because they failed to generate manufacture.[144]

ii. English opposition

A colonial policy of import substitution, of course, flew in the face of English demands that the colonies make and sell (and then only to England and English other colonies) goods that England (or its other colonies) did not provide. English restrictions on colonial manufacturing were part of the mercantile system that sought to secure from the colonies raw materials or finished products needed by England, opposing colonial manufacture of goods or commodities that would compete with English products.[145] Thus, it is not at all surprising that colonial measures seeking to encourage specific industries were disallowed by the London authorities. There are numerous examples. An attempt by Virginia in 1680 to aid shipbuilding, and another in 1682 to promote the manufacture of cloth, were disallowed.[146] Vetoing a Pennsylvania statute of 1706, the Board of Trade remarked: "It cannot be expected that encouragement should be given by law to the making any manufactures made in England in the plantations, it being against the advantage of England."[147] A British law in 1699 prohibited export of wool, woolen yarn or woolen cloth from one colony to another or to a foreign port, although the law probably had little effect given

[142] Clark, supra note 120, at 34 [Footnotes omitted].

[143] See id. at 33. See also Newton Mereness, Maryland as a Proprietary Province 121 (1901).

[144] Clark, supra note 120, at 71-72.

[145] Wright, supra note 49, at 88.

[146] See Chapter One.

[147] Bruchey, supra note 100, at 70-71.

the lack of colonial supply.[148] In 1732, colonial export of hats was prohibited for the benefit of English manufacturers.

English laws and regulations also indirectly restricted colonial manufacturing. For example, customs duties permitted sale of European manufactures in the colonies at prices lower than competing local products. In 1750, England also restricted the free emigration of skilled artisans, machines and tools used in the wool and silk industries, repeating the same for cotton and linen in 1774.[149]

iii. Import substitution generally failed more from economic conditions than from English opposition

The colonial efforts to bring about import substitution (and the ancillary monopoly grants) generally failed not so much because of English opposition or a colonial aversion to monopoly, but more because of local economic conditions.[150] Indeed, after 1750 we hear less of these colonial grants to encourage local production and manufacturing. [151]

The Massachusetts Bay colony provides a good example of the failure of a general policy of import substitution. The major thrust of the General Court's program was to reduce imports, the bulk of which were English manufactured goods. Clothing, shoes, boots, glass and ironware all seemed likely candidates for local manufacture, both because they made up a large share of the total value of imports and because New England possessed the necessary raw materials to produce them. The colonial authorities adopted a broad variety of import substitution measures: monopolies of local markets, land grants, bounties, tax incentives, freedom from military obligations for workers, and even a relaxation of religious regulations.[152] Despite all these measures, the effort to industrialize early New England failed because local economic conditions were not yet favorable. Manufacturing was impeded by scarce and expensive labor, shortages of capital and a small domestic market.[153] To

---

148 Wright, supra note 49, at 88.

149 Id. at 89.

150 Clark concludes that the temporary and local effect of colonial monopolies to encourage manufacture and production may have been at times considerable, but not permanent and general. Clark, supra note 120, at 52-53.

151 See id. at 52-53.

152 McCusker and Menard, supra note 39, at 96.

153 Id. at 97.

cite just one example, a Massachusetts iron manufacturer that received a variety of assistance (monopoly privileges, land grants and tax exemptions) failed after several reorganizations because of high labor costs.[154]

4. *Inventions (patents)*[155] *and author works (copyrights)*

From early in the period, colonial authorities granted exclusive rights to inventors (patents), but often for short terms. Exclusive rights for author works (copyrights) came later during the revolutionary period, with one exception discussed below.

a. Patents

Given the later debates about the power of the federal government to grant patents and copyrights under the federal constitution (discussed in the next chapter), it is important to remember that from the beginning of the settlements, products or processes resulting from invention received privileges as an exception to the general principle disfavoring monopoly.

As early as 1644, Massachusetts excepted inventions from its general ban on monopoly: "No monopolies shall be granted or allowed amongst us, but of such new Inventions as yet are profitable to ye Countrie, & that for a short time."[156] Only two years later in 1646, Massachusetts issued the first patent in the colonies to Joseph Jenks for improved sawmills and scythes. The term was fourteen years. Bruce Bugbee reports an outpouring of Massachusetts patents in the 1640s and 1650s.[157] But not all these patents had the complete exclusivity of modern patents. For example, the General Court granted a patent for a salt-making process to ensure a larger and cheaper supply of salt for consumers and the fishing industry, but the grant provided that during its ten-year term all other salt-making processes were to remain open to public use and other persons were free to import salt.

---

[154] 1 Dorfman, supra note 53, at 46.

[155] As mentioned above, the term "patent" was commonly used in the early 17th century to denote any royal or legislative grant of monopoly privileges, whether or not it involved an invention. Only near the end of the eighteenth century did the term "patent" begin to have a precise and technical meaning.

[156] Quoted in Bugbee, supra note 35, at 61.

[157] Id. at 60.

In 1672, a Connecticut statute declared that "there shall be no Monopolies granted or allowed amongst us, but of such new Inventions as shall be judged profitable for the Country, and that for such time as the General Court shall judge meet."[158] In the 18th century, Connecticut granted a number of awards—most of them with exclusive rights—for industrial processes, including for the manufacture of linseed oil, canvas, steel, potash and glass, with terms ranging from seven to twenty years.[159]

In 1714, New York issued a seven-year grant for "certain New Inventions by [De Graeuw] ... to facilitate the catching of porpoises and fish."[160] Maryland in 1770 granted two patents for ten years concerning threshing machines. William Penn adopted a highly favorable position toward inventions, announcing that "the governor and Provincial Council shall erect and order all publick schools, and encourage and reward the authors of useful sciences and laudable inventions ...."[161]

Although South Carolina had a generic patent provision—the only one in the colonies before the Revolution—South Carolina also granted patents by legislative action like other colonies.[162] South Carolina's first patent was awarded in 1691 for a pendulum engine (but only for a two-year period). The patent terms were quite advanced for the period, providing for licensing and specifying a procedure for legal remedy against infringement.[163]

Colonial patents were granted not only to encourage local production, but also to facilitate transfer of technology into the colony.[164] This echoes the modern use of patents to facilitate transfer of foreign technology, as seen in the case of Japan for several decades after World War II.[165]

---

158 Quoted in Bugbee, supra note 35, at 61.

159 Id. at 69.

160 Id. at 70.

161 Quoted in Bugbee, supra note 35, at 69. But see Clark, supra note 120, at 52.

162 Dotan Oliar, Making Sense of the Intellectual Property Clause: Promotion of Progress as a Limitation on Congress's Intellectual Property Power, 94 Georgetown L.J. 1771, 1803–05 (2006).

163 Bugbee, supra note 35, at 75–76, 82.

164 See Clark, supra note 120, at 47–53.

165 See Akinori Uesugi, Transfer of Technology and Joint Ventures in Japan, in 1982 Fordham Corp. L. Inst. 347 (Barry Hawk ed. 1983).

Colonial patents were fewer in number than the approximately one thousand English patents granted during the same period,[166] although English patents covered the colonies, if so specified.[167] The colonies were predominantly agrarian societies with far less manufacturing than the mother country.[168] Moreover, the cost and time to obtain a colonial patent were greater than in England, making the perceived value of a colonial patent far less.[169] Importantly for later debate during the revolutionary period, there is little to no evidence suggesting that the colonists opposed patent monopoly grants more than their English counterparts. In both England and the colonies, patents were accepted as an exception to the antimonopoly principle.

Let us turn to copyrights which have a different history from colonial patents.

b. Copyrights

The Massachusetts Bay Colony issued the first and only copyright in the colonies before the Revolutionary era. Samuel Green was commissioned by the General Court to print a revised edition of the Massachusetts General Laws and Liberties. After Green published the edition at his own expense, he petitioned for compensation. In 1672, the General Court responded with a law granting him an exclusive right to print copies.[170] A year later, the

---

[166] Walterscheid, supra note 16, at 11.

[167] In 1717, Thomas Masters successfully recorded two English patents for inventions devised by his wife Sybella concerning the "Cleansing, curing & Refining of Indian Corn" and the "Working & W'eaving in a New method, Palmeta, Chip & Straw for covering hatts & Bonnetts." Bugbee, supra note 35, at 72. Both were granted for 14 years, the limit specified by the 1624 Statute of Monopolies, but their territorial scope included not only England but also "the Several plantations in America."

[168] Walterscheid, supra note 16, at 11.

[169] One indication of the relatively low value attached to patents is the fact that no record has been found of any litigation involving colonial patents of monopoly for invention in any colonial or English court. Id.

[170] The law provided in pertinent part:

> "that no printer shall print any more coppies then are agreed & paid for by the owner of the said coppie or coppies, nor shall he nor any other reprint or make sale of any of the same, without the said owners consent, upon the forfeiture and penalty of treble the whole charges of printing, & paper, &c., of the whole quantity paid for by the owner of the coppie, to the said owner or his assignes."

Quoted in Bugbee, supra note 35, at 65-67.

General Court clarified that the term of the grant was seven years. No other copyright has been found in Massachusetts or any other American colony prior to the Revolution. However, every state but Vermont passed a copyright law between 1783 and 1786.[171]

The absence of colonial copyrights contrasts with the English experience. During the 17th century, England passed laws for the purpose of regulating printed works. In 1710, the first true English copyright act became law—the Statute of Anne.[172] The statute was intended to prevent the piracy of printed works, which aimed to encourage the writing of useful books. Authors had the exclusive right to print their works for twenty-one years for existing books, and fourteen years for new books (with one 14-year right of renewal). It was not until the last quarter of the eighteenth century, however, that a common law property right in England clearly took hold.[173] This helps explain the absence of colonial copyrights before the revolutionary period.

This finishes our discussion of the strand of the colonial antimonopoly tradition that concerned government grants of monopoly privileges. As seen in later chapters, this strand and its concerns continued to animate legal and political debate into the 19th century. Since then, however, government grants of monopoly privileges have been replaced by dominant private firms as the principal target of opponents to monopoly—as discussed in Chapter Five.

In the remainder of this chapter, we will look at the historically older strand of the colonial antimonopoly tradition, an agglomeration of policies and forces concerned with an ill-defined group of practices, such as engrossing (cornering the market), forestalling and agreements to fix prices.

IV. "MONOPOLIZATION" PRACTICES

Colonial Americans used the terms "monopoly" and "monopolize" to describe any practices that appeared to corner or interfere with markets and raise prices.[174] Common law condemned

---

171 Friedman, supra note 3, at 256.

172 See Walterscheid, supra note 16, at 17–18.

173 Id. Common law courts had continued to hold that copyrights were perpetual at common law until the House of Lords decided that whatever may have been the case at common law, the Statute of Anne effectively limited the term for which copyright could be enforced at common law to a maximum of 28 years.

174 See Hawk, supra note 1, at 12–81.

them as forestalling, engrossing and price fixing agreements. As discussed more fully below, forestalling was buying goods from the farmer/producer for resale before the goods came to market; engrossing denoted cornering the market. Popular sentiment echoed these condemnations. A prospectus for the Virginia settlement promised investors that the colony would exclude "Monopolists, the very wrack of Merchandizing."[175] "Monopolists" were placed with "Papists" and "bad magistrates" in the forbidden category of excluded persons.[176] A colonial Dante would have put monopolists in the deepest level of hell.

It is important to note that these common law and colonial rules were directed at purely private conduct, unlike the rules concerning government grants of monopoly privileges discussed above. In that sense, the legal rules dealing with engrossing, forestalling and price fixing at first glance might be more easily viewed as precursors of modern antitrust law than Edward Coke's principle disfavoring royal monopoly grants. But critical differences remain between these "monopolizing" practices and modern antitrust infringements. The legal status and economic thinking about the "monopolistic" practices condemned in colonial times have developed quite differently since then. Forestalling is not a concern under modern antitrust law. Engrossing might be roughly analogized to monopolization in modern antitrust law, but they are not at all the same. For example, market or monopoly power is not required for engrossing. Price fixing agreements are treated as a separate category of restrictive agreements. In sum, there is nothing in colonial America (or indeed anywhere in the world before 1880) comparable to modern laws prohibiting and punishing private business conduct found to constitute "monopolization" (section 2 of the Sherman Act) or "abuse of dominant position" (Article 102 of the EU Treaty).[177]

Let us turn to colonial opposition to "monopolistic" practices broken down into engrossing, forestalling (and closed markets) and pricing (just prices, price controls and price fixing agreements).

---

[175] 1 Brown, supra note 57, at 260 quoting a document on the advantages of the Virginia colony addressed to the chief Treasurer of the Colony and the Merchants of the Moscovite and the East India Companies.

[176] It is not entirely clear whether the excluded "Monopolists" were ordinary merchants as distinguished from recipients of government monopoly privileges.

[177] See Hawk, supra note 1, at 20–25.

A. Engrossing

We begin with a caution. The historical record has been muddied by contemporaries and later commentators conflating three practices: forestalling, engrossing and regrating. All were condemned at common law as interference with (local) markets.[178] *Forestalling* was buying goods from the farmer/producer for resale before the goods came to the market, that is, diversion of goods in transit to the market. *Regrating* was buying in bulk and selling piecemeal in the same market. *Engrossing* also concerned buying a quantity of goods for resale, but with the added element of cornering the market.

Here we examine engrossing separately from forestalling (and regrating[179]). As mentioned above, the notion of engrossing as cornering the market has some similarity to the modern concept of monopolization.[180] By contrast, forestalling is directed more to the avoidance of designated or regular markets, with no attention given to quantities purchased or the forestaller's market position.

Philip Bruce argues that engrossing laws were even more important in the colonies than in England.[181] Colonial concerns about engrossing centered on imported goods and commodities. Imports from England rarely satisfied colonial demand; ships were potential bottlenecks for distribution of goods and commodities into the hinterlands. The colonial concern was not simply aimed at protecting local designated markets (discussed more fully below in connection with forestalling), but also concerned bulk buying from the ships and holding for resale when prices increased. For example, in 1677 colonists complained to London that engrossing of imported goods and commodities was so prevalent that it harmed the whole community.[182]

---

[178] For example, Georgia in the mid-18th century prohibited "forestalling, engrossing, and unjust exactions therein" — buying up goods before they reached the market or cornering the market. J.R.T. Hughes, Social Control in the Colonial Economy 127 (1976), quoting Charles Jones, The History of Georgia 479–85 (1883). See also 2 Bruce, supra note 51, at 358–63. This conflation of terms continues into the modern period. See Chapter Five.

[179] Going forward, we will treat forestalling and regrating together under the former term.

[180] As Nathan Dane explains, "Monopoly and engrossing differ only in this, that the first is by patent from the king, the other by act or the subject, between party and party." Nathan Dane, A General Abridgment and Digest of American law, with Occasional Notes and Comments 38 (1823).

[181] 2 Bruce, supra note 51, at 362.

[182] Id. at 361.

The difficulties in enforcement of laws against engrossing, as well as the competing interests involved, are seen in the efforts of Virginia and Massachusetts to combat engrossing of imports in the early years of their settlements.

In Virginia, a wide variety of measures to combat engrossing (and forestalling)[183] of imports were taken over the course of several decades. At first, the authorities were instructed to exercise unceasing vigilance to prevent bulk buying from the ships.[184] Penalties were severe: imprisonment, pillory (offender's head and hands put in wooden frame for public view) and forfeiture of goods. Despite the penalties, ships continued to make sales and future contracts before docking. Then in 1633, resale of certain goods was prohibited (shoes, stockings, and woolen and linen materials for shirts and sheets for servants), with the exception of resale to planters who resided in remote areas. But in 1644, the House of Burgesses repealed these measures with a declaration of free trade policy. The repeal came after powerful opposition of English merchants to engrossing (and forestalling) laws) as well as the increasing supply of imports from England.[185]

Ten years later, however, colonial opposition to bulk buying overrode objections of the English merchants: the House of Burgesses again required ships to transport cargo only to designated port markets to limit engrossing (and forestalling). But this phase of engrossing at Virginia ports ended in 1661 when the House of Burgesses—wishing to conform to the instructions from England but recognizing their impracticability—again passed a law requiring ships to make entry at Jamestown while granting them a license to engage in trade in any part of the colony.

Massachusetts provides another example of early colonial efforts to prevent engrossing of imported goods. In the first years of the Massachusetts Bay Colony,[186] goods were purchased by going directly to a ship and negotiating with the captain or ship's merchants for its cargo. The Massachusetts authorities, like their brethren in Virginia, then prohibited buyers from boarding ships to

---

[183] Both engrossing and forestalling are discussed here because they are closely connected in the Virginia program. For further discussion of forestalling, see below.

[184] Bruce, supra note 51, at 358–63.

[185] See Jones, supra note 64, at 43–44.

[186] See generally Bailyn, supra note 107, at 33–34.

prevent cornering of incoming supplies.[187] In 1631, a regulation was enacted barring purchase from ships without a license from the governor. In 1635, this was followed by the licensing of nine individuals (each from different towns) with exclusive boarding rights that included the further right to buy goods, store them in a local depot and sell them only to each's town residents at a maximum profit of five percent.[188] This licensing scheme also failed.[189]

We should mention another practice often associated with engrossing or cornering of markets—hoarding. In colonial America, it is not surprising to find mentions of a concern about hoarding in connection with engrossing of imports. In 1630, a Virginia law provided that a person buying a greater quantity than necessary was required to dispose of the surplus at the same price.[190] Indeed, sometimes storage was viewed as evidence of engrossing! In 1797, the New York City Council banned hucksters from selling fruit at Fly Market because they were found with a large surplus of produce—a sign that they had been engaged in engrossing.[191]

Public and private storage was common throughout the pre-industrial world[192] to insure against supply fluctuations, while reducing search and transport costs.[193] But storage can also be used as part of a strategy to raise prices. Societies since at least the Mesopotamian cities of the third millennium have struggled to develop rules to distinguish hoarding (a bad thing) from storage (a good thing).[194] The early Islamic world provides detailed examples of the practical difficulties and policy tensions associated with

---

187 See Jones, supra note 64, at 42–45; 1 Weeden, supra note 74, at 118.

188 See id. at 45.

189 Jones argues that a law requiring buyers to stand by idly while nine fortunate individuals monopolized the middleman's profit could not be enforced. Moreover, the buying of goods sufficient to satisfy the needs of a whole town required ready money in amounts above that possessed by the nine licensees. Id.

190 See 2 Bruce, supra note 51, at 358–59.

191 Helen Tagires, Public Markets and Civic Culture in Nineteenth-Century America 19 (2003).

192 The importance of storage is reflected in the name of the Roman god of grain harvest, Consus, which means "storage."

193 Morris Silver, Economic Structures in Antiquity 88 (1985).

194 See Hawk, supra note 1, at 60–66.

hoarding rules.[195] Qing mandarins provide another illustration of the challenges to practical enforcement of hoarding rules.[196]

B. Forestalling and Closed Markets

1. *Closed markets*

Forestalling often was connected with so-called closed markets (e.g., where all trading must take place) which are found in many if not most parts of 17th century colonial America. The early English colonies in Massachusetts and Virginia were small settlements in a predominantly agrarian society supplemented with fishing, fur trading and exchanges with the Indians.[197] Settlers first had to develop a staple crop for needed revenue.[198] Geography was paramount, as local conditions determined the staples. Virginia developed tobacco, Pennsylvania developed wheat and South Carolina developed rice and indigo. New England focused less on a staple crop and more on fishing and maritime trade.

Local marketplaces gradually developed in Virginia, New England and New Netherland.[199] By the late 1630s, for example, Boston and other towns in Massachusetts had already established marketplaces where farmers could sell produce and cattle and buy imported goods. Connecticut followed suit in the 1640s. As larger settlements became towns and small cities, closed markets were created. There were detailed regulations of market activities, and at least in the early Massachusetts settlements detailed regulation of

---

195 See id. Generally, Islamic law condemned hoarding (*iktinaz*) (الاكتناز) of essential foodstuffs. *Iktinaz* refers to the case where shortages are created by holding large stocks of goods in warehouses and withholding them from sale. Intention is critical. Storage becomes hoarding when the motive is to keep supply lower than demand and then profit by selling when the price increases. Zulkifli Hasan, Islamic Perspective on Competition Law and Policy, International Conference on Law and Commerce, International Islamic University Malaysia and Victoria University 8 (2005).

196 Hawk, supra note 1, at 64. Generally, a distinction was made between 1) holding grain stocks off the market until prices rose, which was viewed as tolerable opportunism, and 2) deliberately trying to cause a price increase by withholding stocks, which was viewed as antisocial market manipulation. The distinction rested primarily on the intentions of the hoarders.

197 As noted before, this book uses the contemporary term "Indians."

198 See Allan Kulikoff, From British Peasants to Colonial American Famers 206 (2000).

199 Id.

economic (and social) life generally. For example, much of the 1648 Massachusetts Bay Colony Code was devoted to regulation of business.[200] Indeed, only four lines were devoted to "Governour," but 110 lines to "In-keepers." Detailed regulations specified how much bakers might charge, how fur trade with the Indians must be carried on, and how inspectors of pipe-staves were to be appointed.[201]

This attention to detail also can be seen in the regulation of markets and fairs, particularly during the 17th century when various measures were put in place to require that all trading take place in designated marketplaces. This was common throughout the colonies where authorities designated location, days and hours for the trade of specified goods and commodities.[202] As early as 1633, Boston established a "Thursday market."[203] Its purpose was to regulate more effectively sale of local produce.[204] In 1696, Bristol banned the sale of produce on any but a designated day. Those bringing in country produce were forbidden from selling to local hucksters and peddlers until consumers had been given the opportunity to make their purchases.[205] Although local farm produce constituted the principal goods sold at the markets, a considerable range of other goods—such as fish and household items—also could be found.[206]

Outside of New England, the same pattern of heavily regulated closed markets was common.[207] An annual fair was established in Brooklyn in 1675 and a market house at the New York Battery the next year.[208] Philadelphia was allowed by its 1691 charter to hold two

---

[200] See Thorp L. Wolford, The Laws and Liberties of 1648, 28 B.U. Law Rev. 426, 457–58 (1948).

[201] Interest above eight per cent was deemed usurious and illegal, tobacco was not permitted to be taken nearer than twenty poles from any house because of the danger of fire, bread had to bear the mark of the baker and inspectors of weights for bread and butter were rewarded for all wrong weights they found. Id.

Another example of the legislative attention to household details is a 1655 Massachusetts law directing the selectmen of every town to calculate the number of family members able to spin yarn and time available to do so. The number of spinners and weekly quotas were assigned to each household, with fines for failure to meet the quotas. See Clark, supra note 120, at 31.

[202] See Hughes, supra note 178, at 11.

[203] Bruchey, supra note 100, at 44–45.

[204] Id.

[205] Wright, supra note 49, at 113.

[206] Id.

[207] See Bridenbaugh, supra note 113, at 27–28.

[208] Hughes, supra note 178, at 126–27.

market days each week and three fairs a year.[209] In 1708, Annapolis was allowed to hold a market each week and a fair once a year. In 1745, Baltimore was given the privilege of holding two annual fairs.[210] A 1739 South Carolina law set up a public market for the sale of meat and "other butchery wares" in Charleston. No meat could be sold except at the market during designated hours.[211]

Who could trade was also regulated. Non-residents often were banned from trading in designated markets to protect local producers and artisans from outside competition. At the same time, regulations had to be sufficiently flexible to ensure an adequate supply of craftsmen and laborers.[212]

In 1657, Boston prescribed that only a resident could maintain a shop or set up any manufacture.[213] As with the laws in other colonies and towns, the Boston law was enforced. In 1662, the town of Boston fined Nathaniel Milles and Thomas Alline twenty shillings each for having opened shops in the town before being admitted as residents. In 1675, a mob of Bostonians took the law into their own hands, "forcibly taking an ["interloper" John Langworthy] upon a pole & by violence carrying him from the North end of Boston as far as the Town dock."

There are many other examples of laws (and extra-legal action) restricting local markets to residents. New Haven would not permit a stranger to buy or hire without permission of the court.[214] Ferries were required to charge lower fares to local townspeople than to outsiders. Indeed, even retail trade in urban areas (outside of designated markets) was prohibited in Connecticut in the 1660s, because the emerging retail trade was seen as a threat to incumbent sellers.[215] Prior to 1680, the village of Newport prohibited all except inhabitants who had "liberty" from opening shops there.

---

209 Id.

210 Id.

211 Friedman, supra note 3, at 77, citing James W. Ely, Jr., "Patterns of Statutory Enactment in South Carolina, 1720–1770," in Herbert A. Johnson, ed., South Carolina Legal History 67, 69 (1980). The Charlestown authorities banned purchases by hucksters until the ringing of the nine o'clock bell. See Bridenbaugh, supra note 113, at 350–51.

212 See Bridenbaugh, supra note 113, at 198.

213 Id. at 45–46.

214 See Jones, supra note 64, at 47–48.

215 See Hughes, supra note 178, at 130–31.

Even in the Dutch New Netherland, where there was a Company-mandated preference for free trade as discussed above, one can find examples of limitations on outsiders. A 1648 law initially excluded non-residents from local trade.[216] The law was directed against certain "Scottish merchants and small traders," who undersold Dutch burghers in "wholesale and retail." The law was modified, however, to permit non-residents to trade on payment of a fee.

Closed markets raise questions about the consistency of colonial opposition to monopoly. Closed markets could be viewed as creating local monopolies or restricting competition more generally. Were closed markets consistent with the colonial antimonopoly tradition? Yes and no. One reason for closed markets was the belief that they facilitated market liquidity and "just" prices by limiting commercial exchanges to a marketplace with the maximum number of buyers and sellers. But this hardly justifies exclusion of non-locals who were happy to buy and sell in the designated market. In that sense, exclusion of outsiders looks more like a protectionist measure to protect local producers.

Colonial authorities in fact recognized the monopoly aspect of closed markets. Local towns sometimes failed to get the support of the higher colonial authorities for closed markets. In 1677, craftsmen in Boston complained to the General Court of the Massachusetts Bay Colony of the "frequent intruding of strangers from all parts, especially such as are not desirably qualified." It appears, however, that the General Court never acted on the petition to empower the Boston Selectmen to regulate "this evil" of non-tax paying interlopers.[217]

There is another policy explanation for closed markets (but not necessarily for exclusion of outsiders). Concentration of transactions in a closed market increased revenues for the local authorities, as well as the public and private owners of local markets who frequently held exclusive rights to operate markets.[218] This would be consistent with earlier historical examples where revenues were an important reason for official measures to centralize exchanges in designated marketplaces. Carolingian rulers like Charles the Bold

---

[216] See Bridenbaugh, supra note 113, at 45–46.

[217] Id. at 45–46 and 199.

[218] See William L. Letwin, Congress and the Sherman Antitrust Law: 1887–1890 23 U. Chi. L. Rev. 221 (1956).

restricted trade to authorized markets in order to facilitate collection of taxes and tolls.[219]

But we should not exaggerate the importance of closed markets in colonial America; they were not universal. For example, Virginia apparently never adopted closed markets and New Netherland ended them as early as the 1640s. And the closed market systems in the American colonies probably were never as complete at those in England and Europe. Moreover, the American colonies shifted to an open system before England, in part because of earlier colonial opposition to closed markets from both farmers and merchants. Merchants were among the most vigorous opponents of closed markets in Virginia where the House of Burgesses made repeated but unsuccessful attempts to establish them.[220] Closed markets were thought to interfere with the merchant's interest to sell to the first person offering an acceptable price.[221] Most of these merchants were English with not inconsiderable political influence in London.[222]

The Dutch colony centered in New Amsterdam created open markets in 1641 when Governor Kieft approved annual cattle and hog fairs to be held in the "open spaces" before the Fort. The fair was a "free market," that is, strangers as well as burghers were allowed to retail goods and enjoy exemption from arrest while visiting the market.[223] Later in Philadelphia, closed markets became a political football for several years.[224] In the end, merchants failed to persuade the authorities to establish a closed market system that would prevent "hucksters, Indians, Negroes and mulatto servants" from buying goods and reselling them at exorbitant prices.

By the end of the 17th century, New England farmers were allowed to sell directly to customers outside the designated market days after they complained that the closed market system—and more specifically designated market days—resulted in lower prices for their products. For example, New Hampshire farmers complained that so much produce arrived at one time that it glutted the market,

---

219 See Adriaan Verhulst, The Carolingian Economy 129 (2002).

220 2 Bruce, supra note 51, at 389–90.

221 See id. at 363–64.

222 This might explain royal opposition. Virginia laws appointing and regulating fairs were disallowed on the ground that they encroached upon the prerogatives of the governor. See Dickerson, supra note 14, at 230.

223 Bridenbaugh, supra note 113, at 27–28. See also Syrett, supra note 50, at 541.

224 Bridenbaugh, supra note 113, at 350–51.

forced the farmers to dispose of all their goods by the end of the day and thus placed them at the mercy of townspeople.[225] At other times, farmers were fierce opponents of creditor monopolies and the industrial trusts. This raises a larger point. Opposition to (and support of) monopoly not infrequently rests on short-term self-interests that vary in time and place.

The tension between rural and urban attitudes toward closed markets is also seen in a decades-long dispute in Boston.[226] As William Weeden summarizes: "The market in Boston was opened and closed fitfully several times. The record of petitions and counter-petitions attest the public interest, especially about 1730. ... many wished the market closed. ... Parties for and against public markets were almost equally divided." Town residents also opposed closed markets, sometimes with violence. For example, in 1737 Bostonians destroyed two recently erected markets.[227]

Of course, it was not only opposition to closed markets that caused their demise. A sea change in economic conditions favoring open markets appeared at the same time. The medieval European economic world of small local markets and scarcity of storage facilities was replaced in colonial America with a world of settlements dispersed over a wide area, with commodities shipped between colonies in bulk and overseas.

There was another important difference between the colonies and England/Europe. As discussed above with respect to engrossing, colonials worried more about bottlenecks in import markets than price hikes and exclusion in closed markets.

2. *Forestalling*

Forestalling can be defined as buying goods from a producer or importer for resale before the goods come to the designated or public market. As seen above in the case of imports into Virginia, forestalling and engrossing laws often were combined. This entails some repeating of the story narrated above.

Forestalling bans have an ancient history. Indeed, they pre-date history. Hunter-gatherers believed that misfortune fell on anyone who

---

[225] Weeden, supra note 74, at 406.

[226] See Bridenbaugh, supra note 113, at 194.

[227] Paul Gilje, Rioting in America 28 (1996).

sold her goods outside the normal place of exchange.[228] Islamic commentators condemned *talaqqi* (التلقي), the purchase of goods before they reached the marketplace, for example, stopping a caravan on its way to a town with the aim of purchasing the goods at the lowest possible prices.[229] Forestalling laws are commonly found in medieval and early modern Europe.[230] In 1485, the commune of Vicenza condemned the practice of buying timber from sellers outside the market square and before the ninth hour, and then selling it at more than the fair price (*plus aequo*).[231] English common law and statutes condemned forestalling.[232] Towns in Massachusetts copied the English bans on forestalling,[233] as did Georgia in the mid-18th.[234]

Forestalling laws in England and Europe were used to protect local closed markets. They were used for the same purpose in colonial America. Colonial forestalling laws also were used to address concerns about bottleneck monopolies of imported goods. As discussed above, colonial demand far exceeded English supply. Ships bringing imported goods were potential bottlenecks for the further distribution of goods and commodities.

In Virginia, a wide variety of measures were taken over the course of several decades to combat forestalling of imported goods. In the early Virginia settlement, ships were prohibited from making sales before they came to anchor at Jamestown in order to prevent buyers from meeting the ships as they came up the river to "forestall" the supply before it reached the market.[235] In 1622, a forestaller was legally defined as one who 1) had obtained, under the terms of a contract, actual possession of merchandise or right to its possession before it reached Jamestown, whether introduced by land or by water; or 2) used any subterfuge to enhance the price of goods when offered for sale in the market or who prevented their transport

---

228 See Hawk, supra note 1, at 50.

229 See Yassine Essid, A Critique of the Origins of Islamic Economic Thought 154 (1995).

230 Raymond de Roover, The Concept of Just Price: Theory and Economic Policy, 18 J. Econ. Hist. 418, 429 (1958), and authorities cited therein.

231 Luca Clerici, Market, Civic Virtues, and Civic Bargaining in the Medieval and Early Modern Age: Some Evidence from Sixteenth Century Italy, 59 Intl. Rev. Econ. 459, 463 (2012).

232 See Hawk, supra note 1, at 55–59.

233 See Bruchey, supra note 100, at 44-45.

234 See Jones, supra note 178, at 479–85.

235 See generally 2 Bruce, supra note 51, at 353–63 and 532.

to market. In 1626, colonists were prohibited from boarding a ship on its way to Jamestown without special license from the authorities. A ship also was required to hold its cargo ten days before sale to enable colonists to travel to Jamestown and have equal opportunity to make their needed purchases.[236] Sanctions included forfeiture of goods and imprisonment of the captain. These laws also appear to have been enforced. The planter Michael Wilcox, for example, was fined because he boarded a ship lying at anchor in the James River and purchased twelve pounds of sugar.

Despite the laws, ships continued to make sales and future contracts before docking. To try to stop this, the House of Burgesses in 1631-32 ordered that the English forestalling statutes should be expressly reenacted in Virginia. Penalties were severe, including imprisonment and, for multiple offenses, the pillory and forfeiture of goods. As seen earlier with respect to engrossing, however, the House of Burgesses in 1644 repealed these laws after opposition from English merchants.

It remained too early, however, for free trade to be accepted in Virginia. In 1655, the Virginia Assembly designated marketplaces in each county, usually near a river or creek for greater accessibility.[237] Imported goods were to be brought to these markets from certain prescribed ports, with the exception of goods held for eight months. Forestallers were subject to punishment. But then in 1661, the House of Burgesses eased the forestalling rules by granting vessels the right to obtain a license to engage in trade in any part of the Colony after they arrived in Jamestown.

Massachusetts provides another example of colonial attempts to regulate imports and protect closed markets through bans on forestalling and other measures. Again, as discussed earlier respecting engrossing, colonial authorities viewed the practice of buying directly from ships as increasing prices and monopolizing goods needed by the settlers. In 1631, a regulation prohibited the purchases from ships without a license from the governor.

In sum, the history of forestalling bans in colonial America is replete with ineffective enforcement. Whether or not forestalling bans were ever successful in England and Europe, they often failed in colonial America—certainly as criminal offenses—because of

---

[236] Jones, supra note 64, at 43–44.

[237] 2 Bruce, supra note 51, at 390.

indefinite legal standards and evidentiary difficulty of proof.[238] Nathan Dane concludes, perhaps with some exaggeration, that "probably not one offence of this kind ... has ever been punished or prosecuted .... and ... statutes ... usually they have been a dead letter."[239] Forestalling laws also faced increasing condemnation by economic thinkers in the 18th century, such as the French *philosophes* and Adam Smith who argued that middlemen brought economic benefits, such as stabilization of supply.[240] Indeed, Smith derisively dismissed forestalling bans as witchcraft: "The popular fear of engrossing and forestalling... may be compared to the popular terrors and suspicions of witchcraft."[241]

Forestalling and engrossing laws often were brought into play in England and Europe to meet popular demands for official action against sudden price increases. Price controls were another attempted solution, in colonial America as well. But price controls almost invariably failed—in colonial America and elsewhere. This leads us into a discussion of the notion of a just price, colonial attempts to prevent excessive prices through price controls and price fixing agreements.

C. Pricing Practices

1. *Just prices*

Closed markets and forestalling bans rested on the belief that just prices were facilitated by limiting commercial exchanges to a marketplace with the maximum number of buyers and sellers. The idea of a "just price" has a deep history—not only in the European

---

[238] See Dane, supra note 180, at 33.

[239] See id.

[240] These benefits were recognized in the United States following passage of the Sherman Act:

> "The middleman whose intervention as to certain commodities had been prohibited as entirely mischievous, it was found, had a useful function to perform which facilitated rather than restrained trade. With improved means of communication and transportation this was undoubtedly true. The middleman secured his place in commerce as a result of the specialization of functions which marked the development of modern industry and trade."

United States v. Patten, 226 U.S. 525 (brief of Solicitor General Lehmann) (1913), quoted in Edward A. Adler, Monopolizing at Common Law and Under Section Two of the Sherman Antitrust Act, 31 Harv. L. Rev. 246, 256–57 (1917).

[241] See 4 Adam Smith, The Wealth of Nations (1776).

tradition (beginning with Aristotle), but in other traditions as well.[242] The legal notion of a just price was used under Roman law and developed further in medieval European law. For example, Roman and medieval European law required determination of a just price (*iustium pretium*) in a variety of situations, such as assessment of property as a measure of damages and valuation of estates. Importantly, the just price as ordinarily used in the Roman and medieval legal systems was not based on an abstract standard of value, but rather on actual or estimated market prices, unfettered by monopolistic practices.[243]

Nor was the just price merely a legal notion. The idea of a just price was the subject of moral philosophy for many centuries.[244] Christian theologians—notably Thomas Aquinas in the 13th century—refined the scholastic notion of just price.[245] The just price also had a social dimension in that it was embedded in community values and the comprehensive economic regulation of medieval Europe. Exchanges were considered the responsibility of the community. Pursuit of the common good—rather than an abstract notion of competition—motivated medieval European laws concerning trade and commerce.[246] It is reasonable to conclude that many within the early American colonies brought with them these European notions of a "just price."[247]

---

242 For example, the Islamic theologian Ibn Taimiyah arguably equated fair or just price with market price (*hi l-thaman l-ma'rūf*). See Hawk, supra note 1, at 77 and authorities cited therein.

243 See id. at 76.

244 See id. at 77–79.

245 Aquinas, Summa Theologica II, II, qu.58. The scholastic doctrine applied most clearly to staple products. There was no agreement among scholastics about luxury products (which lacked a regular market) like thoroughbred dogs, birds of paradise and rare pictures.

246 The "market" was viewed as the sphere of society devoted to the collective assessment of the value of goods (the so-called *communes aestimatio* or common estimation) and to the fruitful and legitimate use of wealth, for the benefit of society as a whole. See Luca Clerici, Market, Civic Virtues, and Civic Bargaining in the Medieval and Early Modern Age: Some Evidence from Sixteenth Century Italy, 59 Int'l Rev. Econ. 459, 459–61 (2012).

247 See Bridenbaugh, supra note 113, at 45:

> "Certain economic ideals of medieval England came with the colonists to America. These included the beliefs that the prime function of merchant, craftsman, artisan and laborer was the service of the community, and that careful and minute regulation of all

The Massachusetts Bay Colony offers concrete evidence of early colonial embrace of the notion of just price (and its corollary, excessive price). This is not at all surprising given Puritan morality. For the Puritans, God—as the ultimate lawgiver—demanded a just price. In 1633, John Cotton laid out the principles to distinguish avarice from industry:

> "A man may not sell above the current price, i.e., such a price as is usual in the time and place, and as another (who knows the worth of the commodity) would give for it, if he had occasion to use it. . ..but where there is a scarcity of the commodity, there men may raise their price; for now it is a hand of God upon the commodity, and not the person."[248]

As Bernard Bailyn summarizes: "The [Puritans] assumed that there existed an ideal standard of valuation applicable to every situation. An unjust figure was the result not so much of the mechanical operation of an impersonal market as of some individual's gluttony."[249]

The Puritan mix of morality and law[250] is strikingly illustrated in the case of the merchant Robert Keayne who was condemned in 1639 by both civil and religious authorities for excessive pricing.[251] Keayne was a retailer who sold imported goods to new settlers. He was first accused of overcharging for a bag of nails that he claimed he sold at a perfectly reasonable price. This was followed by complaints

---

phases of commercial life was the proper responsibility of municipal authority. Hence municipal provision for a 'fair customary price' for goods and labor, for wares of a standard quality, for strict supervision of food supply and regulation of weights and measures, for payment of debts when due, and for protection of the community's trade by the exclusion of strangers and interlopers, - all these were medieval legacies to America."

248 Quoted in Bailyn, supra note 107, at 20–21. See also Bruchey, supra note 100, at 45.

249 Bailyn, supra note 107, at 20-21. Arbitration was contemplated if necessary to estimate the just price in a concrete situation.

250 See Bruchey, supra note 100, at 46–47 who argues that the incident reflects numerous restraints imposed on the merchants by the Puritan elders in an effort to protect the means of subsistence and the religious ideals of the larger community.

251 See generally Bailyn, supra note 107, at 41–42; Bruchey, supra note 100, at 46–47.

that he had overcharged on other goods, including "great gold buttons," a bridle and a skein of thread. The General Court convicted Keayne of excessive prices by "taking above six-pence in the shilling profit; in some above eight-pence; and in some small things, above two for one." The Church elders then severely admonished Keayne for selling goods at excessive prices, "to the Dishonor of God's name, the Offence of the General Court, and the Publique scandall of the Country." It took a "penitential acknowledgement" of his sin to regain full membership in the church.[252]

The Puritans were not the only colonists insisting on a just price; we also find complaints of unjust excessive prices in other colonies. Residents in New Amsterdam, for example, complained to the authorities about unjust prices.[253] Medical practitioners in early Virginia were accused of charging such high fees that the colony mandated binding arbitration of disputes about medical fees.[254] Carl Bridenbaugh reports that the period from 1690 to 1720 was notable for provincial and local regulations intended to ensure that artisans and tradesmen charged a "just" price for their goods, gave fair measure and maintained a high standard of quality in their products.[255]

Yet, how was the just price calculated? Did the Puritans and other colonists—like their Roman and medieval European predecessors—look to market prices in determining the just price in a concrete situation? Did the colonists reflect Thomas Aquinas' recognition of the practical difficulties of determining a just price and his distinction between the moral just price and the more proximate legal just price?[256] The answers are not entirely clear from our survey

---

[252] Quoted in Bailyn, supra note 107, at 42. See also Bridenbaugh, supra note 113, at 41–42, citing 2 Bos. Rec. Com., 83, 89; Johnson, Wonder-Working Providence, 211; 2 MHS Procs., I, 238; Mass. Col. Recs., V, 62–63: Bostonians complained bitterly of shopkeepers and merchants who set excessive prices on their goods.

[253] In 1657, New Amsterdam residents protested to Peter Stuyvesant that prices of necessary commodities and household goods were too high.

[254] 2 Bruce, supra note 51, at 233: When a patient had just cause to think that a fee was unreasonable, the physician was required to state upon oath to the court the quantity and value of the medicines which he had administered; a court decided the reasonable fee.

[255] Bridenbaugh, supra note 113, at 201.

[256] II-II, q. 77, a. 1 ad 1: "the just price of things is not fixed with mathematical precision, but depends on a kind of estimate, so that a slight addition or subtraction would not seem to destroy the equality of justice." See Hawk, supra note 1, at 79.

of the historical sources, but it is reasonable to conclude that estimated market prices were the norm.

Although it is difficult to measure the importance and enforcement of colonial laws prohibiting excessive prices, we can more confidently conclude that complaints about excessive prices frequently triggered price controls, a subject to which we now turn.

2. *Price controls (fixing official prices)*

As in many other pre-industrial societies,[257] colonial authorities often resorted to price controls in reaction to complaints about excessive prices. And most colonial price controls failed, just as they did in other societies. Price controls were sometimes placed on a wide or indefinite range of goods and services. For example, in 1633 the Massachusetts Bay General Court declared that prices must not "exceed the bounds of moderation," and that the prices of provisions, clothing and tools must not be more than four pence above the price in England.[258]

The most common goods and services subject to price controls were bread, beer, wine, grain, corn and carters. Each is briefly summarized here to give a flavor of the regulatory atmosphere of colonial America and its ultimate collapse.

Bread, the life staple before the modern era, commonly was subject to colonial price controls. For example, the early Massachusetts Bay Colony adopted the method of adjusting the weight, quality and price of a loaf of bread by a sliding scale harnessed to the current price of wheat.[259]

Beer, wine and **liquor** followed bread as frequent subjects of colonial price controls. The proliferation of drinking houses often prompted close official scrutiny. In 1648, the New Netherland authority complained that "one full fourth of the City of New Amsterdam" had been "turned into taverns for the sale of brandy, tobacco and beer...."[260] Virginia illustrates, however, the difficulties faced in implementing an effective and fair price control system that

[257] See Hawk, supra note 1, at 68–73.

[258] 1 Albert Hart, Commonwealth History of Massachusetts 410, 428 (1927).

[259] Clark, supra note 120, at 64.

[260] Syrett, supra note 50, at 539.

had to be accepted by both suppliers and customers.[261] Beer, wine, cider and liquors were readily available in Virginia taverns, often at what were perceived as exorbitant prices. This was big business in 17th century Virginia. In 1668, there were so many taverns and "tippling-houses" that the numbers in each county were reduced to one or two, unless more were needed for the accommodation of travelers at ports, ferries and important road intersections. Persons who managed drinking shops without a license were fined two thousand pounds of tobacco.

In 1645, the House of Burgesses fixed the prices of wines and liquors sold by retailers and innkeepers. The law failed, however, largely because of the high price volatility of tobacco, the exchange currency. In 1666, Virginia tried again. The difficult task of setting prices fair and acceptable to both buyers and sellers was addressed in a new regulation that allowed the retailer or innkeeper to charge triple his cost, provided that he did not exceed a fixed price. But the prices set in 1666, and readopted in 1667, were found to be too high and had to be reduced only a few years later. Finally, sixty years after the first attempt to set official prices, the prices of foreign liquors in 1705 were fixed in accordance with their import price and adjusted to the fluctuating value of tobacco. This system for foreign wines and spirits continued during the remainder of the 18th century.

Another group of services often subject to colonial price controls concerned **carters and haulers** who were regulated much like modern taxis. The Massachusetts Bay Colony in 1637 or 1638 regulated carters' rates because of complaints about their "excessive prices."[262] New York provides an example of carter resistance to price controls. In 1684, New York carters went on strike to protest the official rates for carting firewood.[263] After fifteen carters went on strike, the authorities "Suspended and Discharged" the strikers, and notified townspeople that all "persons within this Citty have hereby free Lyberty and Lycence to Serve for hyre or Wages as Carmen." When, a week later, the penitent carters pleaded for their jobs back, they were

---

[261] 2 Bruce, supra note 51, at 221–28. According to Bruce, madeira, malaga, canary and fayal wines were probably much more abundant in the Colony than in England at this time and were drunk by classes which in the mother country were content with strong and small beer.

[262] Bridenbaugh, supra note 113 at 44, quoting Stokes, Iconography, IV, 207, 960, 962; S. C.

[263] Id.

required to pay a fine. And so ended perhaps America's first transportation strike.

Rates and prices were set for many other service providers, such as **gravediggers,**[264] **blacksmiths** and **mechanics**. In the early Virginia settlement, blacksmith rates were fixed after complaints that blacksmith had bought small estates with the profits from their excessive prices.[265] In Pennsylvania around 1682, the council approved measures empowering the justice of each county court to set the wages of workmen and servants "at a just rate."[266]

As mentioned above, price controls throughout history often resulted from popular demands for official action when prices spiked in times of drought or war. This was also true in colonial America. In 1715 in Charleston, Indians destroyed crops, slaughtered cattle and drove planters into the town.[267] Prices soared beyond the capacity of the poor to buy. In 1719, Governor Robert Johnson requested the Assembly seriously to consider regulation of prices charged by butchers and the laying of high export duties on foodstuffs. There appears to be no record of the Assembly's action.

Where shortages resulted from military conflict, measures like export bans often were taken by the authorities and formal price controls avoided. One example concerns the abortive Quebec expedition by England in 1709.[268] The gathering of forces at Boston created a severe shortage of grain and other provisions. The Boston selectmen sent an unsuccessful petition to the Governor, calling for a temporary embargo on the export of foodstuffs. The shortage situation again became critical in 1713 when two hundred food rioters wounded officials and their families. This time the town obtained the Governor's proclamation of an embargo on grain and other provisions leaving the port.[269]

Colonial price controls also were used to protect vulnerable or itinerant buyers against excessive prices or prices greater than those charged to local buyers—price controls as a measure to avoid our

---

264 Id., at 202; 2 Bruce, supra note 51, at 415.

265 Id. at 419.

266 1 Dorfman, supra note 53, at 86. As to other colonies and wage controls, see Wolford, supra note 200, at 458.

267 Bridenbaugh, supra note 113, at 197.

268 See id. at 196–97.

269 See also Weeden, supra note 74, at 594.

modern concept of price discrimination. English soldiers stationed in Virginia in 1676 are an example[270] of this historical practice.[271] Soldiers were protected from price discrimination in the Roman Empire. Hadrian issued an edict prohibiting sellers in Ephesus from charging soldiers more than the market price as of nineteen days prior to the sale.[272] In 1158, Emperor Frederic I imposed draconian penalties on sutlers who sold their wares to soldiers at a price higher than the one prevailing in local markets. Punishment included confiscation of their merchandise, whipping and branding with a hot iron on both cheeks.[273] Colonial penalties were modest by comparison.

Colonial price controls did not go uncriticized, despite receiving the support of Harvard students.[274] Benjamin Franklin argued against a proposal of the English government that prices should be fixed in the Indian trade for the sake of peace with the Indians:

> "[It is] contrary to the nature of commerce, for government to interfere in the prices of commodities. Trade is a voluntary thing between buyer and seller; in every article of which each exercises his own judgement, and is to please himself. . . . Where there are a number of different traders, the separate desire of each to get more custom will operate in bringing their goods down to a reasonable price. . . . Therefore . . trade will best find and make its own rates."[275]

---

270 2 Bruce, supra note 51, at 205-07.

271 In the Carolingian world of early medieval Europe, price discrimination laws similarly protected travelers from local sellers. See Hawk, supra note 1, at 66–67.

272 See Kenneth S. Cahn, The Roman and Frankish Roots of the Just Price of Medieval Canon Law, 6 Studies in Medieval and Renaissance Hist. 3, 41–42 (Paul J. Du Plessis, Clifford Ando and Kaius Tuori eds., 1969).

273 See MGH, Legum, Sectio IV, I, 24i, No. I73, art. I7, cited in de Roover, supra note 230, at 434 n.82.

274 In 1725, the candidates for the master's degree at Harvard were asked: "Can the price of articles for sale be regulated by law?" They answered in the affirmative. Next, they were asked: "Is it always lawful to give and take the market price?" They answered in the negative. See Weeden, supra note 74, at 524.

275 See 1 Dorfman, supra note 53, at 188.

Farmers also complained about price controls,[276] claiming for example that farm prices were set at such unacceptably low prices[277] that they failed to keep up with black market prices of shoes, clothing and other necessities charged by peddlers and retailers. Rural seasonal and day laborers protested that their fixed wages diminished in purchasing power as prices rose for basic needs that they had to obtain in the urban markets. Price controls on wages were particularly ineffective in a new country where labor was scarce—many artisans simply relocated or took up farming on their own.[278]

In conclusion, most colonial price controls failed, just like price controls of their ancestors and their heirs. Let us turn to another practice often (and perhaps confusingly to modern antitrust lawyers) treated as "monopolistic" in colonial and earlier times: agreements between competitors to fix prices, that is, cartel agreements.

3. *Price fixing (cartels and guilds)*

In addition to forestalling and engrossing, agreements between competitors to fix prices were included in the colonial list of "monopolistic" practices. Under modern antitrust law, of course, price fixing agreements are treated separately from monopolization. That separation was not clearly drawn in colonial America, although price fixing agreements were the targets of some distinct colonial laws. For example, the colonial bread assizes—which set official prices—were seen as a remedy for the propensity and opportunity of bakers to agree on prices.[279] With that caveat in mind, let us proceed.

The colonists were quite aware of Adam Smith's "natural propensity" of traders to agree on prices and they took action against price fixing agreements, including criminal penalties. In 1680, New York convicted coopers for raising their prices and fined them £2. 10

---

[276] See Cathy Matson, The Revolution, the Constitution, and the New Nation, in 1 Cambridge Economic History of the United States 363, 369-70 (Stanley Engerman and Robert Gallman eds. 1996).

[277] But see Daniel Vickers, The Northern Colonies: Economy and Society, 1600-1775, in 1 Cambridge Economic History of the United States 209, 241 (Stanley Engerman and Robert Gallman eds. 1996) (the price of foodstuffs went almost unregulated in the colonial countryside).

[278] Bridenbaugh, supra note 113, at 49. See also 1 Dorfman, supra note 53, at 63-64.

[279] See 1 Dorfman, supra note 53, at 397.

each.[280] Carl Bridenbaugh reports that coopers in other cities (Boston, Charlestown, Newport and Philadelphia) also agreed on prices.[281] In 1703, the Governor of Charlestown, outraged by the exorbitant prices charged by shoemakers,[282] proposed a law against all combinations to fix prices, a law entitled "Against ye Combination of all Tradesmen."[283]

Refusals to sell—or what may be viewed today as per se unlawful boycott activity—were used as part of cartels or price fixing agreements. For example, farmers boycotted town merchants unless they got higher prices for their goods.[284] And a buyers' cartel was formed in 1741 by Manhattan bakers who refused to bake bread until wheat prices fell.

Although colonial farmers, artisans and merchants had the same human propensity to fix prices, they may have had less opportunity to successfully implement cartel agreements—given colonial market conditions. These conditions included: 1) English restrictions on trade and bans on colonial manufacture (which affected the detection and viability of import and export cartels and limited cartels to domestic goods); 2) the extensive regulation of local markets (which affected the viability of domestic retail cartels); and 3) the frequent colonial attempts to fix official prices to remedy price spikes (and the constant threat of price controls if prices rose by cartel agreement).

The English restrictions on trade and bans on colonial manufacture merit special attention. They affected the detection and viability of cartels and limited the kinds of domestic products that were possible subjects of cartel agreements.

This leads to three observations. First, the colonial market for manufactured goods was largely comprised of imported goods against which colonial producers could not compete. Small unprotected markets kept colonial manufacturers from competing effectively with their British counterparts—even when they evaded

---

280 Bridenbaugh, supra note 113, at 37.

281 See Stokes, Iconography, IV, 319; Pa. Mag., IV, 195; Austin, Journal of William Jefferay, 28; S.C. Statutes, II, 55–57, cited in Bridenbaugh, supra note 113, at 37.

282 The Governor complained that shoemakers were "exacting upon ye people of twelve Royall a pair when leather is Sold at a royall a pound."

283 S.C. Commons Journal, 1703, 95, 110; Pa. Col. Recs., I, 576; Pa. Statutes, II, 61; R.I. Col. Recs., IV, II; II Bos. Rec. Com., 3. 5, 205.

284 Kulikoff, supra note 198, at 212.

English bans on manufacturing in the first place. English manufacturers and merchants sold to a far larger market, produced on a larger scale and succeeded in keeping costs down better than colonial competitors.[285] Cartels of English manufacturers and English merchants were beyond the enforcement powers of colonial authorities (even if they suspected cartel behavior). The importation itself was part of the English restricted system with its own monopoly aspect which also was beyond the purview of colonial authorities.

Second, the residual domestic demand for colonial manufactured goods was more limited and perhaps more transparent than for imported goods. This made price agreements more difficult to maintain.

Third, the colonial export trade was limited to agricultural goods that may have been harder to cartelize successfully; moreover, any cartel among colonial exporters might well have been approved or accepted as an export cartel.

Relatedly, guilds, which in England were condemned as monopolies, also were subject to colonial scrutiny. Guilds were essentially associations (in varying legal forms) of members of the same profession or trade like artisans of ceramic goods, textile producers or merchants.[286] In many periods—like medieval Europe—there were essentially two kinds of guilds: craft guilds of artisans and service providers and merchant guilds of wholesale traders.[287] Guilds generally received privileges from authorities such as the exclusive right to practice their trade, the right to decide who could become a guild member and the right to regulate members' commercial activities.

Sheilagh Ogilvie cites extensive evidence that despite prohibitions on price fixing, medieval English guilds raised prices, limited output, detected and punished cheaters, restricted entry and raised rivals' costs.[288] But guilds in medieval Europe gradually lost their importance as the Middle Ages waned. Beginning in the late 15th century, the power of Dutch and English guilds began to decline. The undermining of the English guild system began with

---

[285] See McCusker and Menard, supra note 39, at 309.

[286] For further discussion, see Hawk, supra note 1, at 38-44.

[287] See Sheilagh Ogilvie, Institutions and European Trade: Merchant Guilds, 1000-1800 (2011) [hereinafter Ogilvie 2011]; Sheilagh Ogilvie, The European Guilds: An Economic Analysis (2019) [hereinafter Ogilvie 2019].

[288] See Ogilvie 2011, supra note 287, at 51-62.

the establishment of independent traders and craftsmen outside the areas of guild and municipal regulations and with the entry of foreign inventors and experts who received free trading privileges as incentives.[289] Craft guilds declined later than merchant guilds.[290]

Guilds were less important in colonial America than in Europe.[291] Michel Guillaume Jean de Crevecoeur, a French observer who wrote shortly before the American Revolution, noted that all mechanics served a regular apprenticeship, but there were few guilds.[292] Still, colonial authorities recognized the anticompetitive potential of guilds and prohibited price fixing by guild members. For example, in 1648 Massachusetts authorized a Shoemakers' Guild for a period of three years. The shoemakers were empowered to issue orders for the regulation of their trade, to prescribe reasonable penalties for their breach and to suppress incompetent workmen. The guilds were prohibited, however, from setting prices and from refusing to make shoes for any inhabitant at a reasonable price. As noted above, however, there are many instances in the 17th century where towns excluded strangers from trading much like the earlier European guilds. Yet, many forces were at work at this time, and the anticompetitive or monopoly potential of colonial craft guilds was reduced by the English policy of discouraging colonial manufacture (let alone a colonial guild monopoly).[293]

A brief word on another institution often associated with guilds—apprenticeships. Although the colonial system of apprenticeships often was rigorously enforced,[294] it does not seem to have been used to promote monopolies.[295]

---

289 Thorelli, supra note 33, at 14; see also Ogilvie 2011, supra note 287, at 31-32.

290 Personal correspondence with Sheilagh Ogilvie (Oct. 18, 2017).

291 See Clark, supra note 120, at 67-68; Ratner et. al., The Evolution of the American Economy: Growth, Welfare, and Decision Making 69 (1979); but cf. Weeden, supra note 74, at 274.

292 Clark, supra note 120, at 67-68, citing Michel Guillaume Jean de Crevecoeur, Lettres d'un Cultivateur Americain, III, 487, 488.

293 See Jones, supra note 64, at 47-48.

294 For example, Massachusetts required a special act to free an apprentice from his obligations even when the master had deserted him. See Clark, supra note 120, at 67-68.

295 See id. See also Weeden, supra note 74, at 274.

As we shall see in the next chapter, both strands of the colonial antimonopoly tradition strengthened during the Revolutionary and Founding periods. Opposition to government grants of monopoly privileges led to independence and wartime inflation intensified resort to action against "monopolizing" practices.

Chapter Three

REVOLUTION AND FOUNDING OF THE UNITED STATES—1763 TO 1800

In 1763, the Treaty of Paris ended the Seven Years' War and expanded England's territory in North America to include all the previously French possessions in Canada and lands west of the Appalachians to the Mississippi. In 1775, American colonists began the Revolutionary War which ended with independence and, ultimately, the founding of the United States. In 1800, Thomas Jefferson replaced the Federalists in the White House. The years from 1763 to 1800 are rich in contemporary sources about American attitudes toward monopoly and laws to deal with monopoly. As discussed below, the history of monopoly during the Revolutionary and Founding period is invoked for many purposes today—interpretation of the federal constitution, support for political programs and legislative agendas, and probably least of all, roots of our antitrust principles and laws.

As seen in the prior chapter, antimonopoly sentiment during the colonial period was directed primarily toward the initial charter monopolies, English trading monopolies and grants of monopoly privileges by colonial authorities. At the beginning of the Revolutionary War, complaints about the English trading monopolies intensified and, indeed, contributed to the movement for independence (section I below). During the war, the colonies resorted to forestalling and engrossing laws, as well as price controls, to combat wartime inflation (section II). After the Revolution, several states elevated their monopoly opposition to the constitutional level by including antimonopoly provisions in their state constitutions (section III). In contrast, the federal constitution (including the Bill of Rights or first Ten Amendments) did not include a ban on monopoly; moreover, the intellectual property clause concerning patents and copyrights was viewed as a legitimate exception to the antimonopoly principle (section IV).

I. ENGLISH TRADING MONOPOLIES AND THE REVOLUTION—BOSTON TEA PARTY

In the Revolutionary and Founding period, complaints about monopoly continued to be voiced about English trading monopolies, notably the East India Company. The primary concern remained the freedom and opportunity to trade and engage in business. For example, the Philadelphia Quaker merchant Tench Coxe extolled the virtues of America in these terms: an immigrant may pursue his calling "without any hindrances from corporation rules or monopolizing companies."[1] Thomas Paine proclaimed a similar ideal: "That there shall be no monopolies of any kind—that all trades shall be free, and every man free to follow any occupation by which he can procure an honest livelihood, and in any place, town and city throughout the nation."[2]

Interestingly, historical complaints about the English trading monopolies are invoked in today's debate about progressive ideals, including on the Senate floor. Hence, this history is relied on in part to demand the strengthening of U.S. antitrust statutes to combat 22nd century monopolies: as Senator Amy Klobuchar writes:

> "Thus, our country's Declaration of Independence from England was not only a political Declaration of Independence from a foreign country but also an act of economic rebellion against monopoly power."[3]

Indeed, some scholars assert that the English trading monopolies were the primary cause of the American Revolution.[4] Is this all hyperbole? Political rhetoric? Academic exaggeration? To answer those questions, we look more closely at the circumstances that led to the Boston Tea Party, an historical icon for today's opponents of private monopoly.

The English government had granted a monopoly of the Chinese tea trade to the East India Company (Company): only the

---

[1] Tench Coxe, View of the United States 442 (1793).

[2] Thomas Paine, The Rights of Man 87 (1791).

[3] Amy Klobuchar, Anti-Trust: Taking on Monopoly Power from the Gilded Age to the Digital Age 21 (2022).

[4] See Steven G. Calabresi & Larissa C. Leibowitz, Monopolies and the Constitution: A History of Crony Capitalism, 36 Harv. J. of Law & Pub. Pol'y 983, 1007 (2013).

Company had the right to import tea into England for consumption or reshipment to the colonies.[5] In earlier years, the tea trade was highly profitable for the Company and generated considerable revenues for the English government. But, over time, the Company steadily increased the supply of Chinese tea shipped to England, while at the same time English and European smugglers saturated the English market with more and more Chinese tea. By 1773, unsold tea reached 17.5 million pounds—more than everyone in England drank in a year. The Company faced bankruptcy due to the oversupply.

In 1773, after the Bank of England refused a loan to the Company to cover its losses, Lord North proposed the Tea Act which was intended to assist both the Company and the Treasury. Parliament would continue to collect the three-penny duty on imported tea and the Company would receive a tax rebate on tea shipped to America. This would allow the Company to offer a lower price to American customers—not a higher price—a result that was expected to generate colonial support.

However, the Tea Act also changed the distribution system to the detriment of American tea merchants. In the past, English and American merchants had been able to compete for tea at auction in London and ship the tea to America for a healthy profit. Now the Company could select its own agents and sell tea directly to the American colonies. To Lord North, this appeared the perfect solution: the Tea Act would reduce the surplus of tea in the Company's warehouses, Americans would buy more tea at lower prices, the Company's profit margins would rise and the British Treasury would increase its cut.[6]

Lord North miscalculated. Colonial opposition was immediate, widespread and violent. And opposition was not limited to Boston. Objections were voiced in the other major cities—Charleston, New York and Philadelphia. The three principal objections were "taxation without representation," the grant of monopoly or special trading privileges to the Company and the funding of salaries of provincial officials from the taxes.

New Yorkers and Philadelphians focused on the first two: taxation without representation and monopoly. The Tea Act

---

[5] See generally Benjamin L. Carp, Defiance of the Patriots: The Boston Tea Party and the Making of America 3-20 (2010); Chester Whitney Wright, Economic History of the United States 164-66 (2nd ed. 1949).

[6] See Carp, supra note 5, at 20-21.

reaffirmed the tax that Townshend had imposed in 1767: for every pound of tea that entered an American port, the merchants would still have to pay three pence. As an anonymous New Yorker wrote in "A Constitutional Catechism:"

> "Why do the Americans refuse the Importation of English Tea at this Time? ... Because it is saddled with a *duty,* which is a *tax for* the Purpose of raising a Revenue from us, without our own consent, and such *tax, or duty,* is therefore *unconstitutional, cruel,* and *unjust.*"[7]

The duty was unconstitutional because it violated "a fundamental maxim of the British constitution:" taxation required consent. The duty was cruel because it treated Americans like enemies. And the duty was unjust because using parliamentary power to seize property without consent resembled "downright robbery." The "Constitutional Catechism" was widely distributed. After appearing simultaneously in two New York newspapers in early December 1773, it was reprinted in other colonies seven more times over the next two months.

But taxation without representation was not the only issue for the colonists. The Tea Act also was viewed as giving the East India Company an unfair competitive advantage in selling tea in America. This second complaint was elaborated and circulated more fully in October by an anonymous New York author—"Hampden"—who published a series of essays called *The Alarm*. Hampden argued that in theory a merchant or company might be granted exclusive trading rights as a reward for the risk and uncertainty when engaging in foreign commerce. The East India Company, however, had obtained its unjustified monopoly through bribes well beyond what was fair to other traders.[8] Hampden dismissed the projected lower American price for tea as a seductive trick to obtain colonial support; the Company could set any price it wanted with its new privileges and would begin fleecing colonial American consumers in due course. The argument resonated with the middle colonies where smugglers and law-abiding merchants objected to any law favoring the Company agents.

---

[7] Mary Beth Norton, 1774: The Long Year of Revolution 12–21 (2020).

[8] Carp, supra note 5, at 20–21.

In Boston, vigorous debate turned violent, and Boston was not alone.[9] The Massachusetts House of Representatives issued a proclamation raising three objections to the Tea Act: taxation without representation, funding of colonial salaries from the taxes and trading monopoly.[10] The last merits closer attention. According to the Massachusetts legislators, the Tea Act granted special privileges to a monopolistic company at the expense of American merchants. Using its unfair competitive advantage, the East India Company could now starve the American people of their livelihood, while imperial courtiers and their cronies schemed to take the remainder. Americans, poorly connected in London, would suffer a fate worse than the Bengalis during the infamous famine of 1770.

Farmers and others in the rural areas of Massachusetts voiced similar fears and outrage.[11] The promise of cheaper tea was intended to lure them into accepting an unjust tax; establishment of a government—that was independent of popular control—would be funded by revenue from the tea; and the East India company's monopoly would crowd out American merchants. The Boston merchants joined the radical leaders of artisans and laborers to organize an economic boycott. Meanwhile other events—such as the presence of British soldiers and the Boston Massacre of 1770—aroused the fury of colonists who were interested less in trading profits and more in their personal liberties.

In December 1773, three ships loaded with Chinese tea arrived in Boston Harbor. The Sons of Liberty were a group of merchants and traders founded to protest the Stamp Act and other English taxes. The group was led by Samuel Adams, himself a tea smuggler. The Sons of Liberty called for mass protests: more than five thousand people responded, a considerable proportion of the local population. On the morning of December 16, thousands convened at the Boston wharf and surrounding streets; at the Old South Meeting House a large group of colonists voted to refuse to pay taxes on the tea or allow the tea to be unloaded, stored, sold or used. That night, a large group of men—many reportedly members of the Sons of Liberty—disguised themselves in Indian dress, boarded the ships and threw 342

---

[9] In Maryland, a ship owner importing tea was coerced into burning his vessel and cargo after threats of tarring and feathering—a now traditional American practice. See Paul A. Gilje, Rioting in America 49 (1999).

[10] Carp, supra note 5, at 20–21.

[11] Id. at 166.

chests of tea into the water. Most participants in the Boston Tea Party were under the age of forty and sixteen of them were in their teens. Thanks to their disguises, only one was arrested and imprisoned—Francis Akeley.

The English government responded with punitive measures—the so-called Coercive Acts. The acts closed Boston Harbor until the tea was paid for, abolished the Massachusetts Constitution, imposed martial law and required quartering of British troops. As we all know, less than a year later, all the colonies except Georgia sent delegates to Philadelphia for the First Continental Congress in September 1774. The next month, the Congress issued a declaration calling for, among other actions, repeal of the Coercive Acts, boycott of English goods and formation of a colonial militia. England rejected the demands and then on April 19, 1775 in Concord, the "shot heard round the world" began the war, ultimately leading to American independence.

On July 4, 1776 representatives from the thirteen colonies signed the Declaration of Independence. English trading monopolies were listed among George III's "injuries and usurpation"—"cutting off our Trade with all parts of the world." In the same year, two colonies listed freedom from monopoly in their constitutions. Maryland declaimed in its Declaration of Rights that "monopolies are odious, contrary to the spirit of a free government, and the principles of commerce; and ought not to be suffered." And North Carolina stated in its Declaration of Rights that "perpetuities and monopolies are contrary to the genius of a free state, and ought not to be allowed." These and other state constitutional bans on monopoly are discussed below.

In sum, by 1776 the aversion to monopoly evidenced already in the early 17th century had developed into a deeply rooted tradition of opposition in the colonies. That opposition was motivated not only by economic concerns over exclusion from trade and high prices, but also reflected a critically important political element—independence. In answer to the questions posed earlier, colonial opposition to the English trading monopolies was an important contributing factor that brought about the American Revolution—England and its monopoly privileges were to be left behind in the new republican world. As Madison later proclaimed: "That is not a just government . . . where arbitrary restrictions, exemptions, and monopolies deny to part of its citizens that free use of their faculties, and free choice of their occupations ...."[12]

---

[12] James Madison, Property (Mar. 29, 1792), in Phillip B. Kurland & Ralph Lerner (eds.), 1 The Founders' Constitution: Major Themes 598 (1987).

In addition to complaints about English trading monopolies, the colonists also addressed the problem of wartime inflation by resorting to traditional laws against "monopolistic" prices, like forestalling and engrossing, as well as imposing price controls. These are discussed in the next section.

II. ENGROSSING, FORESTALLING AND PRICE CONTROLS AT OUR NATION'S BIRTH

Colonial complaints and laws concerning "monopolistic" practices perceived as raising prices—like forestalling and engrossing (cornering the market)—not only continued into the revolutionary and founding period; they increased in volume and intensity. As to forestalling, in 1797 a farmer complained to a Philadelphia newspaper that hucksters aggressively jumped onto farmers' boats before they had landed: "This is one of the many instances of these people's forestalling our markets by which means I believe they raise a tax upon us of one half and sometimes more than one half of the amount of our Market-house."[13] The farmer blamed the absence of market clerks, who had left the city during the yellow fever epidemic. As to engrossing, in 1777 in New York, "monopolizing hucksters" purchased large quantities of potatoes and turnips, stored them in cellars near the dock, and "afterwards introduce[d] them into the market, and dispose[d] them at a very exorbitant price."[14] The mayor ordered the vegetables seized and sent to the public almshouse.

As mentioned in Chapter Two, a distinction between (lawful) storage and (unlawful) hoarding is often difficult to assess in a specific situation. Indeed, sometimes storage itself was viewed as evidence of engrossing. In 1797, the New York City Council banned hucksters from selling fruit at Fly Market because they were found with a large surplus of produce—a sign that they had been engaged in engrossing.[15]

Wartime inflation was closely connected with engrossers and price controls. After only a year, the war was already taking its toll on the colonial economy given the dislocations of supply, increased demand, reliance on depreciating paper currency and high

[13] Helen Tagires, Public Markets and Civic Culture in Nineteenth-Century America 7-8 (2003).

[14] Id. at 8.

[15] Id. at 19.

inflation.[16] Moreover, the Continental Congress and the states were issuing paper money in huge amounts and prices rapidly increased with high volatility. Sterling prices of grain rose 200 to 600 percent in the first two years of the war around Hartford, Providence and Philadelphia.[17] And despite price controls, in Maryland, for example, salt appreciated in value 3,900 percent between 1777 and 1780; wheat appreciated 5,000 percent in the same period.

Like their many predecessors in other countries and times, the colonists blamed inflation on "monopolizers." In Boston, for example, a broadside poster described those withholding goods and charging exorbitant prices as "monopolizers and extortioners, who, like canker worms, are gnawing upon your vitals. They are reducing the currency to waste paper by refusing to take it for many articles."[18] Toward the end of 1778, an Army officer urged the Pennsylvania civil authorities to take measures to protect the poor "as Grain is so dear and the Monopolizers and Forestallers are to blame, for I look uppon them to be worse than the Savages or any Enemy thats against us."[19]

We will examine engrossing, forestalling and price controls during the Revolutionary period in chronological order. Several themes should be kept in mind. First, food riots and violence against the "monopolizers" centered on economic concerns about higher prices,[20] just as they had in medieval and early modern Europe. For example, James Madison declaimed that "[t]he spirit of monopoly" had created "an artificial scarcity of commodities wanted for public use, the consequence of which has been an increase of their price."[21] Even fervent Federalists, like Alexander Hamilton, decried the price-raising effect of monopoly.[22]

---

[16] See E. James Ferguson, The Power of the Purse (1961); Anne Bezanson, Prices and Inflation During the American Revolution: Pennsylvania, 1770–1790 (1951).

[17] Cathy Matson, "The Revolution, The Constitution, and the Early National Economy" in 1 The Cambridge Economic History of the United States 368–69 (Stanley Engerman & Robert Gallman 1996).

[18] Davis Rich Dewey, Financial History of the United States 345–46 (Hart 1922).

[19] Franklin D. Jones, Historical Development of the Law of Business Competition, 36 Yale L. J. 42, 53 (1926), citing 7 Pennsylvania Archives 113 (Hazard's ed. 1853).

[20] See Barry Hawk, Antitrust and Competition Laws 12-17(2020)

[21] Madison essay on "Money" (ca. Sept. 1779–Mar. 1780), quoted in Daniel Francis, Making Sense of Monopolization: Antitrust and the Digital Economy 22, 84 Antitrust Law J. (2022).

[22] See Hamilton, Report on the Subject of Manufactures (Dec. 5, 1791).

But, importantly, the American revolutionaries added a political element to their protests against monopoly: support for independence from England.[23] As "A Farmer" explained in the popular press in 1778: "This is the very same oppression that we complain of Great Britain!"[24] Economic and political matters were closely connected in colonial America in the sense that economic burdens signaled government failure—if not corruption.[25] The link between patriotism and prices already can be seen in the "solemn leagues and covenants" organized to boycott English goods beginning in 1764. As Barbara Clark Smith describes:

> "Elite Americans would abandon genteel imports in order to patronize local artisans; countrywomen would stay home from the store to produce homespun for their households and possibly for urban consumers. Everyone would put aside profit in a common sacrifice: neither merchants nor mechanics would raise prices to reap a windfall from the shortages that nonimportation would cause."[26]

These non-importation and non-consumption pacts made mundane matters—like tea drinking, thread spinning and buying and selling goods—political lightning rods.

Relatedly, the Continental Congress created the Continental Association which consisted of more than a thousand local Committees of Safety or Committees of Inspection throughout the colonies.[27] Like earlier organized embargos on English imports, these Committees brought patriotic support to the local working level. As Joseph Ellis describes, "everyone was touched by the Association .... what prices you charged if you were a merchant or grocer ... all become political statements for which all were held

---

[23] See Barbara Clark Smith, Food Rioters and the American Revolution, 51 William and Mary Q. 3d 1, 6 (1994). Of course, government grants of monopoly privileges were roundly condemned as well as the private monopolizing practices that raised prices.

[24] "A Farmer," Connecticut Courant, Feb. 16, 1778.

[25] See Smith, supra note 23, at 9.

[26] Id. at 14.

[27] See Joseph J. Ellis, The Cause: The American Revolution and Its Discontents 1773–1783 80 (2021). For example, Massachusetts appointed 160 town committees with ten members each. Virginia allocated 20 committed committee members for each of its 61 counties.

accountable."[28] Again, this added a novel and important political element to the ancient opposition to "monopolizers:" a patriot did not charge excessive prices.

Second, colonial food rioters and other protesters demanded an assortment of informal and official actions well beyond prosecution of forestalling and engrossing laws.[29] These included demands that authorities seize and sell certain goods at reasonable prices,[30] boycott monopolists and publish the names of monopolists and hoarders.[31] (More examples can be seen below in our chronology.) Thus, a description of engrossing, forestalling and monopoly during the Revolutionary period that is limited to evidence (or the absence of evidence) of prosecutions and court cases likely understates the opposition to monopoly at the time.

Third, there was a shift in protests from rural to urban areas as the war progressed.[32] During the earlier years, import prices rose more quickly than prices for domestic products. This harmed farmers whose agricultural produce bought fewer imported goods—like sugar—and led farmers to suspect that rural storekeepers were seeking unreasonable profits. By the late 1770s, however, farm prices outpaced imports and food riots occurred in the cities.

Let us turn now to a chronological sampling of protests against the "monopolizers" and the eventual failure of price controls as a response to popular demands for action. We begin in 1776. In March, there were numerous complaints in Pennsylvania that forestallers and engrossers were cornering the supply of salt, sugar, spice, coffee and other provisions. The Committee of Safety fixed prices and provided that anyone failing to observe them should be "exposed by name to public view as sordid vultures, who were preying on the vitals of their country in time of common distress."[33]

In July 1776, a crowd in Longmeadow (Massachusetts) took direct action, rather than troubling the authorities with legal measures. Disguised as "Indians" and their faces blackened, a

---

[28] Id.

[29] Smith suggests that Americans continued to prefer their own stringent standards (and remedies) of fairness rather than those of courts or prosecuting officials. Supra note 23, at 20.

[30] In 1776, local authorities in New York ordered the seizure of tea and resale of the tea at a fixed price. Id.

[31] Id.

[32] Id. at 17.

[33] Jones, supra note 19.

crowd delivered a written ultimatum to two retailers to reduce their "extravagant prices" of West India goods (notably, rum and molasses) and sell them at prices the crowd deemed appropriate.[34] Given an hour to think matters over, the retailers lowered their prices to the levels demanded.[35] But the Longmeadow crowd met stiffer resistance from another reseller of West Indian goods, Samuel Colton. His goods eventually were taken and hidden by the crowd. After a public confession, Colton got his goods back, but he then sold them at higher prices. Impatient with "moderate measures," people then broke into Colton's house, carried away rum, sugar, molasses and salt, and took them to the town clerk who sold them at "reasonable" prices, leaving the proceeds in Colton's house.

In November 1776, Connecticut attributed the "rapid and exorbitant rise of prices" to monopolizers, thereafter enacting comprehensive price controls.[36] In December, Governor Trumbull of Connecticut called for a convention of New England states for the purpose, among others, of suppressing monopoly. The states then agreed upon fixed prices for certain domestic products, profit caps on imported goods and cessation of the issuance of paper money.

In the spring of 1777, Boston saw more disguised collective action. A masked and costumed figure known as "Joyce, Jr."—the symbolic descendant of the Cornet George Joyce who had captured Charles I—led a crowd of five hundred protesters through the Boston streets.[37] The role of Joyce, Jr., was reportedly played by John Winthrop, a prominent merchant and member of Boston's Committee of Correspondence, Safety, and Inspection. The merchants who sat on the Committee hesitated to move forcefully, finding themselves caught between their colleagues' reluctance to abide voluntarily by price ceilings and popular demands for action.[38] The Joyce crowd seized five monopolizing "Tories," took them out of town in a cart and warned them never to return to Boston. As a merchant and patriot committee member, Winthrop may have tried to act as a moderating force between the city's poorer classes and its

[34] See Smith, supra note 23, at 6–7.

[35] Diary of Stephen Williams 9, 117 (July 11, 1776), cited in Smith, supra 23, at 7.

[36] Joseph Dorfman, 1 The Economic Mind in American Civilization: 1606–1865 213 (1966).

[37] Smith, supra note 23, at 16–17.

[38] Id. at 20.

merchants.[39] But many other merchants deplored Winthrop's crowd for the extralegal measures, describing them as "shocking to any One that has the sparks of humanity in them."[40]

These admonitions did not stop popular protests, many of which were led by women, as with food riots in England and France.[41] In July 1777 in Boston, about a hundred women put the merchant Thomas Boylston in a cart, seized the keys to his warehouse and confiscated coffee that he had refused to sell.[42] Women likewise led the charge in Beverly (Massachusetts), breaking into a distillery, seizing sugar, forcing other merchants to hand over their supplies and appointing one of their number to supervise retail sales.[43]

In late 1777, crowds eschewed legal niceties to demand that merchants supply goods at reasonable prices and stop hoarding. For example, in Boston a reputed hoarder (Jonathan Amory), faced with a crowd at his store, sent for three members of Boston's Committee and asked them to intervene on his behalf. In turn, the crowd delegated representatives to confer with patriot leaders, who agreed to distribute the sugar at a price acceptable to both parties.[44]

Violence and resort to extra-legal measures were not limited to New England. For example, in 1779 in Philadelphia, there were outbursts of violence.[45] Crowds of armed men forced shopkeepers to lower prices of foodstuffs, escorted offenders—a merchant, a butcher and a speculator accused of raising prices—to the city jail, seized a merchant suspected of exporting flour, and forced him to sell flour at prices the crowds were willing to pay.[46] A mass meeting created "citizen committees" to investigate flour engrossing and to set price ceilings.[47] Ultimately, the local militia were called in to restore order.

---

[39] Id. at 21.

[40] Isaac Smith wrote: "To be seized when setting down to breakfast and lodged into a Cart with his wife and Children hanging round him, not knowing but what he was a going to the Gallows, must be shocking to any one that has the sparks of humanity in them." Quoted in Smith, supra note 23 at 21.

[41] See Smith, supra note 23, at 9; Gilje, supra note 9, at 50.

[42] See Smith, supra note 23, at 22–23.

[43] Id. at 23, citing Stone, History of Beverly 83–84.

[44] Smith, supra note 23, at 23.

[45] Louis Hartz, Economic Policy and Democratic Thought: Pennsylvania, 1776-1860 7-10 (1948).

[46] Matson, supra note 17, at 369–70.

[47] Smith, supra note 23, at 25.

Later in 1779, the Supreme Executive Council of Pennsylvania condemned forestalling and engrossing as criminal acts employed by "monopolizers" that seriously harmed the poor.[48] But prosecutions apparently were largely unsuccessful.[49]

Over the course of the war, price controls were established in many places at many levels of government with one consistent result: they failed. As early as 1776, the Continental Congress was asked to recommend price controls to the states. Opponents countered that price rises were due primarily to the scarcity of commodities and excessive issuances of paper money; thus, price controls would be another failed attempt to raise the value of money. In a letter signed "A New Jersey Farmer," John Witherspoon even lectured General Washington on the inexpediency and injustice of attempting to fix prices for provisions for his Army.[50]

In February 1777, the Continental Congress recommended that the states hold regional conventions to discuss price controls. And in August, a northern convention recommended the repeal of all price controls as unworkable. But wartime inflation prompted yet another reversal when a new convention again recommended price controls. The problem of inflation was inextricably tied up with the currency problem: independence depended on the success of the army, which in turn depended on the credit of the currency. Price controls were seen as temporary remedies to permit time for the Congress to reduce the amount of the currency in circulation, and thus appreciate it.

Price controls were put in place by many states. In January 1777, Massachusetts fixed maximum prices of more than fifty staple

---

[48] Minutes of the Supreme Execute Council of Pennsylvania 671 (1852). The Council declared:

> "The prices of rum, tea, sugar, flour, coffee have risen without any real cause. The tax laid on us by forestallers and monopolists the last six months has been sufficient to prosecute the war for a year. ... By stepping in between importers and retailers, monopolizers can introduce a scarcity when they choose and, by transporting goods from one state to another, create a scarcity in one or all; and the retailers are practically free to add what profits they please. ..."

Quoted in Dorfman, supra note 36.

[49] The president of the Council reported to the Assembly that a stronger public abhorrence of forestalling and engrossing was needed for successful prosecutions.

[50] Dorfman, supra note 36, at 214.

articles.[51] Concord set detailed prices for meals at taverns: "an extra good dinner, £1; common, 12sh.; best supper and breakfast 15sh.; common, 12sh.; West India flip, 15sh. per mug."[52] Later in 1777, Massachusetts imposed price controls in "an act to prevent monopoly and oppression."[53] The law was disregarded, and new legislation was passed providing varying prices—but again to no avail. John Adams admitted that "rascally upstarts in trade" made great fortunes by monopoly and oppression, but this evil could only be cured by people refusing to buy their goods.[54] Adams warned that civil war in Massachusetts would follow if the price control legislation was not quickly repealed. And indeed, after a few months it was.

In December 1777, New Jersey fixed prices in order "to prevent forestalling, regrating and engrossing."[55] Maximum prices were set on iron, leather, shoes, wheat, corn, flour, butter and other goods. About a month later, the president of the Council of Safety was forced to warn local officials to enforce the law under pain of prosecution and to transmit the names of offenders to state authorities: "evil minded persons ... endeavor to persuade the ignorant or unwary" that the law would not be enforced.

Yet in 1778, the Continental Congress again switched course and recommended that the states repeal all price controls, because they were ineffective. But General Washington remained unconvinced: "Speculation, peculation, engrossing, forestalling with all their concomitants, evidence the decay of public virtue."[56] Others in the Congress shared Washington's sentiments. In November, a Committee of Congress advised the Supreme Executive Council of Pennsylvania: "the dangerous practices of Engrossers have increased .... This seething of the Kid in its Mother's milk calls for

---

[51] Dewey, supra note 18.

"Good well fatted grass-fed beef at 3d. a lb. and stall-fed beef well fatted at 4d. a lb. and beef of inferior quality in equal proportion"; "good merchantable imported salt, at 10sh. a bushel."

[52] Id.

[53] See N. Dane, A General Abridgement and Digest of American Law, with Occasional Notes and Comments 39–40 (1823).

[54] Dorfman, supra note 36 at 421–22, quoting letter from John Adams to Abigail Adams in Letters of John Adams, II, 6 (September 8, 1777).

[55] Jones, supra note 19, at 54, quoting 1 New Jersey Archives, 2d Series 535 (Stryker's ed. 1901).

[56] Dorfman, supra note 36, at 216.

the most exemplary punishment."[57] Price controls and criminal penalties again were recommended.

Wishing to avoid a repeat of previous failures of price control, the Massachusetts General Court in 1779 encouraged Boston merchants to do their best to prevent price increases and not accept gold or silver in any form. In July, a convention at Concord drafted a schedule of prices and agreed to a reduction in all prices—both efforts failed.

Price controls failed during the Revolutionary period for many reasons other than administrative and enforcement difficulties; again, market forces often prevailed. For example, in many instances there was rural opposition from farmers to price controls.[58] Farmers claimed that prices of agricultural goods were fixed at unacceptably low prices and failed to keep up with the rising urban (black market) prices charged by peddlers and stores of needed clothing and goods.

Another conflict of interests—albeit not so directly related to market competition—influenced positions toward price controls and monopoly: the interests of debtors versus creditors. Rural debtors—like farmers—condemned bankers and creditors as monopolizers. For example, in 1777 Massachusetts passed a law depriving Massachusetts bills of their legal-tender status and provided for their exchange into interest-bearing bonds in denominations of £10 or more.[59] This inflamed debtor farmers[60] who berated the selfish "Monopolizers" who "made great gains by oppression."[61] This

---

[57] Jones, supra note 19, citing 7 Pennsylvania Archives 85-88 (Hazard's ed. 1853).

[58] See Oscar and Mary Handlin, Commonwealth - A Study of the Role of Government in the American Economy: Massachusetts, 1774-1871 22-23 (1947); Matson, supra note 17, at 369-70; Cf. Daniel Vickers, "The Northern Colonies: Economy and Society" in 1 The Cambridge Economic History of the United States 241 (Stanley Engerman and Robert Gallman 1996).

[59] See Handlin, supra note 58, at 14.

[60] J. Adams to Gerry, Dec. 6,1777, J. Adams, Works, IX. 470 ff.

[61] A Belcherstown petition was emphatic:

> "whether these People are in Boston or in the country we are not able to Say, but we apprehend they have persuaded your Honours to Call in their Bills—which they have unrighteously gained, and put them upon Intrest & that is to make Money Secarce, and . . . it will greatly answer the End of the monopolizer, and what Little of our Estates will be Left at the End of the war must go to pay the principal & Intrest of s^d^. Contract."

tension between the rural producer/debtor and the urban merchant/creditor played a significant role in the opposition to monopoly later in the 19th century, when the great "monopolizer" was the Second Bank of the United States, as we will see in the next chapter.

Price controls imposed during the Revolutionary War were often criticized as not only ineffective but misguided. John Witherspoon, president of the Presbyterian College of New Jersey (later Princeton), strongly opposed price controls and trade monopolies.[62] In 1776, the same year as Adam Smith's *Wealth of Nations*, Pelatiah Webster published "An Essay on the Danger of Too Much Circulating Cash in a State" in which he defended a "free market" and condemned price controls as "abridgements of natural liberty."[63] Webster condemned the "unhappy expedient" of regulating prices during the war, which in his view had disastrous effects.[64] Few goods were brought to market, resentment was created against sellers and the government, and hoarding increased. These opinions were generally consistent with the positions of thinkers outside the colonies. The French *philosophes* and later Adam Smith were developing economic thinking that favored free markets and disfavored price controls, as mentioned in Chapter Two.

Price controls in the colonies also had become associated with the violent and extralegal actions against the "monopolizers." Like many others, Webster argued that the popular demand for price controls often was expressed in violence and disorder—houses and shops were searched to seize hoarded goods, thus infringing personal liberty and violating property rights. While the authorities eventually acted to suppress this violence and to return to law and order, they typically only followed after excision of the patriotic element of protests against the monopolizers. Patriot leaders gradually turned away from formulations of Revolutionary purpose tied to equitable prices and economic morality.[65] Instead, the people were called on to take their grievances to the courts and to leave the

---

Belcherstown, Billerica Remonstrances, M.A., CLXXXIII, 292ff., 307, quoted in Handlin, supra note 58, at 14.

[62] See E.A. J. Johnson, The Foundations of American Economic Freedom: Government and Enterprise in the Age of Washington 11-29 (1973).

[63] Pelatiah Webster, Political Essays 24 (Philadelphia 1791), see Johnson, supra note 62, at 28-29, See also Johnson supra note 62, at 167-68.

[64] Webster, supra note 63, at 11. See Johnson, supra note 62, at 189.

[65] See Smith, supra note 23, at 24.

matter of punishing monopolizers to the proper authorities.[66] The excision was successful. Ultimately, states began to repeal even longstanding price control measures like bread assizes. For example, Pennsylvania repealed its bread assizes as inconsistent with the rights recognized in the 1790 state constitution.[67]

But, as in England, laws on forestalling and engrossing did not end overnight. Bans on forestalling continued into the 19th century in the United States,[68] as discussed in Chapter Four. But it is fair to conclude that demands for forestalling and engrossing laws against the "monopolizers" reached their peak during the inflationary years of the Revolutionary War.

Let us move away from forestalling and engrossing monopolizers to monopolies and exclusive trading privileges granted by government authorities.

III. STATE (AND LOCAL) MONOPOLY GRANTS AND STATE CONSTITUTIONS

As seen above, in the same year as independence was declared, two states—Maryland and North Carolina—included antimonopoly provisions in their constitutions.[69] The Maryland constitution (Article 41) declared that "monopolies are odious, contrary to the spirit of a free government and the principles of commerce, and ought not to be suffered."[70] Scholars offer various sources for Article 41, including among others, English common law, Coke's commentaries and general opposition to the English trading monopolies.[71] In

---

[66] For an argument that this meant the loss of the social and political frame that made sense of the food or price riot as a political form, see Smith, supra note 23, at 34 ("The elite drew back from its endorsement of popular politics in 1780; the Continental Congress discouraged crowds and courted the support of wealthy and conservative men."). Of course, this all changed in the next century, notably with the election of Andrew Jackson as president.

[67] Johnson, supra note 62, at 306–07.

[68] See Hawk, supra note 20, at 59–60.

[69] The fact that only two of the original thirteen colonies included antimonopoly provisions in their constitutions does not evidence the absence of antimonopolist sentiment in the other colonies and states. See Michael Conant, Antimonopoly Tradition under the Ninth and Fourteenth Amendments: Slaughter-House Cases Re-Examined, 31 Emory L. J. 785, 799 (1982).

[70] Md. CONST. art. 41.

[71] See Dan Friedman, The Maryland State Constitution: A Reference Guide 305 n.257 (G. Alan Tarr ed. 2006).

similar language, the North Carolina constitution (section 34) proclaimed: "Perpetuities and monopolies are contrary to the genius of a free State, and ought not to be allowed."[72] Section 34 was interpreted to mean that "[a] monopoly need not be a perpetuity, nor is a perpetuity necessarily a monopoly; but both, existing either jointly or severally, are within the constitutional prohibition."[73] The Tennessee Constitution of 1796 included almost identical language to North Carolina.[74] Several of the new states also adopted monopoly bans in their state constitutions in the 19th century, as discussed in Chapter Four.

The overwhelming majority of states, however, did not include antimonopoly provisions in their constitutions. Mindful of the more than 150 years of colonial grants of monopoly privileges, states recognized that some monopolies were justified as promoting a public interest—like short-term privileges to encourage local manufacture or to incentivize construction and operation of infrastructure. This argued against a constitutional limitation on state legislatures. Thus, despite the strong opposition to monopolies—like the English trading monopoly that triggered the Boston Tea Party—the colonists recognized that some government grants of monopoly privileges could be justified. In other words, the American antimonopoly principle developed through the end of the 18th century did not condemn all monopolies, or in modern terms, the principle did not condemn monopoly per se. As we shall see, that has never changed—despite recurring calls to do so (even today).

The failure to place monopoly provisions in most state constitutions does not mean that opposition to monopoly was ineffective. Opposition continued even in states lacking a constitutional antimonopoly provision, as discussed later in Chapters Four and Five. Federal constitutional limitations on monopoly—both government and private—present a somewhat different picture from state constitutional limitations, to which we now turn.

---

[72] N.C. CONST. art. 1. §34.

[73] Thrift v. Bd. of Comm'rs, 30 S.E. 349, 351 (N.C. 1898).

[74] Article I, section 22 declared: "That perpetuities and monopolies are contrary to the genius of a free state, and shall not be allowed."

IV. FEDERAL CONSTITUTION

A. No Ban on Monopoly

Like eleven of the thirteen original states, there is no ban on monopoly in the federal constitution (including the first Ten Amendments or Bill of Rights). Explanations cannot be clearly gleaned from the Constitutional Convention of 1787. But one can be easily rejected. William Letwin certainly was correct when he concluded that "no one argued that the prohibition was omitted because the public favored or was even indifferent to monopolies."[75] Perhaps the best explanation for the failure of the Constitutional Convention to include a federal constitutional ban on monopoly is the same as the explanation why eleven of the original states failed to place a ban in their state constitutions: some grants of monopoly privileges promoted a public interest in developing local or critical industries; hence, a constitutional limitation on federal legislative powers was unwise. Indeed, as it turned out, a constitutional ban on federal grants of monopoly privileges would have circumscribed the federal government's role in the 20th century, particularly beginning with the New Deal agenda.

When the draft Constitution was sent to the states for ratification, conventions in three states—Massachusetts, New Hampshire and North Carolina—requested that "Congress erect no Company of Merchants with exclusive advantages of commerce." [76] The New York convention that ratified the Constitution recommended an amendment "[t]hat the congress does not grant monopolies, or erect any company with exclusive advantages of commerce."[77] Some scholars add two more states (Virginia and Rhode Island) to the list of proposers of a constitutional ban on federal grants of monopoly or exclusive trading privileges.[78]

---

[75] William L. Letwin, Congress and The Sherman Antitrust Law, 23 Chicago L. Rev. 221-227 (1956).

[76] See Thomas B. Nachbar, Intellectual Property and Constitutional Norms, 104 Columbia L. Rev. 272, 342 n.289 (2004).

[77] Ratification of the New Constitution by the Convention of the State of New York, 4 American Museum 153, 156 (Philadelphia, Matthew Carey 1789).

[78] See Calabresi & Leibowitz, supra note 4, at 1013 n.178; Conant, supra note 69, at 256–57. See also Donald S. Lutz, The States and the U.S. Bill of Rights, 16 S. Ill. U. L.J. 251, 256-57 (1992) (cataloging amendments proposed by ratifying states).

But only one of these six states (North Carolina) included bans on grants of monopoly or exclusive trading privileges in their own state constitutions. This suggests that the five other states were more concerned about federal grants of monopoly than about state grants of monopoly that had become the practice in their states for more than a century. In other words, the concern was more about the powers of the new federal government (seen perhaps in the light of the English trading monopolies imposed by the distant government in London) rather than about the new states' powers to grant monopoly privileges.[79]

The concern over federal power is also seen in the discussion between two members of the Constitutional Convention (George Mason and James Madison) and Thomas Jefferson about monopoly in general (discussed here) and intellectual property rights (discussed below). It is important to distinguish between monopoly in general and intellectual property rights, particularly as most of the correspondence and other historical sources deal with patents and copyrights and not monopoly in general.

Let us start with George Mason who attended the Constitutional Convention in Philadelphia in 1787. Mason refused to sign the proposed constitution,[80] objecting to potential abuse of two proposed federal powers: use of the commerce clause to regulate navigation in favor of the northern and eastern states against the interests of the southern states; and 2) use of the necessary and proper clause to permit overreaching federal regulation to the detriment of state interests, such as grants of monopoly privileges.[81]

---

[79] Another partial explanation is that the states focused more on the structures of state government than on producing state bills of rights. See Calabresi & Leibowitz, supra note 4, at 1014.

[80] George Mason, Objections to the Constitution of Government Formed by the Convention (1787), reprinted in 2 The Complete Anti-Federalist 11, 12-13 (Herbert J. Storing ed., 1981). Mason wrote:

> "Under their own Construction of the general Clause at the End of the enumerated powers the Congress may grant Monopolies in Trade and Commerce, constitute new Crimes, inflict unusual and severe Punishments, and extend their Power as far as they shall think proper; so that the State Legislatures have no Security for the Powers now presumed to remain to them; or the People for their Rights."

Elbridge Gerry of Massachusetts refused to sign the proposed Constitution for similar reasons.

[81] See generally Nachbar, supra note 76.

This suggests that Mason was not necessarily opposed in principle to government monopoly grants, but rather to potential misuses of federal powers.

Jefferson, who was in Paris at the time of the Constitutional Convention, first expressed his views in correspondence with Madison during the ratification process.[82] Jefferson criticized the failure of the Convention to provide "clearly, and without the aid of sophisms for ... restriction of monopolies."[83] He argued for amendments to the constitution or what became known as a Bill of Rights. In addition to freedoms of religion and press, among others, Jefferson urged freedom from monopolies.[84]

In his initial reply to Jefferson, Madison conceded that monopoly generally was evil, but patents/copyrights (inventions or author works) were legitimate exceptions that merited federal empowerment.[85] With respect to monopoly privileges not involving inventions or author works, Madison's position was more nuanced. Madison did not defend monopoly in all circumstances; rather he argued against a constitutional limitation on the federal power to grant monopoly privileges if the federal legislature and executive chose to do so. For Madison, the risk of harmful government monopoly grants was attenuated by representative government at the federal level; that is, the widely dispersed representative system would itself limit the congressional power to grant (harmful) monopolies: "Where the power, as with us, is in the many not in the few, the danger can not be very great that the few will be thus favored. It is much more to be dreaded that the few will be

---

[82] Jefferson had received copy of the Constitution as it was sent to the states for ratification.

[83] Works, Washington II, 329 (1787), quoted in Johnson, supra note 62, at 188-89.

[84] Letter from Thomas Jefferson to James Madison (Dec. 20, 1787) in 12 The Papers of Thomas Jefferson 440 (Julian P. Boyd ed., 1955): "[It] is better to ... abolish ... Monopolies, in all cases, than not to do it in any ...."

[85] Madison wrote:

> "With regard to Monopolies they are justly classed among the greatest nu[i]sances in Government. But is it clear that as encouragements to literary works and ingenious discoveries, they are not too valuable to be wholly renounced?"

Letter from James Madison to Thomas Jefferson (Oct. 17, 1788), in 14 The Papers of Thomas Jefferson 21 (Julian P. Boyd ed., 1958).

unnecessarily sacrificed to the many."[86] In other words, broad representation at the federal level was thought to protect against the English experience with monopoly. In sum, Madison viewed monopoly grants much like protectionist taxation and legislation—inappropriate and violative of property rights in many but not all circumstances. For example, Madison—perhaps begrudgingly—supported duties intended to discriminate in favor of American shipping.[87]

The views of Jefferson were shared to some extent by "anti-Federalists" who feared a strong central federal government. More broadly, critics like Agrippa believed that monopoly harms came more from government action than from the market.[88] A "Son of Liberty" warned that "monopolies in trade, [would be] granted to the favorites of government, by which the spirit of adventure will be destroyed, and the citizens subjected to the extortion of those companies who will have an exclusive right, to engross the different branches of commerce."[89]

In a sense, the views of Jefferson and Agrippa should be seen in their anti-Federalist context. The absence of an antimonopoly provision in either the original Constitution or the Ten Amendments is more persuasive evidence of the Founders' views toward monopoly. In this respect, Jefferson's statements expressing unqualified rejection of government grants of monopoly rights are more useful today for creative lawyering to support a legal position in litigation[90] than for accurately capturing the complexity of history.

Moreover, the absence of a federal constitutional limitation on monopolies (notably, in the Bill of Rights) cannot be explained away or minimized by attributing the absence solely to one Founder—

---

[86] Id. As Nachbar suggests, Madison did not consider the public choice problems inherent in the power to grant monopolies to be so strong as to systematically endanger the legislative process. Nachbar, supra note 76, at 341.

[87] See 1 Annals of Cong. 198-99 (Joseph Gales Ed., 1789), cited in Nachbar, supra note 76, at 356.

[88] See Calabresi & Leibowitz, supra note 4, at 1012–13.

[89] Id. at 1013, quoting James P. Philbin, The Political Economy of the Antifederalists, 11 J. Libertarian Stud. 79, 104 (1994), quoting 4 The Complete Anti-Federalist, at 492 (internal quotation marks omitted).

[90] Nachbar argues that those objections do not appear to have been reflected in anything approaching the kind of "demonstrable consensus" that an originalist would expect to see before inferring an effect on the meaning of the Constitution. See Nachbar, supra 76, at 344–45.

Madison.[91] It is true that Madison played a key role in the constitutional process. Indeed, he was assigned the responsibility of drafting the Bill of Rights in response to the requests for amendments from the state ratifying conventions. Ultimately, however, the states approved the Bill of Rights without an antimonopoly provision—something that surprised Hamilton given state resistance to a federally chartered national bank. (As we shall see in Chapter Four, the battle over the federal power to create a national bank was fought at the legislative (and executive) level in the 19th century—not at the constitutional level.)

Opposition to monopoly did contribute to the Constitutional Convention's rejection of a federal power to grant corporate charters.[92] Madison proposed to give the federal government the power "[t]o grant charters of incorporation in cases where the public good may require them, and the authority of a single State may be incompetent."[93] Likewise, Charles Pinckney proposed a power "[t]o grant charters for incorporation."[94] Rufus King of Massachusetts objected that a federal corporation might lead to "mercantile monopolies," as with England before the American Revolution.[95] George Mason objected more generally that a federal incorporation power would lead to "monopolies of every sort."[96] Madison and Pinckney's proposals were rejected which was confirmed in the state ratifying conventions in which Massachusetts, New Hampshire, New York, North Carolina and Rhode Island suggested that the draft Constitution be amended as not to allow federal charters conferring "exclusive advantages of commerce."[97] In the end, there would be no incorporation clause in the federal constitution. Incorporation was left to the states where, in the 19th century, state-created corporations generated important constitutional and political issues, as discussed in Chapter Four.

---

91 This is the assertion of Calabresi & Leibowitz, supra note 4, at 1014.

92 See Dotan Oliar, Making Sense of the Intellectual Property Clause: Promotion of Progress as a Limitation on Congress's Intellectual Property Power, 94 Georgetown L. J. 1771, 1800-01 (2006).

93 See Madison's Journal for September 14, 1787.

94 See id.

95 Daniel A. Crane, Lochnerian Antitrust, 1 NYU J.L & Liberty 496, 506 (2005), quoting Daniel A. Farber & Suzanna Sherry, A History of The American Constitution 141 (1990) (internal quotation marks omitted).

96 Id.

97 Oliar, supra note 92, at 1801 n.155.

While there is no federal incorporation power in the Constitution, the Constitutional Convention did expressly empower the federal government to grant patents for inventions and copyrights for author works, as are discussed next.

B. Patents and Copyrights

The intellectual property clause of the Constitution (article I, section 8) empowers Congress to grant patents and copyrights for a limited term. The clause was accepted unanimously at the Constitutional Convention and received little critical attention during the ratification process. There has since been considerable legal debate about the meaning of the clause, including its history and legislative intent. As the Court has stated: "[t]o comprehend the scope of Congress's power under the [Intellectual Property] Clause, a page of history is worth a volume of logic."[98] This was true in 1921 and remains true in today's world of originalist thinking and other schools of constitutional interpretation.[99]

It appears to this observer—unskilled in the intricacies of patent and copyright law—that many courts and commentators have placed too much emphasis on historical statements expressing unqualified condemnations of monopoly, generally, to support a narrow interpretation of the intellectual property clause. Most fail to acknowledge that the colonists and their English parents always excepted inventions from the antimonopoly principle. Conferring on the new federal government the (non-exclusive) power to grant patents for inventions is thus entirely consistent with the colonial and English practice. As discussed in Chapter Two, the colonies commonly granted patents for a limited term for products or processes resulting from invention, the first being granted in 1646. These grants were viewed as an exception to a general rule disfavoring monopoly. The history of copyrights before 1787 is markedly different. Colonial copyrights were pretty much non-existent until the 1780s, as discussed later below.

Given the different colonial histories of patents and copyrights, we will look at them separately.

---

[98] N.Y. Trust Co. v. Eisner, 256 U.S. 345, 349 (1921).

[99] Oliar, supra note 92, at 1779–80.

1. *Patents*

The intellectual property clause was accepted unanimously at the Constitutional Convention and received little critical attention during the ratification process. This leaves considerable room to speculate on the purpose of the clause. According to Bruce Bugbee, the lawyers comprising a majority of the fifty-five delegates at the Constitutional Convention constructed the clause by looking to colonial and more recent state experience.[100] Others like Edward Walterscheid dismiss this experience as "merely part of the evolutionary background."[101] Several observations are offered here.[102]

First, the federal intellectual property clause does not mirror exactly the language of the colonial and state provisions.[103] This makes reliance on the state law patent provisions less robust in addressing specific federal patent issues, such as term limits and criteria for patentability.

Second, it is unpersuasive to rely on statements by Founders—e.g., like Jefferson's general view that monopoly was evil—to support a legal argument about a specific patent issue (like term limits or criteria for patentability).[104] The colonial and state experiences prior to 1787 confirm that patents with limited monopoly rights were clearly recognized as legitimate exceptions to the antimonopoly tradition. It is not at all surprising then, that a federal power to grant patents would be viewed as an uncontroversial exception to the antimonopoly principle. The view is also supported by the new economic learning of Adam Smith which was known at the time. For example, James Kent of New York wrote to Nathaniel Lawrence, a delegate to the New York ratifying convention, explaining: "I have just been reading Smith on the Wealth of Nations & he has taught me to look with an unfavorable

---

[100] See Bruce W. Bugbee, Genesis of American Patent and Copyright Law 2-3 (1967) (most delegates acquired their political preparation in the colonial legislatures).

[101] See Edward C. Walterscheid, To Promote the Progress of Science and Useful Arts: the Background and Origin of the Intellectual Property Clause of the United States Constitution, 2 J. of Intell. Prop 1, 31 n.101 (1994).

[102] These conclusions also pertain to copyrights.

[103] See Bugbee, supra note 100, at 127–29. For discussion of the language in the state constitutions, see Walterscheid, supra note 101, at 30–31.

[104] See discussion below.

eye on monopolies-But a monopoly of the mental kind I take to be laudable & an exception to the Rule."[105]

Accordingly, legal arguments about term limits and patentability are more persuasive to the extent that they rest on historical evidence specific to the issue (for example, term limits in colonial patent grants). This conclusion may strike some readers as inconsistent with the litany of articles and court opinions filled with statements declaring that the federal intellectual property clause must be interpreted in the light of an historical American (and English) abhorrence of monopoly.[106] And to be sure, there was an American antimonopoly tradition firmly established by 1787. But again, that tradition had always recognized the legitimacy of monopoly grants for inventions.

Third, and relatedly, the colonial view of patents as an exception to the antimonopoly principle arguably was expressed—at least implicitly—through the often overlooked Progress Clause.[107] Section 8 begins: "The Congress shall have Power . . . to promote the Progress of Science and useful Arts ...." Unlike every other power-granting clause, section 8 is the only one that specifies the means and purpose to which the power is devoted—Congress was not given the power simply to enact patents (or copyrights).[108]

---

[105] Tyler T. Ochoa & Mark Rose, The Anti-Monopoly Origins of the Patent and Copyright Clause, 84 J. Pat & Trademark Off. Soc'y 909, 928 (2002). In Pennsylvania, "Sentinel" wrote "that monopolies in trade or arts, other than to authors of books or inventors of useful arts, for a reasonable time, ought not to be suffered." Id.

[106] See, e.g., Ochoa & Rose, supra note 105, at 925; Richard Posner, The Constitutionality of the Copyright Term Extension Act: Economics, Politics, Law, and Judicial Technique, 55 Sup. Ct. Rev. 143 (2003). But see Nachbar, supra note 76, at 330–49.; Paul M. Schwartz & William Michael Treanor, Eldred and Lochner: Copyright Term Extension and Intellectual Property as Constitutional Property, 112 Yale L. J. 2331, 2378 & n.271 (2003) ("[T]here is, for example, no particular reason to read into the Clause the view that the Founders were afraid that Congress would engage in the kind of giveaways in which Queen Elizabeth had once engaged.').

[107] There is extensive debate whether the Progress clause limits only the grant of patents and copyrights or limits congressional powers more broadly. See generally Oliar, supra note 92, at 1772–1812. ("[T]he Framers intended to allow Congress to use some means (patents, copyrights) to "promote the progress of science and useful arts," and at the same time not others (universities, encouragements (bounties).").

[108] See Lawrence Lessig, Copyright's First Amendment, 48 UCLA L. Rev. 1057, 1062 (2000-2001).

The Supreme Court in *Graham v. John Deere Co.* declared that the Progress Clause serves to limit the power conferred by the intellectual property clause.[109] To support its interpretation, the Court invoked a general abhorrence of monopolies in the colonies, yet with no reference to any particular Framer, with the lone (and standard) exception of reference to Jefferson's abhorrence to monopolies. In the face of this relatively bald position, the views of Madison and Jefferson toward patents are worth considering in more detail.

The influence of Jefferson on Supreme Court decisions concerning patents (and copyrights as seen in the next section) can hardly be exaggerated. Jefferson's views are expressed in correspondence with Madison during and after the ratification process, as well as in letters written after Jefferson's stint as head of the U.S. patent office. Rather than cite individual sentences, we will reproduce, in chronological order, longer excerpts in order to give a fuller picture of their views.

After receiving a draft of the Constitution at the end of 1787, Jefferson wrote to Madison: "I will now add what I do not like. First, the omission of a bill of rights providing clearly and without the aid of sophisms for ... restriction against monopolies.[110] In July 1788, Jefferson amplified his concern in a letter to Madison: "[I]t is better to ... abolish ... Monopolies, in all cases, than not to do it in any.... The saying there shall be no monopolies lessens the incitements to ingenuity, which is spurred on by the hope of a monopoly for a limited time, as of 14 years; but the benefit even of limited monopolies is too doubtful to be opposed to that of their general suppression."[111]

Madison then defended the intellectual property clause in his reply of October 1788:

> "With regard to Monopolies they are justly classed among the greatest nuisances in Government. But is it clear that as encouragements to literary works and ingenious

[109] 383 U.S. 1, 5-8 (1966) ("Congress in the exercise of the patent power may not overreach the restraints imposed by the stated constitutional purpose."); see also Great Atl. & Pac. Tea Co. v. Supermarket Equip. Corp., 340 U.S. 147, 154 (1950) (Douglas, J., concurring) ("Congress acts under the restraint imposed by the statement of purpose in Art. I, § 8."); See generally Oliar, supra note 92, at 1782.

[110] Letter from Jefferson to Madison (Dec. 20, 1787), in 12 The Papers of Thomas Jefferson 440 (1955).

[111] Letter from Jefferson to Madison (July 31, 1788), in 13 The Papers of Thomas Jefferson 442-43 (1956).

discoveries, they are not too valuable to be wholly renounced? Would it not suffice to reserve in all cases a right to the public to abolish the privilege at a price to be specified in the grant of it?"[112]

After receiving Madison's draft of the Bill of Rights, Jefferson wrote in August 1789:

> "I like it as far as it goes; but I should have been for going further. For instance, the following alterations and additions would have pleased me.... Art. 9. Monopolies may be allowed to persons for their own productions in literature and their own inventions in the arts for a term not exceeding - years but for no longer term and for no other purpose. ... These restrictions I think are so guarded as to hinder evil only. However if we do not have them now, I have so much confidence in our countrymen as to be satisfied that we shall have them as soon as the degeneracy of our government shall render them necessary."[113]

Then in 1790, after passage of the Patent Act, Jefferson expressed a more favorable view of patents:

> "An act of Congress authorising the issuing patents for new discoveries has given a spring to invention beyond my conception. Being an instrument in granting the patents, I am acquainted with their discoveries. Many of them indeed are trifling, but there are some of great consequence which have been proved by practice, and others which if they stand the same proof will produce great effect."[114]

Many years later in 1807, Jefferson repeated his approval of the federal patent grant: "Certainly an inventor ought to be allowed a right to the benefit of his invention for some certain time. ... Nobody wishes more than I do that ingenuity should receive a liberal encouragement."[115]

---

[112] Letter from Madison to Jefferson (Oct. 17, 1788), in 14 The Papers of Thomas Jefferson 21 (1958).

[113] Letter from Jefferson to Madison (Aug. 28, 1789), in 15 The Papers of Thomas Jefferson 367–68 (1958).

[114] See Bugbee, supra note 100, at 148, quoting Letter from Jefferson to Benjamin Vaughan (June 27, 1790) in The Papers of Thomas Jefferson, 578–80 (1961).

[115] Letter to Oliver Evans (May 1807), V Writings of Thomas Jefferson, at 75–76 (Washington ed.).

Finally, some 30 years after the Federalist, Madison looked back and summarized his views on the entire subject area:

> "Monopolies tho' in certain cases useful ought to be granted with caution, and guarded with strictness agst abuse. The Constitution of the U.S. has limited them to two cases, the authors of Books and of useful inventions .... There can be no just objection to a temporary monopoly in these cases: but it ought to be temporary, because under that limitation sufficient recompence and encouragement may be given....
>
> ... [Monopoly grants for useful undertakings] can be justified in very peculiar cases only, if at all: the danger being very great that the good resulting from the operation of the monopoly, will be overbalanced by the evil effect of the precedent; and it being not impossible that the monopoly itself, in its original operation, may produce more evil than good.
>
> In all cases of monopoly, not excepting those specified in favor of authors & inventors, it would be well to reserve to the State, a right to terminate the monopoly by paying a specified and reasonable sum [to the holder.] This would guard against the public discontents resulting from the exorbitant gains of individuals, and from the inconvenient restrictions combined with them.[116]

Some scholars have castigated the propensity of judges and lawyers to selectively cite isolated statements of Jefferson (and other Founders) to support certain legal position. For example, a particularly unhappy complaint comes from Edward Walterscheid: "The Court's selective use of the Jeffersonian record, frequently out of context, as a form of advocacy, creates a mythology at odds with the contemporaneous record."[117] We will limit our own reaction

---

[116] Oliar, supra note 92, at 1800-01, citing James Madison, Monopolies, Perpetuities, Corporations, Ecclesiastical Endowments., in Elizabeth Fleet, Madison's "Detached Memoranda," 3 Wm. & Mary Q. 3d 534, 551-52 (1946).

[117] Edward C. Walterscheid, The Use and Abuse of History: The Supreme Court's Interpretation of Thomas Jefferson's Influence on the Patent Law, 39 IDEA 195, 224 (1999).

here to three questions (and answers): would a professional historian agree that the Jefferson/Madison correspondence is a reliable or robust basis to conclude that the members of the Constitutional Convention shared Jefferson's view of a high patentability standard? No. Would a professional historian agree that the Jefferson/Madison correspondence is a reliable or robust basis to conclude that public opinion, or even the opinions of state ratifiers, shared Jefferson's view of a high patentability standard? No. Would a professional historian agree that the Jefferson/ Madison correspondence is a reliable or robust basis to conclude that Jefferson clearly and consistently disapproved of monopoly grants for inventions? No. In sum, this historical record confirms that both Jefferson and Madison eventually saw and agreed that patent rights for a term were an important and deserved exception to the general abhorrence of monopoly.

Let us turn to copyrights and their historical record.

2. *Copyrights*

Colonial copyrights developed far more slowly than patents, with only one copyright granted before the Revolution. Then in the 1780s, there was a burst of state copyright statutes: twelve states adopted laws following a recommendation of the Continental Congress,[118] although their implementation is doubted by many commentators.[119] The state statutes varied considerably in their terms and coverage. For example, only four statutes covered both previously published and unpublished works. Ten of the statutes required that the copyright holder be either a citizen or resident of the United States. Commentators also differ on compulsory licensing and mandatory price terms.[120]

The state copyright laws, though only recently enacted before the Constitutional Convention, cast some doubt on modern arguments that the federal copyright powers were begrudgingly

[118] Delaware was the lone non-conformist.

[119] See Bugbee, supra note 100, at 2; Oliar, supra note 92, at 26.

[120] Compare Oliar, supra note 92, at 26 and Walterscheid, supra note 101, at 21 (many statutes allowed courts to issue compulsory licenses and compel authors to provide the public with an adequate supply of copies at reasonable prices); Bugbee, supra note 100 (notably absent were such features as working clauses, provisions for compulsory license, cancellation privileges, or arrangements for price control).

granted and should be narrowly interpreted.[121] This may be laudatory advocacy in arguing against extensions of the copyright term period, but it may well strike some observers as poor history. Lawrence Lessig cites no evidence from the Constitutional Convention or the ratification process to support his assertion that the Framers "struggled over whether any power to grant monopolies [copyrights or patents] should be vested in Congress at all."[122] Other advocates of a narrow reading of the federal copyright clause, as well as the Supreme Court on occasion, likewise offer weak historical evidence for their position, as discussed below. First, let us look at what evidence we do have from the Constitutional Convention and ratification process. Unfortunately, there is little.

In April 1787, Madison wrote that the absence of a uniform law on literary property was one of the weaknesses of the Articles of Confederation. For Madison, however, a federal copyright was not a priority item but rather one of "inferior moment."[123] There appear to be no later references to federal copyrights in the personal records and correspondence of other members of the Constitutional Convention. For example, there is no evidence that any state instructed its delegates to seek a copyright clause in the Constitution.[124] This suggests that little can be based on the Framers' intent concerning specific issues arising under modern copyright law—e.g., term extensions. The thin historical record better supports the general

---

121 For example, in arguing against congressional extensions of the copyright terms, Lawrence Lessig invokes the antimonopoly tradition in broad and eloquent language:

> "The great evil in the Framers' mind, second only to the great evil of centralized, monarchical government, was the evil of state-sanctioned monopoly. And though they struggled over whether any power to grant monopolies should be vested in Congress at all, the power upon which they settled spoke volumes about the limitations it was to embrace: Unlike every other power-granting clause, this was the only power-granting clause that specified the means and purpose to which the power was devoted. Congress was not given the power simply to enact copyrights." Lessig, supra note 108, at 1062.

122 Id.

123 See Bugbee, supra note 100, at 125, citing 4 Documentary History of the Constitution of the United States of America, 1786–1870, at 128 (Washington, Draft St. 1894–1905) (noting that James Madison "unburdened himself on paper" regarding weaknesses of Confederation by cataloging list of its defects); see also Walterscheid, supra note 101, at 24.

124 Walterscheid, supra note 101, at 24.

proposition that "the states felt a strong need for national copyright laws to secure for authors their property rights in their works" and that, as a consequence, there was a "strong desire of the framers to include a copyright clause in the Federal Constitution."[125]

As discussed above, the Supreme Court has on various occasions cited history to support a narrow (or broad) interpretation of the patent power. The same is true of the copyright power. In *Eldred v Ashcroft* where the Court upheld a lengthy congressional extension of the copyright term,[126] both the majority and dissenting opinions refer to history to support their positions.[127] Writing for the majority (which upheld the extension), Justice Ruth Bader Ginsburg distinguished the U.S. history from the English experience. In England, "concerns about monopolistic practices remained, and the 18th century English Parliament was resistant to any enhancement of booksellers' and publishers' entrenched position."[128] By contrast, intense competition existed among publishers in colonial America at the time of the Founding and "[t]he Framers guarded against the future accumulation of monopoly power in booksellers and publishers by authorizing Congress to vest copyrights only in 'Authors.' "[129]

Justices Stevens and Breyer, on the other hand, essentially cited two reasons for finding the copyright extension unconstitutional: 1) the general antimonopoly tradition ("the antimonopoly environment in which the Framers wrote the Clause"); and 2) the English Statute of Anne ("the history of the

---

[125] Irah Donner, The Copyright Clause of the U.S. Constitution: Why Did the Framers Include It With Unanimous Approval?, 36 Am. J. Legal Hist. 361, 362-65 (1992), criticized in Walterscheid, supra note 101, at 24.

[126] 537 U.S. 186 (2003).

[127] Even critics of the courts' use of history to limit copyright protection acknowledge the importance of English copyright law and practice. For example, Nachbar argues:

> "Both the pre-constitutional state copyright laws and the congressional resolution that prompted many of them bear a striking resemblance to the Statute of Anne. For instance, the Statute of Anne calls itself a statute 'for the encouragement of learning,' a theme captured in one way or another in ten of the twelve the state copyright laws. Similarly, every one of the state copyright laws provided for grants that, like those of the Statute of Anne, were limited in time." [Footnote omitted] Nachbar, supra note 76, at 330–31.

[128] Eldred v. Ashcroft, 537 U.S. 186, n.5 (2003).

[129] Id.

Clause's English antecedent, the Statute of Anne—a statute that sought to break up a publishers' monopoly by offering, as an alternative, an author's monopoly of limited duration").[130] The first reason is unpersuasive. Yes, there was a colonial antimonopoly tradition, but it recognized an exception for inventions, and perhaps less clearly for author works that came later in time than patents. Indeed, to speak of an "antimonopoly environment" without mentioning the exception is disingenuous at best; the dissent can correctly be criticized for operating at an undue "high level of generality."[131] The second reason to limit copyright protection is not a misstatement; rather it rests on the unproved assumption that the Founders were familiar with the details of English copyright history.[132]

In sum, the Supreme Court and many commentators[133] have placed far too much emphasis on the general antimonopoly tradition in colonial and revolutionary America—especially as it related to patents—without acknowledging that patents (and later in time copyrights) were accepted as legitimate exceptions. A more persuasive historical basis to address a specific issue under today's patent or copyright law would be a colonial's or Founder's views about the specific issue to be decided. For example, the issue in *Eldred v Ashcroft* whether an extension of the copyright term is constitutional would have been better addressed by reference to the fact that all twelve of the state copyright laws adopted before the Constitutional Convention contained grants that were limited in

---

130 Id at 260.

131 See Schwartz & Treanor, supra note 106, at 2363–65.

132 See id:

"As relevant British background, [Justice Stevens] focuses on the rationale offered in a published letter from 1735 that appeared as part of the successful opposition to an amendment to the Statute of Anne. It can hardly be assumed that the Founders both knew of British experience and political thought at this level of detail and were informed by more than half a century later." [Footnote omitted.]

133 See Schwartz & Treanor, supra note 106, at 2332–34:

"With striking unanimity, scholars have called for aggressive judicial review of the constitutionality of congressional legislation in this area. The champions of this position-we refer to them as the "IP Restrictors. .... the IP Restrictors read the Framers' views at a high level of abstraction. This tactic is necessary because of the thinness of the existing historical record supporting their view."

time, with the longest a term of twenty one years.[134] This is a more persuasive basis to limit copyright terms than a general and unqualified reference to the antimonopoly tradition at the time of the Founding. This is not to say that any congressional extension is constitutional. It is to say that the (constitutionally acceptable) length of the copyright term would be more appropriately determined by reference to historical evidence concerning term length—not a reference to the antimonopoly tradition generally.

With those clarifications and cautions in mind about the use of history to solve legal disputes, let us turn to opposition to monopoly after the Founding and up to the Civil War—the antebellum period of American history.

---

[134] Nachbar, supra note 76, at 331, citing Thorvald Solberg, Copyright Enactments of the United States 1783-1906 11-31 (1906) (reprinting all twelve of the state copyright laws enacted prior to the Constitution).

Chapter Four

ANTEBELLUM AMERICA

The first government of the new United States wasted no time in challenging the most criticized monopolies of the colonial period: the English trading companies and their privileges under the English mercantilist system—like the East India Company of Boston Tea Party fame.[1] Of course, colonial shipowners had been encroaching on the trade of the East India Company since the Revolutionary War began. But independence and the new powers of the federal government brought considerably greater weapons to the fight. In the very first year of its existence in 1789, Congress enacted import tariffs, while granting a 10 percent discount on goods brought in ships built and owned by American citizens.[2] The legislation also imposed a lower duty on tea brought from India in American vessels and high duties on tea bought from the East India Company in Europe, even if transported in an American vessel. The trading monopoly of the East India Company was predictably shattered as American shippers developed a competing trade. This clearly was also a victory for opponents of monopoly.

Monopolies, however, did not just disappear in the 19th century world of the new country. There were new perceived monopolies, like banks and chartered corporations. There was also a different cast of opponents. In the past, the most representative figures of a monopoly opponent were merchants claiming that they were disadvantaged by the English trading privileges, as well as street protesters (or food rioters) demanding action against excessive prices charged by sellers of foodstuffs and other necessities. In contrast, the most representative figures of a monopoly opponent during the antebellum period were a farmer, artisan or urban worker who condemned banks and chartered corporations because they exacerbated income inequalities. For example, around 1826, the legislature of Alabama formally declared: "The sponge of monopoly has absorbed nearly the whole wealth of the nation. ... Of 21,000,000 people, less than 300,000 are said to own the whole of the immense

---

[1] See Franklin D. Jones, Historical Development of the Law of Business Competition, 36 Yale LJ 207, 209 (1926).

[2] The Tariff Act of 1789, 1 Stat. 24, 27.

public debt, and nearly the whole of the landed property."[3] As we shall see, Andrew Jackson echoed these sentiments when he vetoed the recharter of the Second Bank of the United States. Hence, sectional and class interests played a large role in opposition to monopoly during the antebellum period.

Let us have a capsulized look at the economic, political and social environment of the antebellum period, an environment markedly different from earlier times—notably a Brobdingnagian expansion of territory, population and economic activity.

If an American living in 1789 were teleported in time to the United States at the eve of the Civil War, she would find a completely different world in almost every way. The agrarian nation of the 18th century was becoming the industrial-mercantile nation that Alexander Hamilton had envisioned,[4] involving immense geographic and political expansion. American territory and natural resources more than doubled, and in 1860 extended beyond the Mississippi to the Pacific and the Rio Grande. By 1828, eleven new states—all but two to the west of the Appalachians—had been added to the original thirteen; before 1860, nine more had been admitted to the Union. Population increased fourfold, fuelled by immigrants who viewed America as the land of opportunity. There also was considerable geographic mobility; in 1860, well over one third of the free population[5] resided in states other than the ones in which they had been born.[6]

Western expansion significantly affected political and social values, including attitudes toward monopoly. The most vivid example is the 1828 election of the first president born west of the Appalachians—Andrew Jackson. Jackson almost singlehandedly destroyed the Second Bank of the United States, which he condemned as a monopoly (discussed below).

The American economy grew exponentially between 1800 and 1860.[7] With independence, English restrictions no longer posed an

---

[3] American State Papers, Finance, v, 849. Quoted in Victor S. Clark, History of Manufactures in the United States 281 (1929).

[4] Robert G. McCloskey, The American Supreme Court 102 (1960).

[5] The great problem of slavery meant that the enslaved portion of the population did not benefit from these changes.

[6] Sidney Ratner, James H. Soltow & Richard Sylla, The Evolution of the American Economy: Growth, Welfare and Decision Making 245–46 (1979).

[7] Alfred D. Chandler Jr., The Visible Hand: The Managerial Revolution in American Business 1–14 (1977).

obstacle to American manufacturing.[8] Manufacturing expanded with the introduction of new technology, more advanced types of machinery and, in latter decades, the factory method—all of which resulted in a diversification and volume of goods that both dwarfed the colonial period and increased exports of manufactured goods.[9]

Significant improvements in transportation and communications fuelled this economic expansion. There were better roads, canals and, later, railroads. Expansion of the postal service, the spread of newspapers and the telegraph greatly facilitated communication.[10] These improvements allowed the interior resources of America to be exploited with the comparative cost advantages of scale and scope.[11] Concomitantly, the growth of credit institutions—chiefly banks—helped to facilitate provision of the capital needed for this expansion of commerce.[12] Barriers to interstate trade were removed as well. Playing its part, the Supreme Court interpreted the Constitution to ensure creation and operation of a "common market" in which legal and other barriers to interstate trade were largely eliminated.[13]

The growth of domestic markets had the robust benefit of accelerating specialization. In the 1790s, the general merchant had still played a key role in the distribution system, often acting as exporter, wholesaler, importer, retailer, banker and insurer. By the 1840s, different firms performed these tasks and merchants began to concentrate on one or two lines of goods, such as cotton, wheat, dry goods and drugs.[14] The great majority of firms were single-unit enterprises, and not yet the multiunit firms of far greater size that would appear after the Civil War and generate antimonopoly feelings anew.

In this chapter, we will discuss the antimonopoly tradition between 1800 and 1865. The Civil War only accelerated the growth of manufacturing as it paralleled the beginning of mass production

---

[8] Manufacturing was the area of economic activity in which the colonies had been least successful. Chester Whitney Wright, Economic History of the United States 311 (2d ed. 1949).

[9] See Douglas C. North, The Economic Growth of the United States 1790–1860 66–67 (1961). The secular movement of the terms of trade became increasingly favorable, reflecting a rapid rise in the price of American exports. *Id.* at 70.

[10] Chester Wright, supra note 8, at 231–32.

[11] Ratner, supra note 6, at 231.

[12] Chester Wright, supra note 8, at 246.

[13] Ratner, supra note 6, at 19 and 231.

[14] Chandler, supra note 7, at 15.

in some industries.[15] Of course, any attempt to define distinct periods in history is bound to be somewhat arbitrary.[16] But the Civil War is a reasonable point to separate the antebellum period from the period that followed, a period marked by the rise of large firms; a shift in concern from state grants of monopoly privileges to the emergence of private monopoly; and the enactment of state and federal antitrust laws—all discussed in the next chapter.

The remainder of this chapter focuses on three propositions. Banks, and to a lesser extent corporations, replaced English trading companies as the principal target of monopoly opponents (section I). Complaints about forestalling and engrossing as "monopolistic" practices continued, although with less intensity (section II). And government grants of monopoly privilege continued at the state level, but often faced successful legal and political challenge (section III).

I. BANKS AND CORPORATIONS

In the antebellum period, banks (such as the Second Bank of the United States) replaced the English trading monopolies (such as the East India Company) as the chief targets of monopoly opponents. The, at times, violent colonial opposition of the debtor community of farmers and small businesses to urban creditor banks and merchants was reinforced when western expansion strengthened the political influence of the debtors. Perhaps surprising today, corporate charters (that is, the corporate form itself of doing business) also were challenged as monopolies in the early decades of the antebellum period, as discussed later in the chapter. Let us first look at the banks.

The economic progress in the 19th century required significant improvements in the colonial financial institutions to provide capital and credit for the expanding commerce.[17] Given their importance, it is not surprising that "greedy bankers" became the favorite targets of antebellum opponents of monopoly.[18] Of course, antimonopoly

---

[15] Hans B. Thorelli, The Federal Antitrust Policy 160–61 (1954).

[16] Chester Wright, supra note 8, at 426–27.

[17] Chester Wright, supra note 8, at 363. In part, changes were due to the need for eliminating the abuses and defects of the colonial and revolutionary period, particularly the reckless expansion of credit which helped to create cyclical swings in business; changes in the banking system were also designed to meet new needs arising from the new economic conditions.

[18] Edgar Augustus Jerome Johnson, The Foundation of American Economic Freedom: Government and Enterprise in the Age of Washington 187 (1973). Cathy

concerns about banks were not born in the antebellum period. In the late 18th century, chartering of the Massachusetts Bank and the Bank of North America (in Pennsylvania) precipitated a bitter denunciation of political favoritism. And the federal chartering of the first Bank of the United States in 1791 was condemned by James Jackson of Georgia as "a monopoly of the public moneys for the benefit of the corporation to be created."[19] James Madison called the first Bank of the United States the shameless creation of "a monopoly" that affects the equal rights of every citizen.[20] Monopoly also became an important political issue in the early 19th century: the anti-Federalists (Republicans) put their opponents at a political disadvantage by stigmatizing them as advocates of a system of political favoritism.[21]

The political controversy about monopoly and banks intensified in 1816 when Congress chartered the Second Bank of the United States (Bank). The inability to finance the war of 1812 precipitated demand for the Bank.[22] It was chartered for twenty years: one-fifth of the capital was subscribed by the government and five of the twenty-five directors were appointed by the President.[23] The Bank, centered in Philadelphia, acted essentially as a central bank for the United States. It regulated the money supply, restrained the expansion of bank credit, supervised the exchanges, protected the investment market and served the Treasury Department.[24] The Bank had significant advantages over commercial banks, including among

---

Matson, The Economy of Early America: Historical Perspectives 47 (Cathy Matson, ed., 2006): "[P]ersistent resentment of rising taxes associated with governments run by 'greedy bankers' all filled the newspapers and pamphlet literature of the era. As popular fears persisted, serious social and political challenges arose against banking, especially central banking, after the War of 1812." [Fn. Omitted].

[19] Quoted in William L. Letwin, Congress and the Sherman Antitrust Law: 1887-1890 23 U. Chi. L. Rev. 221, 227 (1956).

[20] James Madison, The Writings of James Madison, Vol VI, 33 (1791). See also id. pp. 33, 37, 77 [1791].

[21] See C. M. Andrews, "Conservative Factors in Early Colonial History," Authority and the Individual (Cambridge, 1937), pp. 154–169; Eli Heckscher, Mercantilism vol. I, 269–293 (1935).

[22] Edward Kaplan, The Bank of the United States and the American Economy x (1999).

[23] Harold Faulkner, American Economic History 300 (1924). It was expected that the notes of the new bank, redeemable in specie on demand, would force the state banks to resume specie payment or drive them out of business.

[24] Kaplan, supra note 22, at 83.

others, enormous resources provided by the federal government—the Bank's own notes were legal tender for debts owed by or payable to the federal government.[25] After a shaky start, the Bank—under the subsequent leadership of Nicholas Biddle—efficiently handled the fiscal operations of the federal government.

Nonetheless, the Bank was viewed in many parts of the country as a dangerous monopoly in the hands of a few eastern bankers. The Bank's restraining influence on the wildcat currency of the frontier banks contributed to bitter opposition. Although much of the animosity had disappeared by the end of 1820s, there still remained powerful critics who continued to challenge the Bank as an abhorrent monopoly.[26]

With the election of Andrew Jackson in 1828, antimonopolists got their champion in the White House. Indeed, historians describe the ensuing struggle as a war between Andrew Jackson and the Bank.[27] It became personal and bitter on both sides. When Martin Van Buren visited Jackson at the White House, the President lying on a couch, reached out his hand and whispered: "The bank, Mr. Van Buren, is trying to kill me, but I will kill it."[28] Jackson's financial losses from land speculations,[29] his constitutional views and his Western predispositions certainly were factors.[30] But the antimonopolist tradition was the most important: in Jackson's view, the Bank threatened the people's liberty because it concentrated enormous power in private hands and used this power to control legislation and influence elections—a monopoly with special privileges granted by the government.[31]

---

[25] Robert Remini, Andrew Jackson and the Bank War 36 (1967).

[26] See id. at 39.

[27] See, e.g., Paul Kahan, The Bank War (2015); Remini, supra note 25.

[28] Martin Van Buren, The Autobiography of Martin Van Buren 625 (1920), quoted in Remini, supra note 25, at 16. Historians differ considerably on Jackson's war against the Bank. Admirers like Arthur Schlesinger heap praise for the termination of a privileged and too powerful monopoly. See Arthur M. Schlesinger Jr., The Age of Jackson (1946). Detractors see the war an act of spite by an ignorant frontiersman who gravely injured his country. See Thomas P. Govan, Nicholas Biddle: Nationalist and Public Banker, 1786–1844 (1959).

[29] Jackson had lost considerable money in land transactions. Thus, land speculation and paper currency became for him evil practices with only specie as the true money component. Because banks speculated in land and issued paper notes, he came to distrust them. Kaplan, supra note 22, at 101–02.

[30] Remini, supra note 25, at 43–44.

[31] See id.

Biddle dismissed Jackson's antimonopoly complaints: "All this stir about monopolies will blow off like a vapor from a Steam Boat as soon as the question gets fairly under way."[32] Biddle cynically believed that Jackson wanted to turn the Bank into a patronage engine.[33] The Philadelphia patrician expressed his disdain for the western war hero in a letter: "This worthy President thinks that because he has scalped Indians and imprisoned Judges, he is to have his way with the Bank. He is mistaken."[34] In a sense, the Bank War can be seen as a dispute between the populace and its democratically-elected representatives on one side and elitist technocrats on the other.[35] To some observers, this may seem to echo dismissals by many of today's antitrust experts of popular (and political) complaints that U.S. antitrust law has become too narrow in its application to meet the challenges of monopoly in the 21st century.[36]

Opposition to monopoly was not the only reason motivating the attack on the Bank; some opponents had more self-interested motives. Financiers and entrepreneurs, including New York bankers,[37] opposed the Philadelphia-based Bank because it created obstacles to their own enterprises.[38] State banks and their shareholders resented the impact of the Bank's size, wealth and significant impact on their own operations.[39] Westerners and Southerners continued to harbor grievances against the Bank. Strict constitutional constructionists (like Jackson himself) condemned the Bank as unconstitutional (despite a Supreme Court decision to the contrary in 1819[40]).[41] In sum, this was a diverse group of opponents with diverse motives and concerns. Supporters of the Bank, who may well have outnumbered opponents of the Bank,[42] likewise were

---

[32] Biddle to Albert Gallatin, Nov. 30, 1830, Gallatin Papers, NYHS.

[33] Kahan, supra note 27, at 62–63.

[34] Quoted in Kaplan, supra note 22, at 133.

[35] Cf. Kahan, supra note 27, at 154.

[36] See Barry Hawk, Antitrust and Competition Laws 153–56 (2020).

[37] See Kahan, supra note 27, at 52–53.

[38] Carter Goodrich, ed. The Government and the Economy, 1783–1861 311–12 (1967).

[39] Remini, supra note 25, at 39.

[40] McCullough v. Maryland, 17 U.S. 316 (1819).

[41] Remini, supra note 25, at 40.

[42] Remini speaks of a "substantial majority." See id. at 41. Jackson probably won reelection in 1832 despite his stance against the Bank. See id. At 45–46 and 106–07.

not limited to one section or class—with the qualification that the wealthier and more educated may have had greater financial or intellectual incentives to appreciate the benefits of a central bank.

In 1832, a serious political miscalculation began the end of the Bank. Supporters of Henry Clay (candidate of the National Republican party in 1832) prevailed upon Biddle to petition for an early renewal of the charter of the Bank, which did not expire until 1836. Jackson took this as the challenge it was, and indeed as further proof that the Bank was using its power to influence the political process.[43] The Bank had considerable support in Congress—the Senate and House voted to renew the charter—but Jackson vetoed the bill.

Jackson's Veto Message on July 10, 1832 articulated his objections. Jackson first acknowledged that a federal bank "is in many respects convenient for the Government and useful to the people."[44] He continued, however, that the chartered bank went too far, because it enjoyed an exclusive privilege of banking under "the authority of the General Government, a monopoly of its favor and support, and, as a necessary consequence, almost a monopoly of the foreign and domestic exchange." The monopoly was unjustified because it gave monopoly profits to eastern bankers and favored foreign stockholders[45] to the detriment of businesses in the south and west where comparatively few were stockholders. But the more fundamental objection was that the Bank was an organ of special privilege, making rich men "richer by act of Congress."[46] This echoes the class elements seen in the colonial antimonopoly tradition:

> "it is to be regretted that the rich and powerful too often band the acts of government to their selfish purposes.... The humble members of society—the farmers, mechanics,

---

[43] Id. at 77.

[44] President Andrew Jackson, Bank Veto speech (July 10, 1832).

[45] Id.:

> "Every monopoly and all exclusive privileges are granted at the expense of the public, which ought to receive a fair equivalent. The many millions which this act proposes to bestow on the stockholders of the existing bank must come directly or indirectly out of the earnings of the American people. It is due to them, therefore, if their Government sell monopolies and exclusive privileges, that they should at least exact for them as much as they are worth in open market. .... But this act does not permit competition in the purchase of this monopoly."

[46] See Goodrich, supra note 38, at 311–12.

> and laborers—who have neither the time nor the means of securing like favors to themselves, have a right to complain of the injustice of their Government."[47]

The economic class warfare element of Jackson's antimonopoly position did not go unnoticed by defenders of the Bank. For example, Biddle complained that Jackson's veto message was "a manifesto of anarchy such as Marat and Robespierre might have issued to the mobs" during the French Revolution.[48] The veto message, according to Biddle, certainly did not fairly or adequately address the economic issues.[49]

As the National Republicans had planned, the Bank became an issue in the presidential election of 1832. But the public, unlike their earlier elected representatives who had just renewed the Bank's charter, voted for Jackson. His re-election sealed the Bank's fate, although the bank war continued. Jackson did not limit his war on the Bank to veto of its charter renewal. He withdrew government deposits from the Bank. Biddle, in turn, retaliated with a contraction of the money supply and refusal to surrender pension money. The Bank's popular support rapidly declined due to the belief that the bank had caused the financial panic of 1833-1834. The Bank's charter expired in 1836 and Biddle's Bank became a private institution under charter from the state of Pennsylvania.[50]

The failure to recharter the Second Bank of the United States is the most dramatic victory for opponents of monopoly in the antebellum period. Many if not most observers believe, however, that the failure to provide a replacement for the Bank condemned the United States to unsound currency and credit institutions for almost a century.[51] For example, Edward Perkins concludes that the Bank War between Jackson and Biddle so politicized development of the country's financial institutions "that it defied political solution until

---

[47] Quoted in Robert Remini, Andrew Jackson and the Course of American Freedom 1822-1832 368 (1981).

[48] Quoted in id. at 369.

[49] See Remini, supra note 25, at 84: "The message was totally indifferent to the Bank's genuine services to the nation. Indeed, it denied these services existed. As an economic document, therefore, attempting to prove a case, it can be easily shredded for misstating facts and for faulty reasoning."

[50] Goodrich, supra note 38, at 311-12.

[51] See Remini, supra note 25, at 176-77.

the creation of the Federal Reserve" in 1913.[52] Edward Kaplan also condemns the absence of a central bank, particularly after the Civil War.[53] From 1865 to 1910, the money supply grew rapidly, causing long periods of deflation with intermittent intervals of serious inflation, resulting in various recessions. A central bank was needed to provide an elastic money supply for the banking system and act as an agent of the Treasury.

In sum, it is questionable whether the price of Jackson's successful antimonopoly war on the Bank was worth it in economic terms. The failure to provide a substitute for the Bank that would perform the functions of a central bank was a high price to pay for this antimonopoly war. This raises an important lesson: demands for action against monopoly can have seriously harmful unintended consequences if plans are not made in advance as what to do after the monopoly is eliminated. Unfortunately, it is easier to complain than fashion a remedy for monopoly.

Opposition to monopoly during the antebellum period was directed not only at the federal Bank; it also helped shape reform of state and local banks, particularly those in the South and West.[54] At first, a bank could secure a charter only by a special act of the legislature. This often-triggered suspicions of unsavory political influence. To avoid these suspicions, while at the same time preventing any danger of a moneyed monopoly, states enacted free-banking laws under which any group meeting the requirements of a general law could start a bank. The first free-banking law was passed in Michigan in 1837, but soon was repealed; New York followed in 1838; by 1860, sixteen states had free-banking laws. Antimonopoly sentiment, however, worked against a greater development of branch banking which might have lessened decentralization and provided stronger banks in small places—the popular fear of monopolies (and local jealousies) commonly opposed branch banking.[55]

Nor was antimonopoly sentiment against the banks confined to the West and South. One hub of antimonopoly activity was in New York City, centered around what became known as the Loco-Focos,

---

[52] Edward J. Perkins, Lost Opportunities for Compromise in the Bank War: A Reassessment of Jackson's Veto Message, 61 Bus. Hist. Rev. 531 (1987).

[53] Kaplan, supra note 22, at 161.

[54] Chester Wright, supra note 8, at 371.

[55] See id. at 380.

or the Equal Rights Party.[56] The Loco-Focos began in 1835 (and ended two years later) as a mutiny within the Tammany Democratic organization against the domination of a conservative element. The Loco-Focos were active in local political campaigns, held two state conventions and organized mass meetings in New York City. They condemned all monopoly and special privilege. In a sense, the Loco-Focos were the Occupy Wall Streeters of the antebellum era. Or perhaps to put it more accurately, the Loco-Focos might be analogized to today's progressive Democrats,[57] not unlike some New York political figures today. But unlike modern Progressives, the Loco-Focos led public protests that became violent. In 1837 in New York City, Loco-Foco politicians spurred a crowd to action at a rally. The crowd broke into warehouses and seized flour of owners who had demanded high prices.[58]

Banks remained the principal targets of Loco-Foco protests.[59] The Loco-Focos claimed that part of the high prices of the necessities of life came from the bank monopoly system. The banks oppressed the poor by real estate speculating which raised rents and by providing capital to "forestallers" and "engrossers."[60] The chief political element of the Loco-Focos program was the spirit of aggressive radicalism that became ascendant in the national Democratic party between 1837 and 1844.[61] The Loco-Focos of New York were not alone. A large section of the Democratic Party (of which Senator Benton of Missouri was a representative leader) held similar views. Frances (Fanny) Wright, a prominent social reformer, praised Jackson's veto as

---

[56] See Fitzwilliam Byrdsall, The History of the Loco-Foco or Equal Rights Party (1842); Steven Piott, The Anti-Monopoly Persuasion: Popular Resistance to the Rise of Big Business in the Midwest 6-7 (1985); William Trimble, The Social Philosophy of the Loco-Foco Democracy 26 Am. J. Sociology 705, 705–11.

[57] The role of the working class and labor movement is not entirely clear. See, e.g., Selig Perlman, "The Concept of Class in the Development of the American Labor Program," Meeting of the American Historical Association, New York City, Dec. 27, 1940.

[58] Paul Gilje, Rioting in America 71 (1996).

[59] See Byrdsall, supra note 56, at 99–195.

[60] Piott, supra note 56. In 1835, Dr. John W. Vethake issued a manifesto of the "Anti-Monopoly Democrats" that denounced chartered corporations and monopolies. Joseph Dorfman, The Economic Mind in American Civilization 1606–1865 655 (1946). The anti-monopoly Jeffersonian Democrats then selected Dr. Vethake for one of the Democratic Party nominations at the regular meeting at Tammany Hall.

[61] See Trimble, supra note 56, at 708.

starting the process of freeing America from its enslavement to the Bank of England and Parliament.[62] Other critics argued that the greatest evil was the financial monopoly created by the state, whether in the form of requiring specie as a currency or granting exclusive charters to issue paper. This monopoly was said to create an artificial scarcity of medium of exchange.[63]

Let us say a bit more about cultural divides and how they relate to monopoly opposition. As mentioned above, the influence of the West on American politics in the 19th century was immensely powerful.[64] The older Atlantic seaboard states came to be outnumbered by the new states (and their economic interests and political views) in the Senate.[65] The election in 1828 of the first Western president—Andrew Jackson—made this plain to everyone.

Most historians agree that the hardships and relative isolation of frontier life developed initiative, adaptability and individualism. These all were reflected in the more democratic constitutions and other social institutions adopted by the Western states.[66] The West produced fervent adherents to an antimonopoly tradition that had developed earlier in the original colonies along the Atlantic coast.

But sectional differences should not be exaggerated with respect to the antimonopoly tradition. To be sure, there were important differences in economic activity during the antebellum period: the Northeast specialized in manufacturing, commerce and finance; the Northwest raised grain and livestock; and the South grew cotton, tobacco and sugar.[67] And looming most visibly was the specter of slavery, the institution that divided the nation and brought about the civil war. Perhaps the most relevant sectional difference for the antimonopoly tradition was the concentration of wealth and industry in the Northeast. Chester Wright concludes that rivalry at the federal level manifested most importantly in conflict between the wealthy industrial and commercial sections of the East and the poorer agricultural sections of the South and the West. This mirrors

---

[62] Dorfman, supra note 60, at 659.

[63] Id. at 673-74.

[64] See, e.g., Faulkner, supra note 23, at 213. The basic work is Frederick Jackson Turner, The Frontier in American History (1893).

[65] Their sparser population gave the western states less power in the House. Chester Wright, supra note 8, at 270.

[66] See id. at 271.

[67] See id. at 409.

to some extent sectional attitudes toward monopoly. As we have seen, much (but not all) of the opposition to the Bank came from the West and South, with support for the Bank stronger in the Northeast. But opponents and supporters also can be divided along non-sectional lines: rural debtor farmers and artisans opposed monopoly more fervently and consistently than urban creditor merchants and banks. We saw this same debtor/creditor tension in attitudes toward antimonopoly in earlier periods of American history.

It is impossible to measure with any precision the relative weight of sectional, class and debtor-creditor relations in the antimonopoly tradition. To cite one of numerous examples, in 1839 a New York court praised the state corporation reforms in language that would have been well understood and embraced on the prairies and frontiers west of the Mississippi and south of the Mason-Dixon line:

> "Contemporary history ... proclaim[s] another 'mischief,' ... the creation of monopolies, the grant at exclusive privileges, the attendant corruption of legislation, the appliances so often and so successfully used to procure these legislative favors."[68]

In sum, opposition to monopoly during the antebellum period was highly effective in challenging the exclusive privileges of the banks. Challenges of government grants of monopoly privileges in other areas had mixed results, as discussed below in section III. In the next section, we will discuss developments of the second strand of the colonial antimonopoly tradition—complaints and laws concerning "monopolistic" practices perceived as raising prices—like forestalling and engrossing (cornering the market).

II. ENGROSSING, FORESTALLING AND PRIVATE MONOPOLY

A. Forestalling and Engrossing

As earlier discussed, English and colonial laws prohibited "monopolistic" practices like forestalling and engrossing (cornering the market). Indeed, popular demands for action against "monopolizers" who charged excessive prices during the Revolutionary War echo in striking fashion popular demands for

---

[68] Thomas v. Dakin, 22 Wend. 9 (1839).

action against monopolists in Europe. But, as we have seen, the American revolutionaries added a political element: patriots did not charge excessive prices.[69]

Laws against forestalling and engrossing remained on the statute books after the Revolutionary War in at least several states.[70] And Maryland re-enacted a ban on engrossing after the Constitution.[71] Perhaps more importantly, towns and other political subdivisions continued to receive petitions for action under new (and prior) state and local laws concerning forestalling and engrossing. For example, in 1801 the New York City Council received a petition from nine butchers accusing Henry Astor of leaving his market stall in the care of an unlicensed butcher while he rode into the countryside to intercept cattle drovers coming into New York.[72] A later example is found in 1846 when the Kentucky Court of Appeals upheld a fine of four dollars on a Louisville resident for violating a city ordinance prohibiting residents from selling goods not produced or prepared by themselves.[73] Defendant, a city resident, "did on the day mentioned in the warrant, sell in the market, in market hours, large quantities of turkeys, chickens, eggs, &c., and was in the habit of doing so on other market days ...."

In England, changes in economic conditions and developments in economic thinking ultimately resulted in the end of forestalling bans in 1844 when Parliament formally repealed all prior statues and abrogated the common law bans.[74] Adam Smith earlier had derisively dismissed forestalling laws as witchcraft: "The popular fear of engrossing and forestalling... may be compared to the popular terrors and suspicions of witchcraft."[75] In the United States, forestalling laws had a similar but not identical history. American domestic markets became significantly larger and closed (local)

---

69 See Chapter Three.

70 For example, 1 Delaware Laws 183, 249ff; Pennsylvania Laws 225, 226, ch. 1398.

71 Maryland Laws (Kilty), May 1788, ch. 17; 1793, ch. 59.

72 Helen Tagires, Public Markets and Civic Culture in Nineteenth-Century America 7 (2003).

73 City of Louisville v. Roupe, 45 Ky. 591, 1846 WL 3192 (1846). Cf. Mays v. Cincinnati, 1 Ohio St 268, 1853 WL 27 (1853) (market regulation banned huckstering and forestalling).

74 See Barry Hawk, Law and Commerce in Pre-Industrial Societies 57–58 (2016).

75 See Adam Smith, The Wealth of Nations, ch. 5 (1776).

markets rarer during the antebellum period. Middlemen, previously condemned as forestallers, were now seen as facilitators not obstructors of trade.[76] By 1860, products were being sold to distant unknown consumers and purchased in equally impersonal markets.[77] This made forestalling less of an issue as agricultural markets became less localized with reduced transport costs and better information technology. Despite these changes in economic conditions and theory, however, laws on forestalling continued beyond the antebellum era into the 20th century, as discussed in the next chapter.

Engrossing defined as cornering the market had a somewhat different history from that of forestalling. Douglass North suggests that that the general economic conditions of the antebellum years—notably, the expansion of markets—made it difficult for private firms or entrepreneurs to corner markets without legal grants of monopoly privileges.[78] However, legal claims of monopolization can be found before the Civil War, as seen in the next section.

B. Private Firm Monopoly

Private firm monopolies received less attention during the antebellum period compared to their prominence as targets of opposition after the Civil War. This does not mean that private firm monopoly did not exist in the antebellum period. For example, the Massachusetts towns of Lowell and Fall River were controlled by single textile manufacturing companies and their allies who

---

[76] These benefits were recognized in the United States following passage of the Sherman Act:

> "The middleman whose intervention as to certain commodities had been prohibited as entirely mischievous, it was found, had a useful function to perform which facilitated rather than restrained trade. With improved means of communication and transportation this was undoubtedly true. The middleman secured his place in commerce as a result of the specialization of functions which marked the development of modern industry and trade."

United States v. Patten, 226 U.S. 525 (brief of Solicitor General Lehmann) quoted in Edward A. Adler, Monopolizing at Common Law and Under Section Two of the Sherman Antitrust Act 31 Harv. L. Rev. 246, 256–57 (1917).

[77] Ratner, supra note 6, at 235. See also Chester Wright, supra note 8, at 314.

[78] See Douglass North, Aspects of Economic Growth in the United States, 1815-1860, in The Experience of Economic Growth: Case Studies in Economic History 235, 245–51 (B. Supple Ed. 1963).

discouraged, where they did not prevent, independent competitors.[79] Similar arrangements can be found in other towns in southeastern Massachusetts and Rhode Island where wealthy mill-owning families like the Slaters acquired control of groups of factories.

Very importantly for the present debates about U.S. antitrust policy, state legislators and courts before the Civil War recognized the legal difficulties and competing policy tensions raised by complaints about private monopoly.[80] One interesting example of a court decision rejecting an antebellum claim of unlawful monopolization is *Harris v. Tyson*.[81] Tyson purchased the rights to mine chrome on Harris' land. Harris sued to invalidate the deed of sale because, among other reasons, Tyson had not informed Harris of the value of the mineral rights. Harris added the accusation that Tyson intended "to monopolize the chrome business." In an opinion that could have been written today, the court rejected the proffer of any subjective intent to obtain a monopoly,[82] distinguished between lawful and unlawful monopoly, and dismissed the action:

> "If Tyson really thought he could get a monopoly in the proper sense of the **word**, that is, a law forbidding all persons but himself from engaging in such an enterprise, ... his fancy was a very harmless one. If he intended merely to carry on the manufacture of chrome so largely and sell it so cheaply that no one would think it worthwhile to compete with him, then he is a meritorious citizen He has a right to all he can win by his science, labor, and capital honestly employed. Either way, the evidence offered could serve no purpose except to waken prejudices which had better be allowed to sleep."

Private firm monopolization also was the subject of legislative inquiries before the Civil War. In the 1830s, a state legislative committee reported on the danger of monopolization of the

---

[79] See Clark, supra note 3, at 458.

[80] Challenges of monopolization of stock and other corporate interests also can be found in the antebellum era. See, e.g., Barry v. Merchants' Exchange Co., 1 Sand. Ch. 280, 7 N.Y. Ch. Ann. 329 (1844); Stribbling v. Bank of the Valley, 5 Rand. 132, 26 Va. 132, 1827 WL 1194 (1827); The Hager's Town Turnpike Road Co. v Creeger, 5 H. & J. 122, 1820 WL 929, 9 Am. Dec. 495 (1820).

[81] Harris v. Tyson 24 Pa. 347, 1855 WL 7110, 64 Am. Dec. 661 (1855).

[82] See Hawk, supra note 36.

Pennsylvania coal industry,[83] but the committee counselled caution about legislative action which might infringe the "natural liberty" of the entrepreneurs.[84]

The analytical difficulties and policy tensions raised by private monopolies were far less acute in the case of government grants of monopoly privileges. These remained the central focus of the antimonopoly tradition during the antebellum period, a subject to which we now turn.

III. GOVERNMENT GRANTS OF MONOPOLY PRIVILEGES

After independence, opposition to government grants of monopoly privileges strengthened. The post-Revolutionary political and economic conditions, western expansion and developments in economic thought were important factors in ensuring that opposition to monopoly would not only continue but would have significant concrete effects—despite the loss of its principal colonial target: the English trading companies and the English mercantile system. The attack on the federally chartered Second Bank of the United States was one example, as seen above. But attacks on state and local grants of monopoly privileges outside the banking sector also were common. We saw in Chapter Two that colonial authorities granted monopoly

---

[83] Pennsylvania Senate Journal, 1833-1834, II, 497 (1834):

> "A large business will of course require a large capital; and if, in the pursuit of honest industry one class of citizens should become wealthy and amass large fortunes we cannot and ought not to deprive them of the advantages of their wealth; but, the Legislature may and ought to prevent them from uniting with these advantages artificial powers and distinctions which may, if improperly exercised, make 'the rich richer and the poor poorer.'"

Report of the Committee is analyzed in Louis Hartz, Economic Policy and Democratic Thought (1948). See Goodrich, supra note 38, at 363-77.

[84] The committee warned:

> "Natural liberty and human action should be no farther restrained by legislative enactment than is consistent with, or indispensable to the purposes of civil society and republican government; and every citizen, suffering no greater restraints than it may be absolutely necessary for him to yield to these purposes, should be allowed freely to pursue his own true and substantial happiness. Too much legislation is more to be dreaded than the entire want of it. The maxim is true, that 'the world is governed too much.'"

Pennsylvania Senate Journal, supra note 83.

privileges to encourage investment in the production and manufacture of commodities and goods. It is fair to generalize that the antimonopoly tradition during the antebellum period moderated the frequency and terms of these colonial grants. Moreover, many monopolies failed on their own despite government privileges.

The antimonopoly tradition manifested itself in several ways with respect to state and local grants of monopoly privileges. First, many states amended their constitutions to restrict the power of state and local authorities to grant monopolies or exclusive privileges. This was particularly true of the new western states which became a majority by 1860. Second, state legislatures and courts limited the scope of specific monopoly grants. Third, federal constitutional provisions further limited state monopoly grants during the antebellum period, although the federal constraints were more potential than actual.

A. State Constitutional Limits on State (and Local) Monopoly Grants

During the antebellum period, economic regulation (including monopoly grants and other market interventions) was far more significant at the state level than the federal level. That is, more governmental activity in economic life was initiated by the state and local governments than by the federal government.[85] States did not relinquish to the federal government the function of encouraging local manufacture which they had exercised as colonies. They continued to aid new industries in the form of monopolies and other state aids.[86] But, like colonial monopoly grants and state aids, their antebellum successors also often failed to achieve their purpose.[87]

---

85 See Hartz, supra note 83, at 3 (economic life was predominantly agrarian and commercial, and it was not until after 1850 that corporations of genuine national significance began to push problems of federal action into the foreground).

86 Clark, supra note 3, at 263 (E.g.: Nails, Massachusetts, Laws and Resolves, 1790, Acts, Chap. 41. Cotton, id., 1788, Acts, Chap. 43; id., 1796, Resolves (May Session), Chap. 5; White, Slater, 294-296; Bagnall, Textile Industries, 487. Glass, Massachusetts, Laws and Resolves, 1793, Acts, Chap. 3; cf. also Bentley, Diary, II, 28, June 7, 1793.) See also Oscar & Mary Handlin, Commonwealth - A Study of the Role of Government in the American Economy: Massachusetts, 1774–1861 83 (1947).

87 See Clark, supra note 3, at 265 ("We can not point to a single instance, prior to 1860, where the intervention of a State government directly to encourage or regulate industries left permanent results in our manufacturing history.")

After the Declaration of Independence and continuing into the antebellum period, many states included provisions in their state constitutions that restricted the power of state and local authorities to grant monopolies or exclusive privileges.[88] Indeed, states whose amendments were adopted in the period between the Founding and the 1870s provided the strongest protections against government monopolies.[89] State constitutional bans were applied even to invalidate earlier pre-Revolution colonial grants.[90] It is important to note, however, that the state constitutional provisions before the Civil War generally did not apply to private monopolies. The language in which they are couched suggests that they were directed primarily, if not solely, against government grants.

As mentioned earlier in Chapter Three, Maryland and North Carolina—only months after the Declaration of Independence in 1776—included antimonopoly provisions in their state constitutions. In 1798, Georgia limited the power to grant monopolies of land in the western territory.[91] Before the Civil War, more new states included antimonopoly provisions in their constitutions. Examples follow.

In 1836, Arkansas declared that "perpetuities and monopolies are contrary to the genius of a republic, and shall not be allowed; nor shall any hereditary emolument, privileges or honors ever be granted or conferred in this State."[92] A state court later referred to the historical background: "The monopolies which in England

---

[88] See James Hurst, The Legitimacy of the Business Corporation in the Law of the United States: 1780-1970 138 (1970). See also Stephen G. Calabresi and Larissa C. Leibowitz, Monopolies and the Constitution: A History of Crony Capitalism 36 Harv. J.L. & Pub. Pol'y 983, 1023–24.

[89] Calabresi and Leibowitz, supra note 88, at 1084.

[90] The Supreme Court of North Carolina applied its constitutional ban to invalidate a 1776 act of the Colonial Assembly, which granted the right to erect a bridge with exclusion of any bridge or ferry within six miles, violated the state constitution. See McRee v. Wilmington R. R., 47 N. C. 186 (1855).

[91] Ga. CONST. art. 1, § 23 provided:

> "The legislature may give its consent to the establishment of one or more governments westward thereof; but monopolies of land by individuals being contrary to the spirit of our free government, no sale of territory of this State, or any part thereof, shall take place to individuals or private companies, unless a county or counties shall have been first laid off, including such territory, and the Indian rights shall have been extinguished thereto."

[92] Ark. CONST, art. 2, §19.

became so odious as to excite general opposition, and ... infuse a detestation which has been transmitted to the free States of America, were in the nature of exclusive privileges of trade, granted to favorites or purchasers from the crown, for the enrichment of individuals, at the cost of the public."[93]

In 1836, the Republic of Texas—and later in 1845 the state of Texas constitution—condemned monopoly together with primogeniture: "Perpetuities and monopolies are contrary to the genius of a free government, and shall never be allowed; nor shall the law of primogeniture or entailments ever be in force in this State."[94] This provision probably reflected the debtor sentiments of Jacksonians.[95] Florida (1838) followed with a constitutional provision that "perpetuities and monopolies are contrary to the genius of a free State, and ought not to be allowed."[96] Kansas (1857) repeated in similar terms: "That forfeitures and monopolies are contrary to the genius of a republic, and shall not be allowed, nor shall any hereditary emolument, privileges, or honors ever be granted or conferred in the State."[97]

Vigorous opposition to monopoly was not confined to the states that placed monopoly bans in their constitutions. There are many examples of courts relying on antimonopoly principles to invalidate state or local economic regulations. For example, a Connecticut court pronounced in 1856:

> "Although we have no direct constitutional provision against a monopoly, yet the whole theory of a free government is opposed to such grants, and it does not require even the aid which may be derived from the Bill of Rights, the first section of which declares 'that no man or set of men is entitled to exclusive public emoluments or privileges from the community,' to render them void."[98]

---

[93] Ex parte Levy, 43 Ark. 42, 51 (1884).

[94] Tex. CONST. art. 1, §19.

[95] See Alexandra K. Howell, Enforcing a Wall of Separation Between Big Business and State: Protection from Monopolies in State Constitutions, 96 Notre Dame L. Rev. 859, 881 (2020).

[96] Fla. CONST. art. 1, §24.

[97] Kan. CONST. art 15, §17.

[98] The Norwich Gas Light Co. v. The Norwich City Gas Co. 25 Conn 19, 38 (1856).

Courts in other states like Pennsylvania recognized that "we have no general statute which prohibits [monopolies]; but certain monopolies granted by the British crown, were held to be illegal and void at the common law; such, for instance, as an exclusive right to import, buy, sell, make, work, or use, any particular article or thing."[99] There are even occasional references to a preference for competition or the "stimulating influence of rivalry."[100] Indeed, the Pennsylvania Supreme Court in the decade before the Civil War expressly endorsed competition as the guiding principle in modern terms that would sound familiar to today's antitrust aficionados: "Competition is the best protection to the public and it is against the policy of the law to destroy it by creating a monopoly of any branch of business. It cannot be done except by the clearly expressed will of the legislative power."[101]

Opposition to government grants of monopoly was not limited to the West. In 1861, a Mississippi court held invalid a grant of exclusive right to sell liquor in quantities of less than one gallon, relying on the state bill of rights:

> "In some of the State constitutions monopolies are mentioned by name, but our bill of rights uses the broad language–exclusive, separate, public emoluments or privileges from the community. This would interdict the government from conferring the exclusive right to sell corn or whiskey."[102]

Importantly, state constitutions were not interpreted to prohibit all monopoly grants per se. For example, the Massachusetts constitution of 1780 explicitly recognized the legitimacy of certain monopoly grants and established standards for bestowing them in "consideration of services rendered to the public."[103] Many colonials and antebellum Americans would have found the modern idea of monopoly per se delusional, at least with respect to government grants.

---

[99] Commonwealth v The Canal Commissioners, 1843 WL 5057 (1843).

[100] Gales v Anderson, 13 Ill. 413, 1851 WL 4368 (1851) (court prefers competition to exclusive ferry grant and limits charter/license rights).

[101] Sandford v. The Catawissa, W. & E.R. Co., 24 Pa. 378 (1855).

[102] City of Jackson v. Bowman, 10 George 671, 39 Miss 671, 1861 WL 1993 (1861). There are many antebellum cases challenging regulation of liquor sales as unlawful monopoly.

[103] U.S. CONST. amend. VI.

Let us move from state constitutional provisions and general antimonopoly principles to state statutes dealing with government grants of monopoly privileges. First, we will look at an issue that might strike modern observers as rather strange: special corporations or the corporate form itself as raising monopoly concerns. Second, we will look at examples of the application of state statutes to government grants of monopoly privileges.

B. State Legislatures and Monopoly Grants

1. *Corporations as monopolies*

In the early decades of the 19th century, corporate charters were challenged as unlawful government grants of monopoly. Antimonopoly critics complained that corporate charters, even when their public purpose seemed obvious—such as those for the college of Philadelphia—were repugnant to the spirit of American republicanism, "which does not admit of granting peculiar privileges to any body of men."[104] Indeed, the claim that all corporations were monopolies—whether or not they enjoyed exclusive privileges—was frequently voiced by opponents during the Revolutionary era and continuing into the 19th century.[105] Opponents were sometimes successful. In 1787, for example, Connecticut rejected a petition to incorporate a medical society because it was "a combination of doctors ... directly against liberty ... a monopoly."[106] Indeed, there are many examples of opposition to licensing of doctors, lawyers and other professionals.[107]

Despite monopoly opposition, state legislatures increasingly incorporated not just colleges and banks, but insurance companies, manufacturers and operators of bridges and canals. The states issued only eleven charters of incorporation between 1781 and 1785. This number increased exponentially in the early 19th century when the states granted nearly 1800 corporate charters.[108]

---

104 Gordon Wood, The Radicalism of the American Revolution 166 (1991).

105 See Letwin, supra note 19, at 229.

106 Davis, Essays in the Earlier History of American Corporations 384-385 (1917). [cited in id. at 64]

107 In 1869, the New Orleans Picayune opposed legislation prohibiting doctors, lawyers and other professionals from practicing without a license because it placed "the whole community under embargo to a few rich men." Quoted in Ronald M. Labbé & Jonathan Lurie, The Slaughterhouse Cases 103 (2003).

108 Wood, supra note 104, at 171.

The complaint that a corporation was an abhorrent monopoly simply because it was a corporation eventually lost traction. And the connection between monopoly and corporations was severed completely with enactment of statutory reservation clauses and general incorporation laws. Statutory reservation clauses began to appear at the beginning of the 19th century.[109] In 1809, Massachusetts provided that the legislature could "from time to time" repeal or amend any corporate charter simply by giving notice to the corporation. Ultimately, reservation clauses were upheld whether in the charter of each corporation or in a general statute applicable to all future corporations. By 1860, fourteen states had adopted reservation and revocation clauses. For many states, the problem of state commitments to specially chartered corporations became a nonissue, at least if the corporation was chartered after the reservation act was passed. Thus, state-created "corporate monopoly" became an issue largely limited to the original colonies and states which had issued charters during colonial and Federalist times. Let us turn to a more ubiquitous issue that continued to excite political debate and incite legal challenges across the country: state and local grants of monopoly privileges.

2. *State monopoly grants*

Over the course of the antebellum period, it is reasonable to generalize that government monopoly grants were reduced in number and scope. For example, gaslight and railroad companies received charters freely, but their privileges were more limited than those enjoyed by earlier turnpikes and canals.[110] The monopoly elements of many licenses and franchises were eliminated under the "reasonableness" standard.[111] Courts overruled prior decisions that had tolerated exclusionary privileges. For example, in 1815 the Massachusetts Supreme Court restricted the scope of an earlier decision, holding that an exclusive stagecoach franchise was a personal right that could not be inherited or acquired by prescription.[112] Oscar

---

[109] Herbert Hovenkamp, Enterprise and American Law 1836-1937 26 (1991).

[110] See Handlin, supra note 86, at 221–22. Cf., e.g., st. 1822 ch. 41; General Statutes, ch.61, secs. 15-19; supra, p. 194. Cf. Thacher v. Dartmouth Bridge Company, 35 Mass. 501, 18 Pick. 501 (1836); st. 1827, ch. 54.

[111] See Handlin, supra note 86, at 223.

[112] See Morton Horwitz, The Transformation of American Law, 1780–1860 119 (1979).

and Mary Handlin report that monopoly opposition in Massachusetts prevented state aid grants after 1830.[113] An ordinance of the District of Columbia requiring that all fish be landed at one wharf was invalidated as an unlawful "monopoly" in 1841.[114]

States continued to grant monopoly privileges, nonetheless, although they may have been more the exception than the rule. Massachusetts granted monopoly privileges to glass manufacturers.[115] And state aids—a practice sometimes accompanied by monopoly grants—also continued in the antebellum period. For example, bounties were given to help agriculture and resource extraction—like Maine bounties to wheat and corn producers in 1839 and Massachusetts bounties to aid fisheries.[116] Nine states subsidized silk production.[117] In 1828, a Boston regulation of the carting of offal was upheld in face of a challenge that it was a monopoly.[118] Indeed, some courts expressed impatience with invocation of the antimonopoly principle to challenge economic regulations. A New York court in 1820 complained that

> "[i]t is too late to question the great public benefits which have been derived from the steam boats which have been brought into operation under these laws. The validity of the acts were [sic] not questioned at the time; but now, when the advantages to be derived from the privilege granted are established, a cry of monopoly is raised against the exclusive right."[119]

Despite these last counterexamples, it is reasonable to conclude that the antimonopoly tradition—expressed in state constitutions, statutes and general principles—constrained state and local monopoly grants during the antebellum period, albeit to an immeasurable extent. Federal constitutional challenges further limited state monopoly grants, as discussed in the next section. As we shall see in the next chapter, however, state and federal

---

113 See Handlin, supra note 86, at 228–29.

114 Lambell v. The Corporation of Washington, 1 Hay&. Haz. 25 (1841).

115 See Handlin, supra note 86, at 38, 81–82. See also Robert A. Lively, The American System: a review article 29 Bus. Hist. Rev. 81, 88 (1955).

116 See Handlin, supra note 86, at 3, 88–84.

117 See George R. Taylor, The Transportation Revolution, 1815–60 380 (2015).

118 Henry Vandine, 6 Pickering 187 (1828).

119 Bartlett v. Crozier 17 Johns. 439 (1820).

constraints on government grants of monopoly privileges began to decline in the late 19th century with judicial deference to state police powers and a shift to private monopoly as the target of opposition.

C. Federal Constitutional Limits on State (and Local) Monopoly Grants

The development of federal constitutional law further limited state monopoly grants during the antebellum period. Of course, this was a new set of legal constraints that did not exist before 1789. The two principal constraints in the antebellum period were the Constitution's commerce clause and supremacy clause. As discussed below, the commerce clause was interpreted to restrict state power to affect interstate and foreign (and Indian) commerce, with the indirect effect of constraining monopoly grants. The supremacy clause gave the federal government the power to override state monopoly grants if it chose to do so. A third federal constitutional provision—the impairment of contracts clause—played a different role. It was used to defend monopoly grants by limiting state attempts to modify or repeal earlier grants of monopoly. The impairment clause challenge was resorted to essentially as a rearguard action to protect earlier monopolies that preceded state constitutional and statutory restrictions.

As discussed in the next chapter, a host of other constitutional protections were invoked after the Civil War to challenge state power to grant monopolies and exclusive trading privileges, including, among others, the privileges and immunities, due process and equal protection clauses.[120] Let us turn here to the federal constitutional limitations on state monopoly grants during the antebellum years.

1. *Commerce clause and federal supremacy clause*

Before formation of the United States, colonies granted monopoly privileges that excluded traders and competitors from other colonies, such as the Massachusetts fur trading and fishing monopolies discussed in Chapter Two. This practice was no longer lawful when the Supreme Court in 1824 held that the constitutional power of Congress to regulate interstate and foreign commerce (as

---

[120] See Chapter Five.

well as trade with the Indian tribes) prevented the states from interfering with interstate and foreign/Indian commerce. Steamboat monopolies provided the dénouement.

New York and Louisiana granted Robert R. Livingston and Robert Fulton exclusive rights to steamboat navigation in their waters, thus giving the grantees controlling positions in two important ports. Rival states were, of course, deeply resentful.[121] Livingston's and Fulton's assignee (Aaron Ogden) petitioned a New York state court for an injunction against Thomas Gibbons restraining him from operating two steamboats running between New York and New Jersey. The court granted the injunction, which was affirmed by the New York Court of Appeal. In 1824, the Supreme Court in *Gibbons v. Ogden*[122] reversed and held that the state grant of exclusive navigation rights was unlawful under the federal commerce clause.[123] Chief Justice Marshall also declared that the New York grant fell afoul of the supremacy clause, because federal coasting license laws overrode the state legislation.

Gibbons v. Ogden established two important limitations on state grants of monopoly or exclusive privileges: 1) grants must not interfere with the federal power to regulate interstate and foreign/Indian commerce; and 2) Congress through legislation can limit state monopoly grants under the supremacy clause. Although the latter gave antimonopolists a significant weapon to combat state monopoly grants, it is fair to conclude that the weapon has been more potential than actually used. As discussed in the next chapter, neither the federal antitrust laws (starting with the Sherman Act in 1890) nor later federal legislation have significantly limited state grants of monopoly privileges.

---

[121] See McCloskey, supra note 4, at 68–71.

[122] 22 U.S. 1 (1824).

[123] Id. Chief Justice Marshall wrote:

"The power of Congress, then, comprehends navigation, within the limits of every State in the Union; so far as that navigation may be, in any manner, connected with "commerce with foreign nations, or among the several States, or with the Indian tribes." It may, of consequence, pass the jurisdictional line of New-York, and act upon the very waters to which the prohibition now under consideration applies."

2. *Impairment of contracts clause*

The federal impairment of contracts clause played a different role with respect to government grants of monopoly privileges. The impairment clause was used as a rearguard action by grantees to defend privileges given in colonial times or before state constitutional antimonopoly provisions. As mentioned above, this concerned a relatively small set of monopoly grants largely limited to the early states in the Northeast. Indeed, the principal Supreme Court decision case concerned a 1785 Massachusetts grant to build a bridge.

Massachusetts contracted with the Charles River Bridge Company to build and maintain a toll bridge across the Charles River. In 1792, the legislature extended the charter from forty to seventy years. Until the expiration of this term, the company was annually to pay two hundred pounds to Harvard College. In 1828, the legislature permitted another company to build a competing bridge nearby—the Warren Bridge. The Charles River Bridge Company sued Massachusetts, arguing that the permit of the new bridge unconstitutionally both divested its property rights and impaired its contract rights. By the time the suit reached the Supreme Court, sufficient tolls had been received by the proprietors of the new Warren Bridge to reimburse all their expenses, the bridge had become a toll-free property of the state, and the value of the franchise granted to the proprietors of the Charles River Bridge was entirely wiped out.[124]

In the *Charles River Bridge* decision, the Supreme Court held that the Massachusetts legislation creating the new bridge did not unconstitutionally impair claimant's contract with the state, that is, the Court rejected the monopoly grantees' argument that the federal protection against state impairment of contracts supported the inference that the legislature would not authorize a competing bridge.[125] Chief Justice Roger B. Taney, a Jacksonian, held that a contract granting monopoly privileges must be narrowly construed, because monopolies were disfavored. Thus, there were no implied grants of monopoly and states had the power to eliminate or modify prior grants.[126] Freedom of contract—a

---

[124] The Proprietors of the Charles River Bridge v. The Proprietors of the Warren Bridge, 36 U.S. 420, 538 (1837).

[125] Id.

[126] Id. at 548:

concept often asserted by legal scholars to be a critically important legal doctrine of the 19th century—did not override the community interest: "While the rights of private property are sacredly guarded, we must not forget that the community also have rights, and that the happiness and well-being of every citizen depends on their faithful preservation."[127] The Court continued that the more recent history of state grants also supported the rejection of implied privileges.[128] In other words, monopoly privileges had to be expressed in the grant and would not be inferred. Justice Joseph Story's dissent rested primarily on the grantees' need for legal certainty before they invested.[129] Story dismissed the monopoly concerns underlying the majority's strict rule of construction. For Story, monopoly grants were often necessary to encourage or incentivize investment in public improvements.[130]

The Supreme Court's decision in *Charles River Bridge* was important, primarily as strengthening state courts' adoption of the

---

"And when a corporation alleges, that a state has surrendered, for seventy- years, its power of improvement and public accommodation, in a great and important line of travel, along which a vast number of its citizens must daily pass, the community have a right to insist, in the language of this Court, above quoted, 'that its abandonment ought not to be presumed, in a case, in which the deliberate purpose of the state to abandon it does not appear.' The continued existence of a government would be of no great value, if, by implications and presumptions, it was disarmed of the powers necessary to accomplish the ends of its creation, and the functions it was designed to perform, transferred to the hands of privileged corporations."

[127] Id. at 422.

[128] Charles River Bridge, supra note 124, at 551–52:

"In some cases, rail roads have rendered the turnpike roads on the same line of travel so entirely useless, that the franchise of the turnpike corporation is not worth preserving. Yet in none of these cases have the corporations supposed that their privileges were invaded, or any contract violated on the part of the state. Amid the multitude of cases which have occurred, and have been daily occurring for the last forty or fifty years, this is the first instance in which such an implied contract has been contended for."

[129] Id. at 606.

[130] Id. at 608. As discussed below, Justice Story's rationale was well out of line with the state of the law and policy in 1837.

rule of strict construction of state monopoly grants.[131] And it is also true that *Charles River Bridge* freed new businesses from the fear of claims by older businesses that held ambiguously worded charters.[132] But perhaps too much has been made of the decision. Although the *Charles River Bridge* decision has been praised as a great triumph of opposition to monopoly, the decision concerned a narrow legal issue—the rule of construction governing corporate charters. Both the majority and dissenting opinions were more in agreement than not; both accepted the legitimacy of government grants of monopoly privileges for what today would be considered natural monopolies; neither would have recommended monopolies for common manufacturing corporations.[133] They differed only on the rule of construction in the comparatively small class of cases where the parties failed to specify the existence and scope of monopoly rights. Indeed, courts had already adopted a strict rule of construction well before the *Charles River Bridge* decision. For example, the federal district court in Louisiana had done so almost two decades before in 1819: "But the General Assembly do not guaranty a monopoly in every grant. A monopoly is never to be taken by construction. So far as the express terms of the grant go, it is exclusive; but no further."[134]

Monopoly rights were specified in the vast majority of antebellum grants, and *Charles River Bridge* was not relevant. If investor/grantees wanted legal certainty, they were free to negotiate for inclusion of terms in the contract in the first place. Indeed, even after the Civil War, if a charter contained a monopoly provision,

---

[131] Perhaps with enthusiastic exaggeration, Stanley Kutler asserts that *Charles River Bridge* "opened the floodgates and courts now directly confronted and denied exaggerated implied claims of vested rights." Stanley I. Kutler, Privilege and Creative Destruction: The Charles River Bridge Case 137 (1978). See also Calabresi and Leibowitz, supra note 88, at 1023, citing Mohawk Bridge Co. v. Utica & Schenectady Rail Road Co., 6 Paige Ch. 554 (N.Y. Ch. 1837) (bridge proprietor's charter did not prohibit competition from a ferry); Tuckahoe Canal Co. v. Tuckahoe & J.R.R. Co. 11 Leigh 42 38 Va. 42 (1840) (canal company's charter did not give the canal company an exclusive right of way to block railroad bridges). Indeed, Taney later in 1851 applied the strict construction principle to railroad charters. See Richmond Railroad Co. v. Louisa Railroad Co. 54 U.S. 71 (1851).

[132] Staurt Bruchey, The Roots of American Economic Growth, 1607-1861: An Essay in Social Causation 138 (1965).

[133] See Hovenkamp, supra note 109, at 1311-12.

[134] Orleans Navigation Co. v. Schooner Amelia, 7 Mart. (o.s.) 632 (1820).

most states enforced the provision. And monopoly charters continued to be written, even during the height of the antitrust movement in the 1880s.[135]

If *Charles River Bridge* is viewed as a battle between Jacksonian antimonopolists (*vide* Taney) and Federalist supporters of property rights and freedom of contract (*vide* Story),[136] then *Charles River Bridge* was a finishing skirmish with a rout of the retreating Federalists who had already lost the war. Justice Story's dissenting opinion was well out of line with the general state of the law in 1837, as reflected in the proliferation of state constitutions, statutes and court judgments of the period. His was a failed late response to the erosion of state monopoly grants in the antebellum period. By 1837, competition and antimonopoly sentiment generally prevailed over investment incentives in drawing the line between justified monopoly grants and unjustified monopoly grants.[137]

Legislators and courts after the Civil War began to rely more directly on economic theory—notably the concepts of natural monopoly and public utilities—to draw the line between justified and unjustified monopoly grants. In a sense, the consensus acceptance of natural monopoly and public utilities has defused much of the antimonopoly resistance to state grants of privileges in many cases. This is discussed in the next chapter.

---

[135] See Hovenkamp, supra note 109, at 110–14.

[136] For example, see Horwitz, supra note 112 (war between landed incumbent Federalists trying to protect their monopoly grants from Jacksonian newcomers). For a critical view of this characterization, see Hovenkamp, supra note 109, at 1267–68.

[137] See Horwitz, supra note 112, at 138–39.

Chapter Five

MODERN ERA—1870 TO TODAY

The American antimonopoly tradition was completely transformed after the Civil War, as the two earlier strands of the tradition unraveled. First, laws against forestalling, engrossing and other "monopolistic" practices lost most of their prominence. Although remnants of those laws can be found today, they lack the vigor of enforcement and popular attention seen in colonial and revolutionary America. Second, concern about government grants of monopoly privileges declined after the Civil War, almost to the point of irrelevance to today's policymakers, academics and the general public. In place of these two strands of the earlier antimonopoly tradition there arose a near exclusive focus on private firm monopoly unrelated to government grants. As targets of antimonopolist sentiment, large private firms—like Standard Oil—replaced grantees of government privileges, like the Second Bank of the United States. Today, it is the most successful firms—like Big Tech—that raise the hackles of critics of monopoly, rather than recipients of government monopoly privileges.

The shift in attention to private firm monopoly after the Civil War ultimately resulted in state and federal monopolization provisions, including most importantly the Sherman Act. A comprehensive set of laws and enforcement institutions were put in place—all informed over time by sophisticated economic analysis. The modern era began in the 1880s and we are still living in it. Indeed, the modern era's exclusive focus on private firms, together with the failure of statutory and constitutional constraints on government grants of monopoly privileges, mark a significant departure from the history of the antimonopoly tradition we saw from the first settlements in Virginia to the late 19th century.

There are several explanations for this historical shift. First, energy of the 19th century's antitrust movement was directed toward the large, new firms that owed less from government monopoly privileges than earlier recipients. Second, theories of natural monopoly, and industry regulated public utilities, have provided policy and economic rationales for many government grants of monopoly privileges that previously had been challenged.

Third, the courts' deference to states' exercise of police powers has permitted a more tolerant judicial review of state and local economic regulation, including the grant of monopoly privileges.

There are many excellent books and articles on the antitrust laws and their application from 1890 to the present, including recent literature criticizing the courts' interpretation of the statutes as unduly narrow. Indeed, in the last few years, there has been a resurgence of antimonopoly sentiment that is fueling demands for strengthened enforcement, particularly against successful firms in the high tech and digital platform spaces. This chapter has the modest goal of placing the present debate about U.S. antitrust law in the context of the historical antimonopoly tradition. The chapter is divided into the following sections: government grants of monopoly privileges (section I); forestalling and engrossing (section II); antitrust movement in the last decades of the 19th century (section III); and private monopoly under the federal antitrust laws (section IV).

I. GOVERNMENT MONOPOLY GRANTS

A. The *Slaughter-House Cases*

We begin our discussion of government grants of monopoly privileges during the modern era with the story of a well-known federal constitutional challenge of a local monopoly—the *Slaughter-House Cases*.[1] The *Slaughter-House Cases* are notorious in the legal literature for their treatment (or mistreatment) of constitutional law principles.[2] Our interest lies more with the broader history of the affair and its ultimate dénouement. In 1869, Louisiana granted Crescent City Livestock Landing and Slaughter-House Company an effective monopoly for 25 years for slaughterhouse operations in New Orleans. Crescent City was required to erect "a grand slaughterhouse of sufficient capacity to accommodate all butchers," together with stockyards. No stock was to be landed or slaughtered for the New Orleans market, except at Crescent City's facilities. The law required full access to all butchers at a fixed schedule of fees.

Like statutes in other cities, such as New York and Philadelphia, the New Orleans legislation was intended to confine butchers to a

---

[1] See generally Ronald M. Labbé & Jonathan Lurie, The Slaughterhouse Cases (2003).

[2] The decisions have been vociferously condemned by constitutional law scholars over the years.

designated area in order to protect municipal water supplies from offal.[3] Also, like other government grants of monopoly privileges, complaints of bribery and corruption swirled around the grant to Crescent City.

Over 400 members of the Butchers' Benevolent Association challenged the legislation, arguing that it violated a number of federal constitutional provisions – notably the recently ratified privileges and immunities clause of the Fourteenth Amendment. In 1873, the Supreme Court, in a majority opinion by Justice Samuel Miller,[4] upheld the legislation to the dismay of antimonopolists and constitutional scholars ever since.[5] The weight of commentaries complain that the majority opinion takes an overly permissive position, finding no fundamental right to be free of monopolies.[6] In my view, this complaint goes too far. The majority's statement is correct in the sense that the federal constitution has no provision specifically banning or restricting monopolies, unlike many state constitutions. The right to be free from monopoly – whether or not fundamental – has never been absolute in the constitutional sense and has always been qualified. And in this particular case, the antimonopoly principle was tempered by the police power to regulate slaughterhouses.[7] The Court went on to hold that the exercise of the

---

[3] Herbert Hovenkamp adds an economic perspective: "the statute that created the Crescent City slaughterhouse monopoly was a work of great genius, designed to create a public utility from a business that had produced a very expensive market failure because of large-scale changes in technology and population." Herbert Hovenkamp, Technology, Politics, and Regulated Monopoly: An American Historical Perspective, 62 Texas L. Rev. 1263, 1296 (1984).

[4] Slaughter-House Cases, 83 U.S. 36 (1872).

[5] Most constitutional law scholars disagree with the result. See, e.g., Amar: "Virtually no serious modern scholar – left, right, and center – thinks that the decision is a plausible reading of the [Fourteenth] Amendment." Akhil Reed Amar, Substance and Method in the Year 2000, 28 Pepp. L. Rev. 601, 631 (2001).

[6] See generally id.

[7] 83 U.S. at 62:

> "'Unwholesome trades, slaughter-houses, operations offensive to the senses, the deposit of powder, the application of steam power to propel cars, the building with combustible materials, and the burial of the dead, may all,' says Chancellor Kent,[13] 'be interdicted by law, in the midst of dense masses of population, on the general and rational principle, that every person ought so to use his property as not to injure his neighbors; and that private interests must be made

police power was reasonable under the specific facts of the case,[8] which of course is most significant in its invocation of police power to justify government grants of monopoly privileges—even in the face of federal constitutional challenge. Looking forward into the 20th century, the decision presages later state and federal courts' heavy reliance on police powers to justify government grants of monopoly privileges (as discussed later below).

Justice Stephen Field, writing for the dissent, agreed that in principle a legitimate exercise of police powers can justify a government grant of monopoly privileges. He argued, however, that the Louisiana legislation was a "pretence" that infringed fundamental constitutional rights guaranteed under the privileges and immunities clause. Field reasoned that the law "which allows no one but the favored company to build, own, or have slaughter-houses is not a police regulation, and has not the faintest semblance of one."[9] Justice Joseph Bradley, also dissenting, invoked Magna Carta and other English history to argue that the legislation's exclusion of competing butchers was "onerous, unreasonable, arbitrary, and unjust. It has none of the qualities of a police regulation. If it were really a police regulation, it would undoubtedly be within the power of the legislature."[10]

In essence, the basic disagreement between the majority and dissenters concerned the scope of a state's police power, particularly when its exercise arguably ran contrary to the tradition against government grants of monopoly. The fiercest adherents of that tradition—such as Justices Field and Bradley—gave little deference to

---

> subservient to the general interests of the community.' This is called the police power." [Footnote omitted.]

[8] Id. at 64:

> "we are not able to see that these privileges are especially odious or objectionable. The duty imposed as a consideration for the privilege is well defined, and its enforcement well guarded. The prices or charges to be made by the company are limited by the statute, and we are not advised that they are on the whole exorbitant or unjust."

The Court also rejected the argument that the legislation violated the butchers' privileges and immunities guaranteed by the Fourteenth Amendment, a rejection that has been passionately criticized by constitutional scholars but has never been overturned.

[9] "It is one of those arbitrary and unjust laws made in the interest of a few scheming individuals, by which some of the Southern States have, within the past few years, been so deplorably oppressed and impoverished." Id. at 120.

[10] Id. at 119-20.

the legislature's judgment about the exercise of its police powers, and they invoked history to support their fierceness. The majority, like later courts, gave greater deference to the legislative exercise of police powers and gave less weight to Magna Carta.

The Supreme Court victory for the monopolist Crescent City was short-lived, however. In 1879, Louisiana amended its constitution to prohibit state and local governments from granting monopoly rights over slaughterhouse activities, including the right to build slaughterhouses and engage in the business of butchering in New Orleans.[11] New Orleans, in turn, immediately passed an ordinance that made slaughtering competitive and the Butchers' Benevolent Association prepared to reenter the market. As expected, Crescent City then challenged the loss of its monopoly privileges as an unconstitutional impairment of contracts, seeking an injunction against the marketplace entry of other butchers. But, as in the *Charles River Bridge* case decades earlier, in 1884 the Supreme Court rejected the impairment claim.[12] The Court held – again in an opinion by Justice Miller – that the earlier Louisiana legislature that had granted the slaughterhouse monopoly did not have the constitutional authority to prevent a later legislature's attempt to regulate public health or public morals.[13]

---

[11] Article 248 of the Louisiana Constitution provided:

> "The police juries of the several parishes, and the constituted authorities of all incorporated municipalities of the State, shall alone have the power of regulating the slaughtering of cattle and other livestock within their respective limits; provided, no monopoly or exclusive privilege shall exist in this State, nor such business be restricted to the land or houses of any individual or corporation; provided, the ordinances designating the places for slaughtering shall obtain the concurrent approval of the Board of Health or other sanitary organization."

La. CONST. of 1879, art. 248.

[12] Butchers' Union Slaughter-House & Live-Stock Landing Co. v. Crescent City Live-Stock Landing & Slaughter-House Co., 111 U.S. 746 (1884).

[13] Justices Bradley and Field, who concurred in the decision to reject the impairment of contracts claim, took the opportunity to repeat their antimonopoly objections to the early legislation – seemingly to suggest that all monopoly grants are unlawful, including the licensing of professions and occupations. Justice Bradley declaimed that "It cannot be that a state may limit to a specified number of its people the right to practice law, the right to practice medicine, the right to preach the gospel, the right to till the soil, or to pursue

The Crescent City monopoly was ended, but the saga of slaughtering in New Orleans continued. Health concerns returned, and the local authorities responded by creating a de facto monopoly by zoning a restricted area in which slaughterhouses could be established. They then licensed only a single slaughterhouse to operate in the zone. In 1892, the Louisiana Supreme Court upheld this response as a valid exercise of police power that did not violate the Louisiana constitution's monopoly ban,[14] citing the majority reasoning of the Supreme Court in the *Slaughter-House Cases*. The Louisiana Supreme Court took the view that the legislation did not confer "monopolous or exclusive privilege" nor restrict "the business of slaughtering to the land or houses of defendants."[15] The court continued: "The most that can be said is that the ordinances do not expressly confer upon others than the defendants the present right to establish slaughterhouses within the limits designated." In sum, a liberal construction of the facts and scope of state police power to regulate public health trumped the state constitutional ban on slaughterhouse monopolies.[16]

The courts' upholding of the New Orleans slaughterhouse laws was a harbinger of the future of legal challenges to government grants of monopoly privileges: they generally were unsuccessful. As discussed below, increasing judicial deference to state exercises of police power, as well as the theory of natural monopoly, have provided economic and legal rationales for many government grants of monopoly privileges that previously had been questioned or even invalidated.

---

particular business or trades, and thus parcel out to different parties the various vocations and callings of life." 111 U.S. at 758.

[14] Darcantel v. People's Slaughterhouse & Refrigerating Co., 44 La. Ann. 632 (1892).

[15] Id. at 641.

[16] The court declared:

> "Considering the importance of the police power over this subject and that the whole police power of the State over it is delegated to the city, we are bound to give it a liberal construction and to respect the discretion of the city in a matter so important to the health and well-being of the citizens, unless convinced, upon complaint of parties whose rights are infringed, that it operates the creation of a monopoly or exclusive privilege in violation of the Constitution."

44 La. Ann. at 643.

B. Natural Monopoly and the Theory of Public Utilities

In colonial times and throughout much of the 19th century, legislators and courts categorized a group of services as permitting monopoly privileges, such as bridges, ferries and turnpikes—and later canals and railroads. These services were based largely on historical precedent ("common right" or a "prerogative of the King" in Blackstone's system[17]) rather than on any coherent economic analysis.[18] But services based on new or changes in technology—like delivery of gas in city pipelines—were difficult to assess under the historical precedents. As Herbert Hovenkamp sarcastically summarizes, "Throughout the [19th] century, the state-created monopoly was an economic institution in search of a legal doctrine that would predictably justify or condemn it."[19] In the 20th century, legislators and courts found that legal doctrine when they began to rely more directly on economic theory—notably the concept of "natural monopoly"—to draw the line between justified and unjustified monopoly grants, and relatedly, to rationalize the regulation of industries.[20]

Although the concept of natural monopoly was considerably refined in the 20th century, the idea itself is not entirely new. An earlier reference to natural monopoly can be found in Matthew Hale's 1670 treatise *De Portibus Maris* concerning government regulation of seaports.[21] Natural monopolies also were recognized by economists like Henry Carter Adams and Richard Ely in the late 19th century,[22] as well as by several courts.[23]

Natural monopolies are industries with pervasive economies of scale (and scope): the greater the output, the lower the costs of production per unit. Costs decline as output increases throughout the

---

[17] 3 W. Blackstone, Commentaries on the Laws of England (1765–1769).

[18] Hovenkamp, supra note 3, at 1285.

[19] Id. at 1281–82.

[20] See id. at 1308 n. 257. Market failures other than natural monopoly—such as free rider problems in national defense—also can explain the legislative decision to confer monopoly rights. See id. at 1274.

[21] See also John Stuart Mill, The Principles of Political Economy (1848) (public utilities). For a brief history of the concept of natural monopoly, see William W. Sharkey, The Theory of Natural Monopoly 14–20 (1982).

[22] See Hans B. Thorelli, The Federal Antitrust Policy: Origination of an American Tradition 124 (1955).

[23] E.g., Munn v. Illinois, 94 U.S. 113 (1876).

entire output range in which buyers are willing to pay a remunerative price. The notion is that natural monopolies require a scale that cannot be achieved with multiple suppliers (a so-called "market failure"). Once a type of market has been recognized as a natural monopoly, the state is likely to intervene and regulate entry and pricing in order to provide the monopolist with a fair rate of return.[24]

It is often difficult, however, to identify an industry as a natural monopoly by a simple measure of economies of scale (or scope).[25] Economists have developed a wide array of complex technical tools to identify natural monopolies and fashion optimal regulatory schemes to deal with them.[26] For example, for most of the 20th century, electric utility companies operated and owned their own generation, transmission and distribution resources within their service area.[27] This model of ownership rested on the oft-debated assumption that a utility inherently is a natural monopoly. In the last several decades, however, the electrical industry has shifted from one that institutionalized the natural monopoly characteristics of a fully integrated utility to one that facilitates competition through open access transmission and generation dispatch markets. Today, regulated, unregulated and partially regulated electricity system models exist across the country.[28] As a policy matter, however, the natural monopoly debate continues and touches on issues concerning Big Tech and its potential regulation.

In sum, many earlier monopolies that generated legal challenge and popular controversy may be viewed as natural monopolies today.[29] And they are regulated at both the federal and state levels.

---

[24] See Hovenkamp, supra note 3, at 1274.

[25] Sharkey, supra note 21, at 20.

[26] See, e.g., Sharkey, supra note 21; Kenneth E. Train, Optimal Regulation: The Economic Theory of Natural Monopoly (1991); Michael Waterson, Recent Developments in the Theory of Natural Monopoly, 1 J. of Econ. Survs., 59 (1987). Some proposals essentially eliminate the need for regulation. See Train xiii, 297-315.

[27] Jada F. Garofalo, An Electricity Regulation Primer—The History of Electricity Regulation in the United States, 2 https://Ssrn.Com/Abstract=3974880.

[28] Id. at 38-39.

[29] Hovenkamp maintains that "most of the great, infamous monopolies of the nineteenth century were the products of new technology or economies of scale and the resulting market failures. In my view, those monopolies that caused the largest amount of public hostility toward concentrated economic power were 'natural monopolies,' most of them necessitated by technological change." Hovenkamp, supra note 3, at 1273.

Monopoly concerns continue to exist, however. The economic concept of natural monopoly has not eliminated the traditional concern that government monopoly grants not only can lead to a misallocation of resources, but they also run the risk of political corruption. And indeed, widespread corruption was common under municipal franchise agreements – municipal officials extorted utilities to maximize their income and utilities bribed municipalities in order to stay in business.[30] To meet this problem, states created administrative bodies at the statewide level to regulate public utilities. Today, there also is regulation at the federal level.

From the historical perspective, it is fair to conclude that regulation, albeit never entirely free from criticism, has reduced complaints about government grants of monopoly privileges in many important industries. For example, a report of the Congressional Budget Office (1997) noted that, in the 1930s, the potential for a natural monopoly existed in both the distribution and generation of electric power, particularly for hydropower.[31] Many observers at the time were concerned that allowing a private business to generate, distribute and sell all the electricity in a region would not serve the interests of the public: monopolists could charge customers more than a socially efficient price for power.[32] The federal government addressed these concerns with four types of intervention: 1) the Tennessee Valley Authority and power marketing entities entered directly into competition with private suppliers; 2) the ability of local distribution companies to compete with private wholesalers was strengthened; 3) the Federal Power Act of 1935 established a regulatory framework for federal and state control of prices and services; and 4) the Securities and Exchange Commission was charged with overseeing and limiting the ability of private companies to extend market power through holding companies. But industries and markets are not static. For example, at the end of the 20th century, the natural monopoly concept had less traction in the electricity industry as new infrastructure was built

[30] Garofalo, supra note 27, at 3–4.

[31] Cong. Budget Off., Should the Federal Government Sell Electricity? (1997).

[32] Id. at 15. For an earlier critique of the power industry as a monopoly, see Gifford Pinchot, The Power Monopoly: Its Make-Up and Its Menace (1928). See also Walter Adams & Horace Gray, Monopoly in America: The Government as Promoter (1955). See generally Lawrence Potamkin, Public Power and the Federal Government, 30 Neb. L. Rev. 375 (1951).

and as the traditional rate formula began to have unwelcome economic effects.[33] In sum, federal and state regulation has moderated antimonopoly complaints in many industries characterized as natural monopolies.[34] The debate about natural monopoly has become highly technical and complex.[35] There always will be a school of thought that the "invisible hand" of the true market will better allocate supply and demand to the benefit of consumers and suppliers alike.

Most markets, of course, are not natural monopolies or even close to it. Let us turn to federal and state constitutional constraints on state and local grants of monopoly privileges in those markets. As the *Slaughter-House* decisions portended, constitutional antimonopoly provisions have been limited in their effect on state and local grants of monopoly privileges—at least when compared with the periods before the Civil War. Perhaps ironically, the monopoly tradition as expressed in federal and state constitutional limitations has been significantly attenuated since the late 19th century.

C. Federal Constitutional Constraints on Monopoly

In 1824, the Supreme Court in *Gibbons v. Ogden*[36] recognized two federal constitutional limitations on state and local grants of monopoly privileges: 1) grants must not interfere with the federal power to regulate interstate and foreign commerce (and commerce with the Indians); and 2) under the supremacy clause, Congress through legislation has the power to limit state and local monopoly grants. Despite this early recognition, the commerce and supremacy clauses have not imposed significant constraints on state and local monopoly grants—especially in the face of the exercise of their police powers. Other federal constitutional limitations also have not been

---

[33] Joseph P. Tomain, The Persistence of Natural Monopoly, 16 Nat. Res. & Env't 242, 246 (2002).

[34] When state and local authorities expressly grant a monopoly to one firm, it often concerns a natural monopoly like an electric utility and is accepted as a legitimate exception to the constitutional ban. One exception appears to be Texas where courts have been aggressive in reviewing municipal contracts for water, gas and electricity. See Alexandra K. Howell, Enforcing a Wall of Separation Between Big Business and the State: Protection from Monopolies in State Constitutions, 89 Notre Dame L. Rev. 859, 882 (2020).

[35] To sample the technical complexities, see, e.g., Sharkey, supra note 21; Train, supra note 26.

[36] Gibbons v. Ogden, 22 U.S 1 (1824). For further discussion, see Chapter Four.

effective instruments to curtail state and local grants of monopoly privileges. As seen above, the 14th Amendment's privileges and immunities clause was rejected as basis for a challenge to the New Orleans butchers' monopoly in the *Slaughter-House Cases.* And, like state constitutional challenges discussed below, federal challenges usually fail once a reasonable exercise of police power is shown.[37]

As to the federal commerce and supremacy clauses specifically, they have not fulfilled their potential as antimonopoly instruments, a potential suggested by early 19th century decisions like *Gibbons v. Ogden.*[38] At the risk of oversimplification, with respect to the commerce clause the Supreme Court over time and in various contexts has essentially granted state and local authorities considerable leeway to regulate commerce—both intrastate and interstate commerce. This regulation can include grants of monopoly privileges. It appears that only state and local measures that expressly discriminate against citizens of other states fall afoul of the federal commerce clause.[39]

The supremacy clause also has failed as an effective instrument to curtail state and local monopoly grants. Congress generally has not used the supremacy clause to combat monopoly privileges granted by states or local authorities. Likewise, neither the federal antitrust laws (starting with the Sherman Act in 1890) nor later federal legislation have been successfully invoked to limit state grants of monopoly privileges in a meaningful way. The failure of the Sherman Act to constrain state and local monopoly reflects the

---

[37] The Supreme Court has stated: "[The grant of monopoly, if otherwise an appropriate exercise of police power, is not void as denying equal protection of the law." Pacific St. Box & Basket Co. v. White, 296 U.S. 176, 184 (1935). See also City of New Orleans v. Dukes, 427 U.S. 297 (1976). For an argument that the Ninth Amendment constrains state grants of monopoly or exclusive privileges, see Michael Conant, Antimonopoly Tradition Under the Ninth and Fourteenth Amendments: Slaughter-House Cases Re-Examined, 31 Emory L.J. 785, 786–789 (1982). See also Howell, supra note 34, at 865.

[38] 22 U.S 1 (1824).

[39] Pike v. Bruce Church, Inc., 397 U.S. 137, 142 (1970) (articulating test that courts employ to assess non-discriminatory laws that burden interstate commerce). See also Alexandra B. Klass & Jim Rossi, Revitalizing Dormant Commerce Clause Review for Interstate Coordination, 100 Minn. L. Rev. 129, 158 (2015) (noting that "it has been more than 25 years since the Supreme Court has invalidated a state law based on *Pike* balancing"); Alan J. Meese, Federalism, Free Competition and Sherman Act Preemption of State Restraints, 16 Va. L. & Bus. Rev. 115, 156–57 (2021).

modern antitrust focus on purely private conduct and the concomitant dilution of monopoly opposition with respect to government monopoly or government grants of monopoly privileges to private operators.

A state is not prohibited under federal antitrust law from creating and running its own monopoly. This has been clear since the 1943 decision in *Parker v. Brown*.[40] Similarly, a local municipality is free under the Sherman Act to create and run a monopoly if there is a "clear articulation" of government policy to displace competition.[41] Indeed, even grants of monopoly privileges to private actors are permitted under the Sherman Act where the challenged conduct is "clearly articulated and affirmatively expressed as state policy" and the challenged restriction or conduct is "actively supervised" by the state.[42] Only the private actor is liable under U.S. antitrust law if the two conditions are not met; the state bears no liability.

This carve out of antimonopoly prohibitions rests on what many view as bedrock considerations of "federalism and state sovereignty," each of which is said to counsel against Sherman Act preemption of state-imposed or state-authorized monopoly grants. The underlying premise is that preemption would unduly interfere with states' ability to serve as laboratories of democracy or their choice how to regulate their own economies.[43] It is probably fair to say that most antitrust scholars agree.[44] Bluntly speaking, federalism and state

---

[40] Parker v. Brown, 317 U.S. 341 (1943) (California scheme to reduce the state's raisin output and increase the price of interstate raisin sales).

[41] See, e.g., City of Columbia v. Omni Outdoor Advert., Inc., 499 U.S. 365 (1991); Community Commc'n Co., Inc. v. City of Boulder, 455 U.S. 40 (1982).

[42] Cf. California Retail Liquor Dealers Ass'n v. Midcal Aluminum, Inc. 445 U.S. 97 (1980).

[43] See Meese, supra note 39 at 120.

[44] See, e.g., William H. Page, Antitrust, Federalism, and the Regulatory Process: A Reconstruction and Critique of the State Action Exemption, 61 B.U.L. Rev. 1099, 1107 (1981) ("To give full preemptive effect to the Sherman Act would go far beyond a prohibition on parochial legislation; given the virtually unlimited jurisdictional reach of the Sherman Act, it would effectively forbid all state regulation of price and entry. For example, professional licensing, a primarily local activity, would certainly be held to affect commerce enough to confer federal jurisdiction."); Milton Handler, The Current Attack on the Parker v. Brown State Action Doctrine, 76 Colum. L. Rev. 1, 15 n.71 (1976) (reversal of Parker would authorize Sherman Act scrutiny of state statutes "regulat[ing] price and entry in such diverse fields as insurance, taxicabs, railroads, sale of prescription drugs, bank branching, buses, milk, sign posting and agricultural

rights have trumped the historical American concerns over government grants of monopoly privileges. In a sense, post-Founding principles of federalism have attenuated—perhaps perversely to some observers—federal protections against state and local grants of monopoly privileges.

D. State Constitutional Constraints on Monopoly

Constraints on state and local grants of monopoly privileges are now more readily found at the state level than at the federal level. As we saw in earlier chapters, a number of states have antimonopoly provisions in their state constitutions. Before the Civil War, these provisions were directed at government grants of monopoly privileges. During the antitrust movement in the late 19th and early 20th centuries, state constitutions added provisions directed at private monopoly. Today, twenty-one states explicitly reference monopolies or monopoly power in their constitutions.[45] And fifteen states have constitutional provisions banning the state from granting any corporation or group special privileges or immunities that are not equally granted to other citizens.[46] These comprehensive constraints are further strengthened with constitutional bans on the granting of irrevocable special privileges or immunities.[47] Specific industry bans also can be found, such as Alaska's constitutional limitations on extraction of natural resources, like fishing.[48]

Lumping together all these provisions, forty-five states have some form of constitutional limitation on government grants of monopoly. At first glance, this evidences a strong and continuing

---

products"). But see Rebecca H. Allensworth, Foxes at the Henhouse: Occupational Licensing Boards Up Close, 105 Cal. L. Rev. 1557, 1582–1600 (2017) (advocating intensified Sherman Act scrutiny of state occupational licensing regimes); Meese, supra note 39.

45 Steven Gow, Calabresi et al., Individual Rights Under State Constitutions in 2018: What Rights Are Deeply Rooted in a Modern-Day Consensus of the States?, 94 Notre Dame L. Rev. 49, 105–109 (2018).

46 Id. at 106. For example, the Virginia constitution provides that "[t] he General Assembly shall not enact any local, special, or private law... [g] ranting to any private corporation, association, or individual any special or exclusive right, privilege, or immunity." Va. CONST. art. IV, § 14.

47 See Gow, supra note 45 at 107. For example, Idaho's constitution provides that "no special privileges or immunities shall ever be granted that may not be altered, revoked, or repealed by the legislature ...." Id. CONST. art. I, § 2.

48 Ak. CONST. art. VIII §§ 3, 15 and 17.

expression of the antimonopoly tradition at the state (constitutional) level. This does not mean, however, that government grants of monopoly have been eliminated. State and local regulations that directly or indirectly confer exclusive privileges (where not a complete monopoly) continue to exist. While there are innumerable court decisions over the course of more than a century (we will not try to summarize them here),[49] we offer a few general observations.

State constitutional challenges to state and local regulations granting monopoly privileges have been unsuccessful usually for two related reasons: judicial deference to legislative purpose and a broad definition of the state's police power with respect to health, safety and public order. Licensing rules and regulations—notably occupational licensing—generally have been upheld as serving a justifiable public interest like protection of the public against incompetents and imposters.[50] The Tennessee Supreme Court upheld a limitation on the number of liquor stores even though, "[a]s a practical matter, such limitation has a tendency to accomplish that which is monopolistic" because "an incidental monopoly" does not "offend[ ] the anti-monopoly clause of our Constitution, if the actual and real tendency of such ordinance or statute is to effect the purpose of protecting the safety, health and morals of the public."[51] Other examples of judicial deference to state regulations that include monopoly or exclusive privileges may strike some readers as more dubious. The Arkansas Supreme Court upheld regulations of juke boxes as a valid exercise of its police power "to protect the morals and general welfare of society," given the possible harms of their use in "dance halls [and] drinking places."[52] The North Carolina Supreme Court upheld restrictions on sales of food and drinks within one-half mile of a local fair.[53] According to Alexandra Howell,

---

[49] For a recent summary and analysis, see Howell, supra note 34.

[50] For example, see State v. Call, 28 S.E. 517 (N.C. 1897):

> "To require [a medical license] is an exercise of the police power for the protection of the public against incompetents and impostors, and it is in no sense the creation of a monopoly or special privileges. The door stands open to all who possess the requisite age and good character and can pass the examination which is exacted of all applicants alike."

See generally Howell, supra note 34, at 875-77.

[51] Landman v. Kizer, 255 S.W.2d 6, 7 (Tenn. 1953).

[52] Brown v. Cheney, 350 S.W.2d 184 (Ark. 1961).

[53] State v. Stovall, 8 S.E. 900, 900(N.C. 1889):

Texas courts have been so deferential to legislative creations of monopoly through economic regulation that they have never invalidated a state or local law under the Texas constitutional monopoly provision.[54]

Given the general deference to legislative judgment and the broad definition of police powers, there are relatively rare instances of successful challenges to government grants of monopoly privileges. The Maryland Court of Appeals invalidated a law requiring that government notices be published only in newspapers that set the type within Montgomery County because it served no public purpose: "Newspaper readers are no more concerned in where the type from which the paper is printed was set up than they are in the birthplace of the typesetter ...."[55] In broad language, the court declared that the antimonopoly ban limited the state's public procurement rights.[56] North Carolina courts expressed "serious doubt" about the constitutionality of a law that required producers

---

> "Organizations such as the Roanoke and Tar River Agricultural Society are justly considered of public benefit, and large numbers of people congregate at their fairs, and from the very nature of such assemblies, regulations for the preservation of order are necessary, and the Legislature has the power to enact such laws and provide for such regulations as will preserve the good order and promote the interest and comfort of those who assemble for purposes of pleasure or for the advancement of agricultural interests."

[54] Howell, supra note 34, at 884.

[55] Raney v. Montgomery Cnty Com'rs, 183 A. 548, 553–54 (Md. 1936). A similar Oklahoma Territory statute was held contrary to a federal statute prohibiting the territories from granting special privileges to a printing company. See Guthrie Daily Leader v. Cameron, 41 P. 635 (Okla. 1895). For another Maryland case, see City of Havre De Grace v. Johnson, 123 A. 65 (Md. 1923) (city ordinance that gave residents a monopoly of the car hire business held invalid as unreasonable and discriminatory).

[56] The court stated:

> "But if it be conceded, as it must be, that the power of the Legislature to determine through what agencies and means the work of the government is to be carried on and administered is necessarily broad and comprehensive, nevertheless that power is not unlimited, for it, as well as all other branches of the government, is restrained by the Constitution. ... It could not, therefore, be doubted that the Legislature would not have the power to declare that all public work in Baltimore City should be done by residents of some one of the counties, or that no public work of the State should be done except by contractors residing in Baltimore City." Id. at 554.

of reconstituted milk to make an equalization payment to regular milk producers who sold at a higher price.[57] And the Arkansas courts that had upheld jukebox regulations, invalidated a law regulating delivery of ice, which was deemed "a business not inherently dangerous to the public welfare or morals, so "the benefit to the public would be remote and problematical."[58] In *Fishburn v. City of Chicago,* an ordinance requiring that the city purchase road materials only from one company was held to constitute an unlawful monopoly.[59]

Some state courts have followed Sherman Act precedents when interpreting their constitutional provisions. The Texas Supreme Court relied on *Grinnell*'s definition of monopolization (monopoly power in a relevant market and the willful acquisition or maintenance of that power) in upholding a state law requiring prescriptions from optometrists or ophthalmologists for lenses to consumers.[60] The existence of 2600 optometrists licensed in Texas suggested to the court that, absent a price fixing conspiracy, competition would prevent them from charging excessive prices for contact lenses. The state also provided a reasonable public health rationale for the statute's distinctions between licensed optometrists and unlicensed dispensers such as the plaintiff.

Last, we do not know how many monopoly grants—either state or federal—were ended or not granted in the first place because of antimonopoly principles. It is reasonable to believe that court decisions understate the effect of the antimonopoly tradition on state and federal monopoly grants. Nor does the low rate of successful court challenges to state monopoly grants necessarily mean that the constitutional bans have had no effect on state legislatures; the threat

---

[57] In re Arcadia Dairy Farms, 259 S.E.2d 368 (N.C. 1979). See Howell, supra note 34, at 784–85.

[58] Cap F. Bourland Ice Co. v. Franklin Utils. Co., 22 S.W.2d 993 (Ark. 1929).

[59] 49 N.E. **532, 532**-33 (Ill. 1898):

> "It does not appear from the face of the ordinance that the effect is necessarily to so prevent competition or create a monopoly; but the proffered proof, which the court excluded, unmistakably disclosed that the asphaltum required by the ordinance to be used in making the street was a product which could only be obtained by purchase from a single corporation. The direct effect of the requirement, therefore, was to create a monopoly in favor of that corporation, and to restrict competition in bidding accordingly."

[60] Lens Exp., Inc. v. Ewald, 907 S.W.2d 64 (Tex. 1992).

of challenges and the legal rules probably have constrained government monopoly grants to some (immeasurable) degree.

Let us finish our discussion of government grants of monopoly privileges with a brief mention of federal grants.

E. Federal Grants of Monopoly Privileges

As mentioned before, the U.S. constitution has no provision banning or limiting monopoly. Despite that absence, the most significant victory of antimonopolists in the antebellum era was Jackson's veto of the Second Bank of the United States. Although Jackson himself was partly motivated by constitutional considerations, the end of the Bank resulted from a political decision, not a legal challenge.

Since the Civil War, popular and political concerns about federal grants of monopoly privileges have declined in importance, both in absolute terms and relative to concerns about private monopoly. Some of this may be explained by shifts in the constituencies and general political economy views of opponents to monopoly. After all, it was Jacksonian Democrats who fought the federally chartered Second Bank of the United States in the 1830s. Democrats today, and throughout most of the 20th century generally, have prioritized the benefits of federal (and state) economic intervention over the (potential) harms of government grants of monopoly. In that sense, the near exclusive focus on private firms by modern Progressive Democrats or neo-Brandeisians is consistent with this prioritization. In contrast, a colonial American or Jacksonian Democrat might view the modern antitrust movement as essentially saying that big (*vide* monopoly and attendant regulation) government is good, but big (*vide* monopoly) business is bad. To understand better whether or not this characterization has any validity, we will discuss the modern antitrust focus on private monopoly in sections III and IV, below. Before we do so, let us look at what is left of forestalling and engrossing laws in the modern era – it is very little.

II. FORESTALLING AND ENGROSSING LAWS

In 1844, the British Parliament abrogated the common law and statutory rules on forestalling and engrossing. And in the early 20th century, some courts announced the death of those rules in the

United States. For example, in 1911 Chief Justice White in *Standard Oil* declaimed:

> "From the development of more accurate economic conceptions and the changes in conditions of society, it came to be recognized that the acts prohibited by the engrossing, forestalling, etc., statutes did not have the harmful tendency which they were presumed to have when the legislation concerning them was enacted, and therefore did not justify the presumption which had previously been deduced from them, but, on the contrary, such acts tended to fructify and develop trade."[61]

This echoes earlier federal court decisions that described laws on forestalling and engrossing as "archaic"[62] and "obsolete."[63] A common perception is that these laws were subsumed into modern antitrust laws. In 1906, a Maryland court stated that new offenses like "corners" and "trusts" simply are old offenses under new names, because they are frequently attempts by a combination of persons to monopolize an article of trade or commerce in order to enhance its price.[64] But, like the death of Mark Twain, announcements of the death of laws against forestalling and engrossing are premature. They continue to be found in places, although with nothing like the vigor and passion seen in colonial and revolutionary America.

Forestalling and engrossing rules continue to appear as part of state antitrust statutes. Mississippi[65] and Tennessee[66] are examples.

---

[61] Standard Oil Co. v. United States, 221 U.S 1, 55 (1911).

[62] State of Minnesota v. N. Sec. Co., 123 F. 692 (D. Minn. 1903).

[63] Davis v. A. Booth & Co., 131 F. 31 (6th Cir. 1904).

[64] Klingel's Pharmacy v. Sharp & Dohme, 64 A. 1029 (Md. 1906). See also State v. Duluth Bd. of Trade, 121 N.W. 395 (Minn. 1909) ("The old offenses of regrating, engrossing, and forestalling are no longer known to the law; but modern Legislatures are still seeking a solution of the same problem—how to maintain the right to freely buy and sell the necessaries and conveniences of life in a market which is free from artificial and conventional restrictions.")

[65] See Georgia Pac. Co. v. Cook Timber Co., Inc., 194 So. 2d 118 (Miss. 2016) (subsection (c) prohibits a business from "engross[ing], forestall[ing] or attempt[ing] to engross or forestall any commodity"); Standard Oil Co. of N.J. v. State, 61 So. 981 (Miss. 1913).

[66] State v. Nashville Ry. & Light Co., 268 S.W. 120 (Tenn. 1925) (1903 antitrust statute comprehends the common law offenses of "forestalling" and "engrossing" directed against conduct that unfairly raises the price of

Forestalling and engrossing remain statutory offenses in other states, as in the Georgia Penal Code.[67] Forestalling and engrossing rules also can be found in local and state regulation of marketplaces. This last point merits further elaboration.

Rules on forestalling and engrossing have often been part of local ordinances regulating markets. Most of these rules have been upheld as legitimate exercise of police power, not unlike the grants of monopoly privileges embedded in market regulations seen earlier. Examples are found in Florida,[68] Oregon,[69] Pennsylvania,[70] New York,[71] Tennessee[72] and Virginia.[73] As early as 1904, a Pennsylvania court explained, quoting an earlier decision:

> "[E]very municipal corporation ... may fix the time or places of holding public market for the sale of food, and make such other regulations concerning them as may conduce to the public interest." [This includes] the right to regulate the sales at a market, the sale of some articles prohibit and of others permit; to provide for special inspection of articles offered for sale; to regulate the days and hours for keeping open the market to the public; and adopt such regulations as are reasonable and necessary for the preservation of the public health and conducive to the public interests."[74]

---

commodities that pass in the channels of commerce to the consuming public). Cf. Dutton v. City of Knoxville, 113 S.W. 381 (Tenn. 1908) (interpreting 1907 charter provision prohibiting forestalling of agricultural products).

67 Penal Code 1910, § 707, Penal Code 1933, § 26-7404. See Scott v. State., 185 S.E. 131 (Ga. Ct. App. 1936). See also Brown v. Jacobs Pharmacy Co., 41 S.E. 553 (Ga. 1936) ("Engrossing, forestalling, and regrating still stand in our Code as criminal offenses, and the presiding judge is required to give the law in reference to these offenses specially in charge to the grand jury at each term of court.").

68 See Blanchard v. Ivers, 24 So. 66 (Fla. 1898).

69 Cancilla v. Gehlar, 27 P.2d 179 (Or. 1933).

70 See, e.g., Easton v. Messinger, 13 Just. 289 (Pa. Ct. Com. Pl. 1915); City of York v. Hatterer, 48 Pa. Super. 216 (1911) (upholding and applying municipal ordinance to defendant, who had purchased onions in a city market with the intention of reselling them in her stand, which was also in the same market); Meadville v. Miller, 14 Pa. D. 27 (Ct. Com. Pl. 1904).

71 People v. Weller, 143 N.E. 205 (N.Y. 1924).

72 Dutton v. City of Knoxville, 131 S.W. 381 (Tenn. 1908) (interpreting 1907 charter provision prohibiting forestalling of agricultural products).

73 See Chambers v. City of Roanoke, 78 S.E. 407 (Va. 1913).

74 Meadville v. Miller, 14 Pa. D. 27 (Ct. Com. Pl. 1904).

Courts have upheld such market regulation rules, though sometimes with reservations about their wisdom. For example, in 1924 the New York Court of Appeal upheld a ban on scalping theater tickets in deference to the legislature:

> "Experience and modern economic opinion based on that experience have so demonstrated the unwisdom of many of these statutes that a court to-day might hesitate to sustain as a reasonable exercise of the police power some of the restrictive statutes which seemed obviously proper centuries ago, yet the power of the Legislature in a proper case to 'promote the public welfare' by regulating or restricting acts which interfere with free negotiation between the consumers and producers of a commodity in common use and impede the operation of the laws of supply and demand should not be doubted."[75]

Challenges to market regulations have also been upheld where they are found to be discriminatory[76] or unreasonable.[77]

In sum, however, the passionate popular demands for enforcement of laws against forestalling, engrossing and "monopolistic" practices voiced during the colonial and revolutionary eras no longer resonate in today's world. They have been replaced by demands for enforcement of antitrust laws against successful private firms, a subject to which we now turn.

III. THE EARLY ANTITRUST MOVEMENT

As mentioned before, large firms replaced government grants of monopoly and forestallers as the principal targets of antimonopolists after the Civil War. Indeed, the wartime conditions accelerated the growth of large firms like meatpackers and shoe manufacturers. Farmers, artisans and small entrepreneurs vociferously complained about the new firms whose size, geographic reach and vertical integration dwarfed businesses of the

---

[75] People v. Weller, 143 N.E. 205 (N.Y. 1924).

[76] See Roach v. Ephren, 90 So. 609 (Fla. 1921) ("charter powers of a city 'to restrain and punish the forestalling and regrading of provisions' does not warrant an arbitrary and grossly unreasonable discrimination in imposing license taxes.")

[77] See Central Mkt. Co. v. City of Erie, 44 Pa. Super. 191 (1910).

pre-industrial world.[78] Some of the most prominent of these large firms took the legal form of the trust, which explains why the antimonopolist tradition was embedded in the "antitrust movement" and, then, the "antitrust laws." As we will see, this had the enormous effect of cabining the antimonopoly tradition in a law enforcement model that ultimately would be restricted to economics concerns that minimized (if not emasculated) broader social and political concerns that had previously animated the tradition. But let us first look at the antitrust movement concerning monopolies as it developed after the Civil War.

The movement began with complaints primarily by farmers in the South and West about the railroads. They accused the railroads of engaging in practices, such as price discrimination, stock-watering and bribery.[79] Like colonial and antebellum businesses, railroads also received monopoly privileges from state and local governments. Railroads were condemned for receiving unwarranted government measures, like land grants, rights of way, tariff protection and "sound" money.[80] Farmers added complaints about tariff-protected manufacturers, local storekeepers and farm implement dealers.[81] This spurred the creation of Granges as Anti-Monopoly political parties. The millennial-old cry against "monopolizers" was repeated by farm groups. They were joined by small businesses and artisans who railed against not only the railroads, but also industrial firms like Standard Oil.[82] Some (but not all) organized labor groups[83] added their antimonopoly complaints. In 1883, 10,000 members of the Central Labor Union walked New York City streets with banners proudly declaring: "We Must Crush Monopolies Lest They Crush Us."[84] Journalists and the popular press added passionate

---

[78] See Barry E. Hawk, Antitrust and Competition Laws 71 (2020).

[79] The strongest expression of antimonopoly feeling and some of the most radical proposals came from Western farmers and Southerners in both houses of congress.

[80] See Thorelli, supra note 22, at 568.

[81] See id. at 60.

[82] See id. at 149.

[83] For example, the National Labor Union condemned the national banking system as "the parent of all monopolies---the very root and essence of slavery." Quoted in id. at 147. But the later American Federation of Labor took a more moderate position. See id. at 148.

[84] Quoted in id. at 147.

condemnation of monopoly. To cite one of countless examples,[85] an editorial in the Chicago Tribune Daily Tribune declaimed:

> "The methods by which the Vanderbilts, Goulds, Fields, Rockefellers, Mackays, Floods, O'Briens, and the coal and iron and salt Pashas are heaping up enormous fortunes are methods, not of creation of wealth, but of the redistribution of the wealth of the masses into the pockets of the monopolists."[86]

In sum, it is fair to generalize that the late 19th century antitrust movement was more widely based than the current outcry against monopoly. The 19th century antitrust movement was rooted in a broader range of constituencies and targeted a broader range of industries than today's movement which focuses on the digital world and the "sharing economy."

There, of course, were dissenters to the 19th century antitrust movement, at least to its more radical proposals. Most importantly for our subject, critics condemned the notion that all monopolies were undesirable. For example, in 1888 George Gunton—like many before and after—reasoned that monopoly is bad only if "procured through the arbitrary exclusion of competitors."[87] If derived from superior efficiency, monopoly is "a positive advantage to the community."[88] This same reasoning can be found in Sherman Act monopolization cases—notably Learned Hand's opinion in *Alcoa*[89]—which rejects monopoly per se and condemns only monopolies created or maintained through anticompetitive conduct. That

---

[85] See the following unsigned editorials of the Chicago Daily Tribune: "Cable Monopolies, Dec. 22, 1882; "A Stiff Monopoly," Dec. 31, 1882; "Why Coal is Dear," Jan. 6, 1882; "The Match Monopoly in Congress," Jan. 8, 1883, and "A Silent Monopoly," Jan. 14. 1883. These editorials were filed by Lloyd as having been written by him. Cf. Carol Lloyd, Henry Demarest Lloyd, 1847-1903, A Biography, Vol. 2 (1912), 355 f.

[86] "American Pashas," unsigned editorial in the Chicago Daily Tribune, Dec. 30, 1881. Other editorials of a similar tenor include "Anti-American Millionaires," Feb. 11, 1883; "Corporations not Sovereigns," Apr. 12, 1884; and "The Beauties of Watered Stock, Dec. 8, 1884.

[87] George Gunton, The Economic and Social Aspects of Trusts, 3 Pol. Sci. Q. 385 (1888).

[88] Id.

[89] United States v. Aluminum Co. of Am., 148 F.2d 416 (2d Cir. 1945).

rejection is consistent with the American antimonopoly tradition since its beginnings in the 17th century.

The antitrust movement of the late 19th century did share one important concern underlying earlier opposition to the English trading companies and colonial government monopoly grants: the unfair exclusion of actual and potential competitors. This can be seen in the complaint that firms and entrepreneurs – unwilling to give up their independence – often were forced to join combinations in the face of exclusionary practices – like the predatory pricing commonly attributed to Standard Oil.[90] There also was a lesser voiced concern about higher prices, although this later became the economists' chief concern about monopoly. Exclusion of competitors and higher prices (or lower output and less quality/innovation) can be analyzed and measured in economic terms. Thus, these concerns have played the principal roles in application of the federal antitrust laws, particularly since the late 1970s (as discussed below).

But the 19th century antitrust movement voiced broader concerns that do not fit as neatly into modern economic based "antitrust law" analysis. For example, state antitrust actions in the last decades of the 19th century were motivated by the loss of local jobs and employment opportunities, as much as – if not more than – concern about higher prices.[91] Another frequently voiced concern was about the sheer size and geographical and product reach of the new firms. Indeed, distrust of monopoly often was viewed from the perspective of firm size and scope. That distrust rested more on political and social concerns than on economic notions of monopoly prices, let alone "consumer welfare." Thus, as in earlier times, the 19th century antitrust movement was motivated in part by the perceived political and social harms that come with monopoly privileges. Like the opponents of colonial monopoly grants and Jacksonian Democrats, many if not most members of the antitrust movement viewed large firms as corrupting democratic institutions.[92] In a significant sense, these sentiments underlie

[90] Cf. Standard Oil Co. v. United States, 221 U.S 1, 55 (1911).

[91] See Wayne D. Collins, Trusts and the Origins of Antitrust Legislation, 81 Fordham L. Rev. 2279 (2013).

[92] See Martin J. Sklar, The Corporate Reconstruction of American Capitalism, 1890-1916: The Market, the Law, and Politics 154, 393 (1988).

Brandeis' concern with concentration of power, which in turn partially drives the neo-Brandeisians today.[93]

Class elements were also important in the antitrust movement, again not unlike earlier antimonopoly movements such as Jackson's war against the Second Bank of the United States. Critics believed that the large industrial firms engaged in "monopolistic" practices that harmed or destroyed the real producing class in the economy — farmers, workers and smaller entrepreneurs. A political and social ideal of America as a nation of small businesses, farmers and an energetic working class motivated much of the late 19th century antitrust movement.[94] Understandably, "fairness" frequently was invoked by the antimonopolists. Geographic differences were also important to the antitrust movement. Expansion into the West reinforced an American distrust of power — both public and private — with sectional objections to economic and social inequalities. Residence in the Northeast of heads of large firms, as well as many members of the financial community, triggered claims of irresponsible and anonymous "absentee" management and ownership from farmers in the South and West.[95]

In sum, the early antitrust movement was driven by a wide variety of not necessarily consistent concerns. For example, concern over lower prices — often driven by scale — could conflict with protection of small businesses. But the very variety of concerns and member constituencies gave a strength to the antitrust movement — despite its internal inconsistencies — which enabled a significant political success: state and federal laws that zeroed in on the large firms. In other words, the collective weight of the antitrust movement was more important for its political success than the relative weights of the individual (and not always mutually consistent) concerns. This makes identification of the relative importance of specific concerns hazardous.

Political success was further helped by the antitrust movement's focus on concrete targets — the dreaded "trusts" like Standard Oil and the Sugar Trust. This illustrates a general point: antimonopoly movements have been most successful (politically) when they have targeted specific firms or institutions like the East India Company or

---

[93] James Keyte, Frederic Jenny & Eleanor Fox, Buckle up: The Global Future of Antitrust Enforcement and Regulation, 35 Antitrust 32 (2021).

[94] This echoes complaints in the first half of the 19th century about the social effects of the factory system. See Chester Whitney Wright, Economic History of the United States 314-15 (2nd ed. 1949).

[95] Thorelli, supra note 22, at 564.

the Second Bank of the United States. This was also true of the 19th century antitrust movement. Whether history will repeat itself with respect to Big Tech and other firms is too soon to tell, especially under the exacting standards of current antitrust law.

The initial legal response to the demands of the antitrust movement came from the states when they introduced antimonopoly provisions into their state constitutions and enacted antitrust laws.[96] By 1915, the number of states and territories with antitrust provisions reached a total of at least thirty-five.[97] Many provisions were actively enforced. In the decade before the Sherman Act, states successfully brought actions against the intrastate activities of six trusts, obtaining annulment of their business privileges or dissolution of legal "trust" connections. Between 1890 and 1902, twelve states brought a total of twenty-eight antitrust actions, while in the same period the United States instituted only nineteen Sherman Act cases.[98] State enforcement was not limited to local firms. Ten states and the Oklahoma Territory brought twenty four actions against members of the Standard Oil Trust between 1890 and 1906; other state antitrust actions challenged the beef, sugar and tobacco combinations.[99] Somewhat surprisingly, private actions were even more numerous than government actions.[100] If success of enforcement is measured by the scale of fines and penalties, then state enforcement in the thirty years after the Sherman Act compares favorably to federal enforcement.[101] This early state antimonopoly response is often under-estimated in antitrust lore, where Theodore Roosevelt's federal trust-busting is given pride of place.

---

[96] Prior to passage of the Sherman Act in 1890, at least fourteen states introduced antimonopoly provisions into their state constitutions and at least thirteen states enacted legislation. Iowa (1888), Kansas (1889), Maine (1889), North Carolina (1889), Nebraska (1889), Texas (1889), Tennessee (1889), Missouri (1889), Michigan (1889), Mississippi (1890), North Dakota (1890), South Dakota (1890) and Kentucky (1890). See Hawk, supra note 78, at 90.

[97] See James May, Antitrust Practice and Procedure in the Formative Era: The Constitutional and Conceptual Reach of State Antitrust Law, 1880–1918, 135 U. Pa. L. Rev. 495, 499 (1987).

[98] Id. at 500–01.

[99] Id. at 501.

[100] See id. at 503 (citing New York State Bar Association, Report of the Special Committee to Study the New York Antitrust Laws 4a (1957).

[101] By the end of 1919, criminal fines under the Sherman Act amounted to $765,822. In a single case against one Standard Oil affiliate, Texas collected over

Let us turn to the federal response to the antitrust movement which began in 1890 with passage of the Sherman Act. The Sherman Act introduced new substantive laws, procedures and institutions to deal with monopoly. Section 2 prohibits monopolization, conspiracy to monopolize and attempt to monopolize. There also was now a permanent set of government officials tasked with investigating entire industries and armed with criminal penalties, injunctions and other remedial options. Private actions for treble damages became part of the enforcement fabric. Unlike colonial and antebellum antimonopoly laws, as well as state constitutional provisions, the Sherman Act was directed toward private firms without express reference to government grants of monopoly privileges.

We saw above that by 1890, the antitrust movement reflected a broad variety of economic, political and social concerns. What was each of their roles in passage of the Sherman Act? The answer is not at all clear. The speeches and statements of the members of Congress do not provide the best evidence for what was going on in America in the decades after the Civil War. More specifically, they are not the best evidence to explain the antitrust movement and its success not only in obtaining federal legislation but also the state constitutional and legislative action in the decade before. The most persuasive explanation for the nearly unanimous approval of the Sherman Act can be seen in two steps.

First, the vast majority of the members of Congress concluded that a) the public demanded action against the trusts, b) the states were responding to those demands with legislation that was being enforced (as seen above), and—importantly c) federal action was needed for two contending reasons—opponents of the trusts viewed federal legislation as necessary to remedy perceived weaknesses of state law (such as constitutional limitations on the territorial scope of state antitrust laws)[102] and sympathizers of the trusts viewed federal action as a more palatable measure than either the proliferating

---

$1.6 million in fines. In 1915, courts in Missouri alone imposed fines of $678,000 against five defendants. May, at 502. Enforcement of state antitrust law continued for several decades after passage of the Sherman Act, but then declined as federal antitrust enforcement became predominant.

[102] State antitrust laws had been successfully challenged under several federal constitutional grounds, notably, the commerce, due process and equal protection clauses. For example, federal and state courts held that states could not constitutionally regulate anticompetitive activity within interstate commerce.

state antitrust laws or a federal incorporation statute that would place the multistate firm's structural decisions under federal control.[103] As would be expected, the legislative record is silent on the positions of trust sympathizers. Second, having decided that something had to be done (albeit for opposing reasons), Congress did what it has often done: enact an ambiguously worded statute and pass the buck to the courts to deal with its interpretation. This view of the Sherman Act's adoption makes reliance on details of its legislative history even more slippery than usual.

But, irrespective of the shrouded legislative history of the Sherman Act, we can confidently conclude that the American antitrust movement was markedly different from the response of European states to the large new firms of the industrial world.[104] After all, large firms, economic concentration and wealth inequalities all existed outside the United States. But it was only after World War II that European law began to challenge monopolies, beginning at the EU level and in Germany.[105]

The reason why the United States in the late 19th century took a different and earlier path derives from the breadth and strength of the American antimonopoly tradition, which went back several centuries to the initial founding of the Virginia and Massachusetts colonies, as seen in earlier chapters. It was a popular tradition that not only was expressed in learned treatises and political pamphlets, but also implemented in statutes and constitutions. The American opposition to monopoly had far more concrete effects than any found in Europe, including England. Perhaps the most important explanation was the greater American distrust of power – both public and private power. This distrust complemented other monopoly concerns about exclusion from trade and higher prices. The American distrust of private power seen in the late 19th century antitrust movement had its counterpart in the Founders' distrust of public power reflected in the constitutional framework of checks and balances. By contrast, outside the United States, there was far greater acceptance of both private and public power, and certainly not the degree of distrust found in the United States. It is important to note, however, that the American distrust of public power declined significantly with the New Deal and later acceptance of extensive

---

[103] See Hawk, supra note 78.

[104] See id. at 88–90.

[105] See id. at 184–89.

government intervention into the economy. This has had the perhaps unintended effect of refocusing the historical antimonopoly tradition away from government to private firms.

The 19th century antitrust movement ultimately was implemented primarily through enactment of the Sherman Act (and later antitrust laws like the Clayton and Federal Trade Commission Acts).[106] Law enforcement was the institutional model selected to combat private monopoly; government monopoly grants were given far less attention as targets. Moreover, antitrust law eventually focused on what might appear to the uninitiated as legal and economic minutiae—to the exclusion of broader political and social concerns that previously animated the American antimonopoly tradition. Is this perception correct? To begin to think about an answer, let us turn (ambitiously, no doubt) to a capsulized summary of the application of the Sherman Act to monopoly over the last 130 years.

IV. PRIVATE MONOPOLY UNDER THE FEDERAL ANTITRUST LAWS

Since 1890, enforcement of the antitrust law with respect to monopoly has been cyclical, with periods of relative action and inaction. There are several explanations for these cycles, which inform the present debate about strengthening the antitrust laws. The modern pivot from government monopoly grants to private monopoly also raises questions—hotly debated at present—whether antitrust law should condemn all monopoly "per se" or only those without justification.

A. Cyclical Enforcement

Enforcement of the monopolization provisions of the Sherman Act has seen periods of intense activity and periods of comparatively little activity.[107] This can be put into the following periods: Trustbusting (1890 to 1920), Hibernation (1920 to 1937), Expansion (1945 to 1970s), Retrenchment (1980 to 2020) and Renewal (today).

---

[106] Enforcement of state law to combat private monopolies was relatively quiet during most of the 20th century, but it has significantly accelerated in the last few years.

[107] Hawk, supra note 78, at 90–181.

1. *Trustbusting (1890 to 1920)*

After a slow start, section 2 was used to successfully challenge many of the large firms that had become the poster children of the 19th century antitrust movement. *Northern Securities* set the precedent to seek relief against monopolies achieved through horizontal acquisitions and mergers.[108] The government later obtained divestitures or breakups of a number of large firms like Standard Oil[109] and American Tobacco Co.[110] that had achieved a monopoly through not only acquisitions and mergers but also predatory business practices. This period of highly aggressive enforcement—initiated by Theodore Roosevelt—has become known in history as the great trustbusting era of antitrust. But not everyone at the time was satisfied.

Despite the court victories, Progressives led by Woodrow Wilson and encouraged by Louis Brandeis demanded more action against monopoly.[111] Progressive demands rested more on social and political concerns than economic concerns in the modern antitrust sense; equal opportunity and the protection of political freedom were more important than lower prices.[112] For the Progressives, Theodore Roosevelt's "trustbusting" had more psychological effect than any meaningful effect on the continued consolidation of monopoly.[113] The election of Woodrow Wilson led to creation in 1914 of a new statute prohibiting "unfair methods of competition." But the war in Europe blunted any Progressive crusade against monopoly.

2. *Hibernation (1920 to 1937)*

In 1920, trustbusting came to an abrupt end when the Supreme Court rejected the government's request to break up U.S. Steel for unlawful monopolization.[114] Antitrust law challenges of

---

[108] N. Sec. Co. v. United States, 193 U.S. 197, 357–60 (1904).

[109] Standard Oil Co. of N.J. v. U.S., 221 U.S. 1 (1911).

[110] United States v. Am. Tobacco Co., 221 U.S. 106 (1911) (ordering divestiture of Du Pont's stock holdings in General Motors).

[111] See Richard Hofstadter, The Age of Reform: From Bryan to F.D.R. 222–48 (1955).

[112] Id. at 222–23.

[113] Id. at 237.

[114] United States v. U.S. Steel Corp., 251 U.S. 417 (1920).

monopoly—and the antimonopoly tradition—went into hibernation during the good times of the Roaring Twenties; cooperation—not competition—was the aim of U.S. economic policy during Franklin Roosevelt's first term.

3. *Expansion (1937 to 1970s)*

In 1937, the pragmatic president Franklin Roosevelt shifted U.S. economic policy from business cooperation back to competition. The change in course reflected the view that the Depression and slow economic recovery resulted from domination of industry by a small number of large firms. This initiated an era of aggressive antitrust challenges to monopoly, which lasted well into the 1970s.

After the successful challenge to Alcoa's aluminum monopoly,[115] government actions against monopolies increased following World War II. Monopolization cases were won against successful U.S. firms like United Shoe,[116] but lost against others like du Pont.[117] Some court opinions appeared so broad in their condemnation of monopoly that some observers in the antitrust community began to believe that monopoly was coming close to being condemned per se—that is, no "monopolizing" conduct was required for a violation of section 2. But this was not to be the case. Monopoly per se was rejected by the Supreme Court in 1968 when the Court reconfirmed that unlawful or monopolizing conduct was required for a section 2 violation.[118] As discussed below, monopoly per se in the lawyers' jargon—or more popularly, "all monopolies are bad"—has never been accepted doctrine in American history.

Toward the end of the 1960s, and extending into the next decade, another wave of government challenges to large firms followed the recommendations of President Johnson's Task Force on Antitrust Policy which sought to restructure large sectors of the

---

[115] United States v. Aluminum Co. of Am., 148 F.2d 416 (2d Cir. 1945).

[116] United States v. United Shoe Mach. Corp., 110 F. Supp. 295 (D. Mass. 1953), aff'd, 347 U.S. 521 (1954) (per curiam).

[117] See, e.g., United States v. E.I. duPont de Nemours & Co., 251 U.S. 377 (1956) (holding that cellophane is "reasonably interchangeable" with other materials, comprising the relevant market for flexible packaging materials; this case is commonly known as the "cellophane fallacy" decision). This was one of the few instances where the courts rejected government antitrust claims.

[118] United States v. Grinnell Corp., 384 U.S. 563 (1966).

American economy.[119] The first "big case" was the 1969 Justice Department challenge to IBM's position as the country's major computer manufacturer.[120] The case was settled in 1982—well after the allegedly unlawful practices had become moot. The costs and time[121] taken to reach this result have been criticized by many.[122] Others believe that the litigation may have had a procompetitive deterrent effect on IBM's business conduct. Whether deterrence warranted the public and private costs, or whether deterrence could have been achieved at lower costs, is open to debate. In any event, the IBM case demonstrated that antitrust law challenges to monopoly generate considerable costs and time, at least under the modern U.S. litigation system.

In the 1970s, after pressure from the Congress to do something about monopoly, the FTC initiated investigations and proceedings under section 5's prohibition of "unfair methods of competition" in a broad variety of sectors, including petroleum, tires and breakfast cereals. There was no single monopoly in most of these industries, so the FTC advanced a novel theory of "shared monopoly." Not one FTC action was successful in the courts. In retrospect, this ended aggressive FTC enforcement against monopolies until the recent investigations and actions against firms in the digital sector.

There was one highly successful use of section 2 against monopoly that was initiated in 1969—the *AT&T* litigation. In contrast to the IBM saga and the FTC's failed crusade against shared monopoly, the government's successful challenge of AT&T's monopoly in the provision of long-distance telephone services had a

---

119 See Hawk, supra note 78, at 126.

120 United States v. IBM Corp., [1961–1970 Transfer Binder] Trade Reg. Rep. (CCH) 45,069 (S.D.N.Y. filed Jan. 17, 1969) (complaint alleging monopolization and attempted monopolization).

121 The case spanned lasted 13 years. The number of trial days reached 700, and the trial transcript exceeded 104,000 pages. See Post-Mortem on IBM Case Provides Forum for Conflicting Perspectives, 42 Antitrust & Trade Reg. Rep. (BNA) 310–11 (1982).

122 William Mulligan (then on the Second Circuit) to remark that this "Frankenstein monster" of litigation was "lasting longer than World War II" and would cost as much. Larry Kramer & John Kennedy, Justice Willing to Discuss IBM Settlement, Wash. Post (Sept. 15, 1979), https://www.washingtonpost.com/archive/business/1979/09/15/justice-willing-to-discuss-ibm-settlement/e67870dc-6924-4f35-9a48-bbc6d92d8b1c/; Connie Winker, IBM, Justice Urged to Settle 'Monster' Suit, Computerworld, Sept. 24, 1979, at 5; Connie Winkler, U.S. vs. IBM Feared as Lengthy as World War II, Computerworld, Oct. 22, 1979, at 8.

dramatic effect on the telecommunications industry. The outcome in 1982—the break-up of AT&T (by consent)[123]—has generated decades of consumer benefits with new entrants and numerous opportunities for new competition.[124]

President Jimmy Carter organized the National Commission for the Review of Antitrust Laws and Procedures. In 1979, the Commission recommended that Congress study adoption of no-fault monopolization or monopoly per se, partially because "existing litigation practice under Sherman Section 2 has not dealt effectively with the problem of persistent monopoly power ...."[125] Looking more to the past than to the future, the Commission's underlying assumption about the persistence of monopoly power was not borne out: many if not most of the firms challenged as "monopolies" in the 1970s no longer even exist today, let alone remain dominant. Others, like Xerox, have lost any monopoly power that they once may have had.

The timing of the Report's recommendation was not felicitous for proponents of aggressive section 2 enforcement against large successful firms. A retrenchment era of antitrust law was beginning, an era in which successful firms were largely tolerated.

4. *Retrenchment (late 1970s to 2020)*

With the exception of the breakup of AT&T in 1982 (in a case initiated in 1969), government challenges to monopoly were sparse between 1980 and 2020, certainly when compared with the trustbusting and post-war expansionary periods. The most important government case against monopoly since the AT&T litigation was the Justice Department's action against Microsoft in the 1990s. The complaint alleged that Microsoft engaged in

---

[123] United States v. AT&T Co., [1970–1979 Transfer Binder] Trade Reg. Rep. (CCH) 45,074 (D.D.C. filed Nov. 20, 1974) (complaint alleging monopolization, attempted monopolization, and conspiracy to monopolize), settled by consent decree, 1982-2 Trade Cas. (CCH) 64,900 (D.D.C. 1982).

[124] A minority of commentators argue that the remedy merely transferred AT&T's monopoly power to several regional monopolies that in turn led to industry regulation and further antitrust interventions.

[125] National Commission for the Review of Antitrust Laws and Procedures, Report to the President and the Attorney General 162 (Jan. 22, 1979). The Commission also concluded that "that (1) dissipation of persistent monopoly power is the chief goal of the Sherman Section 2 monopolization offense, [and] (2) that where persistent monopoly power is shown, deliberate conduct designed to create or maintain that power can be presumed ..."

practices—notably self-preferencing, coercive tying and bundling—in order to prevent or deter nascent rivals from gaining a foothold in the market for operating platforms which Microsoft dominated.[126] The circuit court upheld most of the claims and found that Microsoft had violated the Sherman Act.[127] The court applied structural criteria (that is, market share and entry barriers) to conclude that Microsoft had monopoly power (in concededly dynamic markets), and that its aim and effect were to deter the development of "middleware" that could evolve into a full-blown substitute for its operating system.

Yet, for the two decades after the *Microsoft* decision, the picture was grim for those advocating more vigorous government enforcement against private monopoly. The Justice Department—from the George W. Bush (2001-2009) through the Obama and Trump Administrations—was cautious in bringing section 2 cases, while the FTC was a bit more active, particularly with actions against pharmaceutical companies for section 2 violations.

With the more recent focus on Big Tech, as well as the arrival of neo-Brandeisians in agency leadership positions, the retrenchment era is over. Both the Justice Department and the FTC, as well as state antitrust authorities, have recently begun a number of investigations and brought monopolization actions against firms, particularly in digital platform and other high-tech markets. A new era has begun.

What explains this century-long cycle of monopoly enforcement? What are the implications for the future of the present campaigns against monopoly? We explore these questions next.

B. Reasons for the Cycle of Enforcement

There are several explanations for the cyclical history of antitrust law and monopoly since 1890: political support, popular demand for action, changes in facts (economic conditions), changes in economic theory, legal process concerns and the predominance of consumer welfare analysis. Let us look at each one.

---

[126] United States v. Microsoft Corp., 253 F.3d 34, 64 (D.C. Cir. 2001) (en banc) (per curiam); Government's Complaint, United States v. Microsoft Corp., 87 F. Supp. 2d30 (D.D.C. 2000) (Nos. 98-1232, 98-1233).

[127] United States v. Microsoft Corp., 253 F.3d 34 (D.C. Cir. 2001) (en banc) (per curiam).

1. Political support

Executive support and congressional funding were critical in both the trustbusting era and the expansionary era. Their importance cannot be exaggerated; they often are minimized or omitted in the antitrust literature which focuses on antitrust "schools" to explain historical developments. The strong political support of the Administrations of both Roosevelts and Lyndon Johnson—and the more tolerant view of monopoly shared by the Administrations of Ronald Reagan and George W. Bush—were important factors in our antitrust history. By contrast, the present policies of the Biden Administration—which embraces Progressive views on antitrust enforcement—is the most recent example of the importance of political shifts in support of antitrust policy.

Political support for aggressive antitrust enforcement does not need to come from a deeply held opposition to monopoly. Franklin Roosevelt restarted the antitrust engine primarily for pragmatic reasons. Roosevelt expressed his general pragmatism in 1932: "It is common sense to take a method and try it. If it fails, admit it frankly and try another. But above all, try something."[128] In his first term, FDR tried business cooperation and not competition; when that failed, in 1937 he shifted to stepped up antitrust enforcement. The ultimate result was the most aggressive antimonopoly period since the Administration of his fifth cousin.

What is the implication for the future? The recent renewal of aggressive enforcement by the federal agencies will continue—subject to constraining antitrust standards in the courts—until there is another change in antitrust policy generated most likely by elections. This does not mean that aggressive enforcement will lead to the kinds of serious remedies advocated by the more fervent opponents of monopoly. That will depend to a great extent on the courts, and if necessary, Congress.

2. Popular support

Popular support less clearly correlates with aggressive enforcement. To be sure, popular support was an important motivator during the trustbusting era. As seen earlier, there was a broad-based

---

[128] Quoted in Richard Hofstadter, What Happened to the Antitrust Movement? Notes on the Evolution of an American Creed, in The Business Establishment 307 (Earl F. Cheit ed., 1964).

national movement demanding action against the large firm monopolies. But since the end of World War II, popular attention to monopoly – either for or against – has considerably weakened, at least compared with the early decades of antitrust law. And today, the most visible supporters of antimonopoly action are politicians and academics in sharp contrast to the farmers, small business and workers who formed the 19th century antitrust movement.

Indeed, there has been no truly popular "antitrust movement" in over half a century, as public opinion toward big business has changed considerably since the end of the initial trustbusting era. Earlier Progressive concerns about big business never materialized in the minds of most people, especially after World War II. Social mobility and economic advancement increased in the United States from 1900 to the mid-20th century,[129] and large corporations were viewed as offering more in the way of economic opportunity and social mobility.[130] In 1964, Richard Hofstadter attributed the public acceptance of big business to the remarkable performance of the U.S. economy since the beginning of World War II.[131] Stated more baldly, those who lived through World War II may well have associated large firms more with the production of the thousands of tanks and airplanes that significantly helped win the war than with potential monopoly harms like undue political influence, social dislocation or deadweight welfare loss. When Winston Churchill erupted with joy after the news of Pearl Harbor and the likely entry of American industrial capacity into the war, he was thinking about General Motors and other large firms, not the small shopkeepers cherished by Brandeis. And, even today, the general population appears happy to get "free" platforms and relatively low-cost apps; their basic livelihoods are hardly at stake.

Observers outside the antitrust industry may ask how antitrust law survived and prospered in the expansionary period without public support? Richard Hofstadter answered somewhat cynically in 1964: "[T]he fate of antitrust is an excellent illustration of how a public ideal, vaguely formulated and often hopelessly at odds with stubborn realities, can become embodied in institutions with elaborate, self-serving rules and procedures, a defensible function, and an equally

---

[129] See Richard Hofstadter, The Paranoid Style in American Politics, and Other Essays 218 (1964).

[130] See Sklar, supra note 92, at 26.

[131] Supra note 129, at 215.

stubborn capacity for survival."[132] But cynicism does not capture the expertise, devotion and idealism of those who toil in government and private institutions to secure a reasoned application of antitrust law.

What are the implications for the future? Popular support certainly can generate political support for antitrust enforcement. But aggressive antitrust enforcement against monopoly does not depend on popular support—antitrust has become more the specialty of politicians, academics and the antitrust industry generally.

3. Facts/economic conditions and assumptions

Changes in economic conditions—changes in the facts—are also important in understanding the enforcement cycles. The best example is comparison of the post-war expansionary period and the retrenchment period. The competitive position of U.S. firms had improved significantly by 1945. U.S. firms were relatively free from foreign competition, given the still existing trade barriers to entry and the economic weakness of potential foreign competitors. A reasonable assumption was that any market power enjoyed by U.S. firms would persist. And the success of U.S. firms after 1945 reduced the risks that aggressive enforcement might chill innovation or other procompetitive behavior.

By the end of the 1970s, however, entry of foreign competitors into U.S. markets—previously characterized as single firm monopolies—strongly suggested relaxation of the previous assumption that market power persists without antitrust law intervention. For example, any assumption that large successful U.S. firms like General Motors and du Pont would continue to enjoy market power without antitrust intervention became increasingly untenable. The retrenchment era assumption held that markets (and monopolies) tend to self-correct, making antitrust intervention necessary in only rare circumstances of "market failure." That assumption had significant effect not only on the outcome of decisions, but also on formulation of more tolerant legal rules for dominant firm conduct—such as predatory pricing.[133] The Court in

---

[132] Richard Hofstadter, What Happened to the Antitrust Movement?, in The Business Establishment (Earl Cheit ed. 1964).

[133] As seen below, the new assumption about persistence of market power was not the only consideration. A desire for clear administrable legal rules also was a factor in formulating the new legal test for predatory pricing.

early landmark cases like the 1911 *Standard Oil*[134] and *American Tobacco*[135] decisions condemned predatory pricing under a broad rule of reason inquiry.[136] This contrasts with the modern (administratively simpler) test for predatory pricing focused on below cost prices and the ability to recoup,[137] – a test based partially on the assumption that market power will generally erode if market power were persistently exercised.[138]

What are the implications for the future? The recent renewal of aggressive antitrust enforcement should have been expected because the facts have changed since 1980; that is, the economic conditions of the digital world are significantly different and raise new concerns. It also is interesting to note that foreign competition was absent in the two most important successful monopolization cases during the retrenchment era – *AT&T* and *Microsoft*.

The current monopolization actions against digital platform and other tech firms will test the retrenchment assumption that monopoly, once attained, will go away or how fast it will go away. It can be expected that state and federal government challengers, as well as private plaintiffs, will argue that allegedly monopolistic U.S. firms face no significant or constraining foreign competition. One very important question then is whether the legal process concerns discussed below will trump any new assumptions that support claims of unlawful monopolization.

4. Developments in economic theory

The great trusts like Standard Oil and American Tobacco were condemned as monopolists without deep economic analysis of harm to consumer welfare. But economic theory, as it continued to develop

---

134 Standard Oil Co. of N.J. v. United States, 221 U.S. 1 (1911). For differing views of the actual predation in those cases, compare John S. McGee, Predatory Price Cutting: The Standard Oil (N.J.) Case, 1 J. L. & Econ. 137 (1958), with James A. Dalton and Louis Esposito, Predatory Price Cutting and Standard Oil: A Re-Examination of the Trial Record, 22 Res. L. & Econ. 155 (2007).

135 United States v. Am. Tobacco Co., 221 U.S. 106 (1911).

136 These also included business espionage, rebates and preferences with railroads.

137 Brooke Group Ltd. v. Brown & Williamson Tobacco Corp., 509 U.S. 209 (1993).

138 For a critical view of this historical development, see Nicola Giocoli, Predatory Pricing in Antitrust Law and Economics: A Historical Perspective (2014).

throughout the 20th century, gradually increased its role in antitrust law over the decades. Economic theory played a far more important role in the post-1945 expansionary period than in the earlier trustbusting period. Developments in economic theory also were significant factors in shifting from expansion to retrenchment.

In the 1950s, economic theory supported aggressive antimonopoly enforcement, notably structuralist theories holding that market structure (concentration and monopoly) leads to harmful market performance (higher prices, less output and lower quality goods or innovation).[139] Economists, such as Carl Kaysen and Donald Turner (later to head the Antitrust Division under President Johnson),[140] proposed de-concentration measures based on studies suggesting a strong correlation between concentration and profitability.[141] In a sense, "concentration" and not simply "monopoly" became the target of antitrust law concern.

The "new learning" in the early 1970's challenged both the underlying economic assumptions of the structuralists and eroded empirical support for de-concentration.[142] Superior performance was said to account for the attainment and maintenance of monopoly. Economists also emphasized the importance of efficiencies and criticized antitrust law's inattention to business justifications for allegedly monopolistic behavior.

As it turned out, the antitrust analysis that has prevailed in recent decades focuses on (often short-term) price, output, quality and innovation effects. Exclusionary or foreclosure effects on

---

[139] Structuralism rested on four theoretical and empirical propositions:

1. assumption of a strong link between the number of firms in a market and the propensity of prices to rise above cost
2. large aggregations of capital which were not necessary to achieve economies of scale
3. barriers to entry, broadly defined
4. inevitability of poor performance in highly concentrated markets.

See Daniel A. Crane, Antitrust and Democracy: A Case Study from German Fascism, U. Mich. Law & Econ. No. 18-009, 5 n. 19.

[140] Carl Kaysen & Donald F. Turner, Antitrust Policy: An Economic and Legal Analysis (1959).

[141] See generally Leonard W. Weiss, The Concentration-Profits Relationship and Antitrust, in Industrial Concentration: The New Learning 184, 184-272 (H. J. Goldschmid, H. M. Mann, & J. F. Weston eds. 1974); Almarin Phillips, Market Concentration and Performance: A Survey of the Evidence, 61 Notre Dame L. Rev. 1099 (1986).

[142] See Hawk, supra note 78, at 121.

competitors have been minimized in contrast to historical concerns about monopoly privileges focused on any form of exclusion or foreclosure. This, no doubt, has made it more difficult to successfully challenge monopolies in the courts. The government or private plaintiff (often a competitor) often must prove more than harm to competitors; there must be proof of harmful effect on prices, output or innovation. Thus, the prevailing mantra of the antitrust community: "It is competition, not competitors, which the [Sherman] Act protects."[143] This makes monopolization litigation even more costly and time consuming than it had been.

From the perspective of economic theory, the focus on short-term effects in monopolization cases has been criticized for its failure to consider longer-term business strategies of firms like raising rivals' costs[144] and strategic behavior in markets with network effects. Strategic theories were relied upon by the Supreme Court in a private monopolization action in 1992.[145] But lower courts have largely confined the *Kodak* judgment to its facts.[146] And the Supreme Court in 1993 rejected strategic game theory models in favor of a cost-based test for predatory pricing under section 2, a rule that fits comfortably with "static" economic theory and meets the Court's concern about clear administrable rules.[147] On the other hand, the *Microsoft* decision in 2001 demonstrates that courts are not

---

[143] The phrase was first used in Brown Shoe Co. v. United States, 370 U.S. 294, 344 (1962). The phrase was reconfirmed in Brooke Grp. Ltd. v. Brown & Williamson Tobacco Corp., 509 U.S. 209 (1993) and more recently restated in Volvo Trucks v. Reeder-Simco, 546 U.S. 164 (2006).

[144] See Thomas G. Krattenmaker & Steven C. Salop, Anticompetitive Exclusion: Raising Rivals' Costs to Achieve Power over Price, 96 Yale L.J. 209 (1986).

[145] Eastman Kodak Co. v. Image Tech. Servs., Inc., 504 U.S. 451 (1992). The Court relied on concepts such as imperfect information and customer "lock-in" as sources of market power in holding that a trial was necessary to assess Kodak's ability to exploit its installed base and evaluate the business justifications for the challenged practices.

[146] See generally David A.J. Goldfine & Kenneth M. Vorrasi, The Fall of the Kodak Aftermath Doctrine: Dying a Slow Death in the Lower Courts, 72 Antitrust L.J. 209 (2004).

[147] Brooke Group Ltd. v. Brown & Williamson Tobacco Corp., 509 U.S. 209 (1993). The Supreme Court declared that "recoupment is not possible in oligopoly markets," despite economics literature that suggests the opposite. See Herbert J. Hovenkamp and Fiona Scott Morton, Framing the Chicago School of Antitrust Analysis 7-8 (Faculty Scholarship at U. Penn Law No. 2113, 2019), available at https://scholarship.law.upenn.edu/faculty_scholarship/2113.

necessarily predisposed against strategic economic theories.[148] The circuit court carefully considered the economics literature and the parties' arguments based on strategic theories; the court did not confine itself to short-term effects. Indeed, the court condemned conduct that it found had squashed nascent competitors[149] – a theory of harm quite important in today's challenges of allegedly unlawful monopolies.

Linked to developments in economic theory, the retrenchment era ushered in a new set of related assumptions (a new worldview or *weltanschauung*): 1) efficiencies explain most business arrangements; 2) market power self-corrects and competition is robust; 3) governments (including courts) are less capable than markets to address perceived competition problems; and 4) the risks of false positives are greater than risks of false negatives.[150] These assumptions generally are attributed to the Chicago School of antitrust, notably Robert Bork, Frank Easterbrook and Richard Posner.[151]

Proponents of strengthened antimonopoly enforcement challenge these assumptions, especially in the era of Big Tech.[152] These disagreements are healthy, no doubt, as any assumptions should constantly be reconsidered in order to ensure that antitrust law continues to adapt to changes in economic conditions and developments in economic theory.[153]

What are the implications for the future? One key question is whether challengers of monopoly can persuade courts to accept strategic theories of harm as the D.C. Circuit court did in *Microsoft* or decline to do so as the Supreme Court did in *Brooke Group*. The

---

148 United States v. Microsoft Corp., 253 F.3d 34 (D.C. Cir. 2001) (en banc) (per curiam).

149 253 F.3d at 79.

150 For further discussion, see Hawk, supra note 78, at 129–37.

151 See Robert Bork, The Antitrust Paradox (1978). The Chicago School was part of a broader intellectual movement that expressed confidence in markets and skepticism in government. Chicago included a heavy dose of legal process concerns about false positives, administrability of legal rules and judicial capabilities, as discussed below.

152 See, e.g., Eleanor M. Fox, The Efficiency Paradox, NYU Law & Economics Research Paper Series Working Paper No. 09-26 (July 2009); Marina Lao, Ideology Matters in the Antitrust Debate, 79 Antitrust L.J. 649 (2014); Steven C. Salop, What Consensus: Why Ideology and Elections Still Matter to Antitrust, 79 Antitrust L.J. 601 (2014).

153 Cf. Hovenkamp & Morton, supra note 147, at 3, 7.

answer may well depend on the courts' legal process concerns that we discuss next.

5. Legal process concerns about litigation costs, administrability and certainty of legal rules, court (and jury) capacities and false positives

Concerns about litigation costs, administrability of legal rules, the capability of jurors and judges to fully understand complex facts and economic theories, and the magnitude of chilling effects on investment and efficiency-enhancing conduct when legal rules are overly broad have been critical factors in narrowing application of antitrust law to monopoly. Legal process concerns now pose high hurdles to challengers of monopoly. More tolerant substantive standards favorable to defendant firms for predatory pricing and predatory bidding have replaced tougher standards.[154] A more draconian expression of the desire for administrability and legal certainty is the Court's rejection of whole categories of claims under section 2, such as price or margin squeezes.[155] Critics claim that courts often impose almost impossibly high burdens of proof on plaintiffs to avoid an exaggerated risk of false positives.[156] Other critics argue that courts have been too cautious toward strategic theories that would aggravate concerns about administrability and litigation costs.[157]

Legal process concerns certainly are legitimate subjects for the attention of the relevant decisionmakers – the courts chosen in 1890 as the (ultimate) institution to implement the law enforcement model of dealing with private monopoly. It should not be surprising, therefore, that judges would consider fundamental juridical issues when deciding antitrust cases. Legal bans on forestalling in colonial times

---

154 Brooke Grp. v. Brown & Williamson Tobacco Corp., 509 U.S. 209 (1993); Weyerhaeuser Co. v. Ross-Simmons Hardwood Lumber Co., 549 U.S. 312 (2007).

155 See, e.g., Pac. Bell Tel. Co. v LinkLine Commc'ns, Inc., 555 U.S. 438 (2009).

156 See A. Douglas Melamed, Antitrust Law and Its Critics, 83 Antitrust L. J. 269 (2020). See also Harry First & Spencer Weber Waller, Antitrust's Democracy Deficit, 81 Fordham L. Rev. 2543, 2572 (2013). *But see* Douglas H. Ginsburg & Joshua D. Wright, Philadelphia National Bank: Bad Economics, Bad Law, Good Riddance, 80 Antitrust L.J. 377 (2015) (costs of false negatives emphasized by the progressives are lower than would be the costs of false positives if the law were revised to permit more aggressive enforcement).

157 See generally David A.J. Goldfine & Kenneth M. Vorrasi, The Fall of the Kodak Aftermath Doctrine: Dying a Slow Death in the Lower Courts, 72 Antitrust L.J. 209 (2004).

often were blunted when defendants were tried before courts who insisted on legal requirements like precision of the conduct condemned. Courts make the same demands today in monopolization cases. It is the price we pay for a rule of law that obviates resort to food riots and other extra-legal demands for action against "monopolizers."

What are the implications for the future? Critics of monopoly must expressly and forcefully assuage courts' legal process concerns if antitrust law challenges to monopoly are to be successful.

6. Consumer welfare to the exclusion of historical political and social concerns about monopolies

For the last half century, consumer welfare analysis has dominated antitrust law—to the apparent exclusion of a variety of political and social concerns underlying the original antitrust movement, which generated the state antitrust laws and then the Sherman Act in the first place. For example, some of the political and social concerns of the 19th century antitrust movement—undue political influence, protection of small business[158] and fairness—generally are excluded from antitrust law today—though they are quite on the table in the Biden Administration and in various legislative proposals. In sum, political and social concerns have been sacrificed for analytical rigor, as discussed below.

Take the ambiguous—but important—concept of fairness. Courts generally are unsympathetic to arguments that monopolies are unlawful because they are unfair. And most economists dismiss fairness as a "distributive" value and limit the antitrust analysis to efficiency considerations. This is markedly different from the pre-industrial past when notions of fairness and social justice motivated complaints about monopolizers. Even in the modern world,

---

[158] Small businesses were strong supporters of state and federal antitrust legislation in the late 19th century. And in the early decades of the Sherman Act, protection of small business was frequently cited by the courts as a legitimate policy concern when interpreting the Sherman Act. Justice Peckham in *Trans-Missouri Freight Ass'n* referred in dictum to the Sherman Act as protecting "small dealers and worthy men. United States v. Trans-Missouri Freight Ass'n, 166 U.S. 290, 323-24 (1897); see also Chicago Bd. of Trade v. United States, 246 U.S. 231 (1918). Of course, there has always been tension between the interests of small businesses and consumers. In the last half century, the courts have resolved any tension between small business and consumers (consumer benefits in the form of lower prices, higher output and better product quality or innovation) in favor of consumer welfare.

consumers and citizens may regard monopolistic exploitation as unfair in some sense, whether or not they are the victims. [159] This reinforces the disconnect between modern technical antitrust law – beloved by the *cognoscenti* of the antitrust community – and popular perceptions of the law against monopoly.

The predominance of economics and the apparent discard of political and social concerns in antitrust law has come about for several reasons. At bottom, antitrust law examines economic activity, and the modern discipline of economics offers the most relevant and consistent framework for a predictable jurisprudence. Modern economics has also increased analytical rigor and legal precision in monopolization cases, and has enabled courts to create specific legal rules for different kinds of practices that for centuries had been lumped together or conflated under the rubric "monopolizing" practices (as seen in Chapters Two and Three). This certainly is a welcome advance over the past analytical confusion. It does mean, however, that the economist's definition of monopoly makes it quite different from popular and historical notions of monopoly and "monopolizers."

In antitrust cases, monopoly power ordinarily (at least in static terms) is measured by share of a relevant geographic and product market, subject to entry barriers that prevent markets from being contestable. This definition of monopoly is far more precise and considerably narrower than the popular (and historical) understanding. Indeed, many monopolies condemned in op-eds and political speeches would not be considered monopolies under the Sherman Act.

It is important to recognize that courts have not explicitly excluded from modern antitrust law the social and political concerns voiced in the 19th century antitrust movement. These concerns evaporated more subtly, as they were subsumed (and critics would say emasculated) under an economic concept of competition and a desire for precision and legal predictability, with "social and political goals ... relegated to rhetorical declamations."[160] And, no doubt, a member of the 19th century antitrust movement teleported to today might well believe that the movement has been hijacked by the economists and lawyers who interpret the Sherman Act in a such a narrow way that it no longer serves as an adequate instrument to combat private

[159] *See* Daniel Kahneman, Jack L. Knetsch & Richard Thaler, Fairness as a Constraint on Profit Seeking: Entitlements in the Market, 76 Am. Econ. Rev. 728 (1986); Daniel Kahneman, Thinking, Fast and Slow 306 (2011).

[160] Herbert Hovenkamp, Enterprise and American Law 1836–1937 303 (1991).

monopoly. A card-carrying member of today's antitrust establishment might reply that reliance on economics has been worth the costs and that antitrust law can still serve as an adequate instrument to meet concerns about modern monopoly, especially if the focus is on the interests of ultimate consumers.

Antitrust law is entering a new phase—or at least a renewal—with the challenges raised in the 21st century digital world.[161] As seen above, courts have shown themselves capable of adjusting to new facts and new economic theories; *Microsoft* in 2001 is just such a case. In the litigation wars that have been unleashed by federal and state authorities against successful firms, courts might devise legal presumptions and allocate burdens of proof that incorporate social and political considerations to meet demands for precision and predictability. Or Congress might legislate new legal rules that reflect political and social concerns. Indeed, the current demand for strengthened legal action against monopoly in digital industries might well generate a legislative solution similar to the one chosen by the Congress in 1890: new rules to be applied by the courts supported both by fervent antimonopolists and by sympathizers who fear more draconian constraints on business conduct.

That leads us to our final questions: how do you distinguish lawful from unlawful private monopolies and not kill the goose that lays the golden egg? How do you break up a successful firm (or change its business models) without depriving happy customers who prefer its prices and services, as evidenced by their copious purchases of those products and services?

C. The Fundamental Conundrum Concerning Private Monopoly

The modern pivot from government monopoly grants to private monopoly has brought to the fore questions that remained largely in the background before the antitrust movement of the 19th century: how do we apply laws dealing with private monopoly so as not to stifle entrepreneurial drive? should the law condemn all monopoly per se or only those without justification for their conduct?

Before the state antitrust laws and the Sherman Act in 1890, the primary focus of the American antimonopoly tradition was on

---

[161] See, e.g., Lina M. Khan, The Ideological Roots of America's Market Power Problem, 127 Yale L.J.F. 960 (2018); Zephyr Teachout, Break 'Em Up (2020); Tim Wu, The Curse of Bigness: Antitrust in the New Gilded Age 106 (2018).

government monopoly grants and "monopolizing" practices like engrossing and forestalling. The analysis of the conduct (for example, was the grant justified? did forestalling occur?) and the remedy (for example, voiding of the government grant or punishment for forestalling) were clearer and simpler to apply than modern cases challenging the often competitively ambiguous practices of successful firms. The latter require 1) complex legal and economic analysis of business practices (what is "competition on the merits?" what is "exclusionary" behavior?) and 2) fashioning of an appropriate remedy (dissolution of the monopolist, divestiture of business operations or injunction against certain business practices?).

The legal rules on what constitutes unlawful monopolization — and an appropriate remedy — remain elusive under modern antitrust law, despite the greater analytical precision brought by modern economics. Of course, there is a simple solution: condemn all monopolies per se (without a finding of anticompetitive or exclusionary conduct). This would certainly simplify the legal and economic analysis and expand application of the antitrust laws against (perceived) monopolies. But the cost to society, and in particular innovation, would likely be enormous.

Calls for monopoly per se, of course, have been voiced from the early days of the Sherman Act. In 1889, the Populist William Jennings Bryan declaimed:

> "I do not divide monopolies in private hands into good monopolies and bad monopolies. There is no good monopoly in private hands. There can be no good monopoly in private hands until the Almighty sends us angels to preside over the monopoly. There may be a despot who is better than another despot, but there is no good despotism."[162]

Much later, in 1979 the National Commission for the Review of Antitrust Laws and Procedures recommended a congressional inquiry into amending the Sherman Act to provide for no-fault monopolization or monopoly per se.[163] Today, critics of large firms

---

[162] Chicago Conference on Trusts 497 (quoted in Thorelli, supra note 22, at 336).

[163] National Commission for the Review of Antitrust Laws and Procedures, Report to the President and the Attorney General 162 (Jan. 22, 1979): "(1) dissipation of persistent monopoly power is the chief goal of the Sherman Section 2 monopolization offense, (2) that where persistent monopoly power is

in digital platform markets and other high-tech sectors have called for reexamination of per se monopolization.[164]

History, however, stands against demands for per se monopoly—for very good reasons. Even in England at the time of the initial condemnation of royal grants of monopoly in the early 17th century, English courts did not condemn all monopoly grants, but only those resulting from abuse of procedures or that served no public purpose (or more accurately, under a varied and shifting reasonableness standard).[165]

In America since colonial times, legislators and courts also have consistently rejected condemnation of all monopolies, despite a very strong antimonopoly tradition. To cite one example, in 1856 the Pennsylvania Supreme Court—in an opinion that could have been written yesterday—distinguished between lawful and unlawful monopoly:

> "If [defendant] intended merely to carry on the manufacture of chrome so largely and sell it so cheaply that no one would think it worthwhile to compete with him, then he is a meritorious citizen. He has a right to all he can win by his science, labor, and capital honestly employed. Either way, the evidence offered could serve no purpose except to waken prejudices which had better be allowed to sleep."[166]

It is fair to generalize that over the past four centuries, calls for condemnation of all monopolies have been rejected. For example, even during the robust antitrust movement that led to the antitrust laws, one labor leader cautioned that monopoly is bad only if "procured through the arbitrary exclusion of competitors;" if monopoly is derived from superior efficiency, then it is "a positive advantage to the community."[167] Learned Hand echoed this reasoning almost a century later in *Alcoa* (1945) when he rejected a per se monopoly rule because it would disincentivize and punish

shown, deliberate conduct designed to create or maintain that power can be presumed, and (3) that existing litigation practice under Sherman Section 2 has not dealt effectively with the problem of persistent monopoly power …."

[164] For example, see Robert Lande, The No-Fault Approach to Monopolization: Terrific, Terrible, or Textualism? Antitrust Magazine (Aug. 2021).

[165] See Chapter Two.

[166] Harris v. Tyson, 34 Pa. 347 (1855).

[167] George Gunton, supra note 87.

successful competitors: "[t]he successful competitor, having been urged to compete, must not be turned upon when he wins."[168]

And Justice Scalia proclaimed in *Trinko:*

> "The opportunity to charge monopoly prices—at least for a short period—is what attracts 'business acumen' in the first place; it induces risk taking that produces innovation and economic growth. To safeguard the incentive to innovate, the possession of monopoly power will not be found unlawful unless it is accompanied by an element of anticompetitive conduct."[169]

A similar sentiment can be found in the Sherman Act discussions. Senator John Kenna asked whether a citizen who obtained control of a market "by virtue of his superior skill" would violate the proposed legislation, Senator George Edmunds replied that, absent exclusionary conduct, the answer was no.[170] Most colonists and antebellum Americans would probably have agreed with Senator Edmunds.

Today's antitrust battles are being fought with the technical weapons of modern economics and more precise legal standards and doctrines. But it is naïve to believe that the application of economic concepts and legal rules to the conflicting and complex facts offered

---

[168] United States v. Aluminum Co. of Am., 148 F.2d 416, 430 (2d Cir. 1945). Nonetheless, Alcoa was found to have unlawfully monopolized by anticipating growing demand and preparing itself to meet that demand.

More recently, courts have rejected monopoly per se on the basis of the consumer welfare standard: "[s]uccess alone is not enough to sustain an antitrust claim or the antitrust laws would have their greatest impact on the most efficient entrepreneurs and would injure rather than protect consumers." U.S. Football League v. Nat'l Football League, 842 F.2d 1335, 1359 (2d Cir. 1988); see also Trans Sport, Inc. v. Starter Sportswear, Inc., 964 F.2d 186 (2d Cir. 1992).

[169] Verizon Communications Inc., v. Law Offices of Curtis V. Trinko, 540 U.S. 398, 407 (2004).

[170] 21 Cong. Rec. 3151-52 (Apr. 8, 1890):

> "[A] man who merely by superior skill and intelligence, a breeder of horses or raiser of cattle, or manufacturer or artisan of any kind, got the whole business because nobody could do it as well as he could was not a monopolist, but that it involved something like the use of means which made it impossible for other persons to engage in fair competition like the engrossing, the buying up of all other persons engaged in the same business."

by the adversaries in litigation operates in an algorithmic fashion that produces a clearly evident result. It is often the case that reasonable people disagree about the outcome, including the courts that decided the case. This suggests that deeper convictions or views about monopoly may very well influence case outcomes. In brief, the historical yin and yang of monopolies are 1) concern about exclusion of competitors and competitive rivalry, and 2) praise for success and the entrepreneurial spirit. On the one hand, Americans for centuries have condemned both public and private monopoly, primarily because it reduces opportunity to compete—or in modern antitrust terms, its exclusionary or foreclosure effects on actual and potential competitors. On the other hand, Americans historically have prized a vigorous entrepreneurial spirit that embraces competition as a race that inherently produces winners and losers—Americans generally applaud winners.

These fundamental (yin and yang) views of monopoly can influence case outcomes—sometimes dispositively. Parties in litigation commonly proffer different facts and propose differing economic theories. Whether the judge leans to the yin (opportunity to compete) or the yang (entrepreneurial spirit and success) can affect which facts to find and which economic theories to select. These underlying views often are not expressly articulated in court opinions. Rather, they remain hidden or obscured by the discussion of the technical legal and economic arguments of modern antitrust law. But the yin and yang exist and indeed may well be the decisive element that determines the outcomes of today's monopolization challenges to successful firms.

BIBLIOGRAPHY

John Adams, Works

Walter Adams & Horace Gray, Monopoly in America: The Government as Promoter (1955)

Edward A. Adler, Monopolizing at Common Law and Under Section Two of the Sherman Antitrust Act, 31 Harv. L. Rev. 246 (1917)

"A Farmer," Connecticut Courant, Feb. 16, 1778

Rebecca H. Allensworth, Foxes at the Henhouse: Occupational Licensing Boards Up Close, 105 Cal. L. Rev. 1557 (2017)

Akhil Reed Amar, Substance and Method in the Year 2000, 28 Pepp. L. Rev. 601 (2001)

Antitrust Act, 31 Harv. L. Rev. 246 (1917)

C. M. Andrews, Conservative Factors in Early Colonial History, Authority and the Individual (1937)

Charles M. Andrews, The Colonial Period of American History: England's Commercial and Colonial Policy 15 (1938)

1 Annals of Cong. (Joseph Gales Ed., 1789)

Aquinas, Summa Theologica

Aristotle, Politics and Ethics

Bernard Bailyn, The New England Merchants in the Seventeenth Century (1979)

Belcherstown, Billerica Remonstrances (1803)

Anne Bezanson, Prices and Inflation During the American Revolution: Pennsylvania, 1777–1790 (1951)

3 W. Blackstone, Commentaries on the Laws of England (1765–1769)

Robert Bork, The Antitrust Paradox (1978)

Carl Bridenbaugh, Cities in the Wilderness - The First Century of Urban Life in America 1625–1742 (2013)

Brodhead, History of the State of New York (1853)

Alexander Brown, The Genesis of the United States (1890)

James Bryce, The American Commonwealth (1889)

Stuart Bruchey, The Roots of American Economic Growth, 1607-1861: An Essay in Social Causation (1965)

Phillip Alexander Bruce, Economic History of Virginia in the Seventeenth Century (1896)

Bruce W. Bugbee, Genesis of American Patent and Copyright Law (1967)

Martin Van Buren, The Autobiography of Martin Van Buren (1920)

Fitzwilliam Byrdsall, The History of the Loco-Foco or Equal Rights Party (1842)

Kenneth S. Cahn, The Roman and Frankish Roots of the Just Price of Medieval Canon Law, in Studies in Medieval and Renaissance Hist. (Paul J. Du Plessis, Clifford Ando & Kaius Tuori eds. 1969)

Steven G. Calabresi et al., Individual Rights Under State Constitutions in 2018: What Rights Are Deeply Rooted in a Modern-Day Consensus of the States?, 94 Notre Dame L. Rev. 49 (2018)

Steven G. Calabresi & Larissa C. Leibowitz, Monopolies and the Constitution: A History of Crony Capitalism, 36 Harv. J. of Law & Pub. Pol'y 983 (2013)

Calendar State Papers Colonial, America and West Indies

Benjamin L. Carp, Defiance of the Patriots: The Boston Tea Party and the Making of America (2010)

Alfred D. Chandler Jr., The Visible Hand: The Managerial Revolution in American Business (1977)

Victor S. Clark, History of Manufactures in the United States (1929)

Luca Clerici, Market, Civic Virtues, and Civic Bargaining in the Medieval and Early Modern Age: Some Evidence from Sixteenth Century Italy, 59 Intl. Rev. Econ. 459 (2012)

Wayne D. Collins, Trusts and the Origins of Antitrust Legislation, 81 Fordham L.Rev. 2279 (2013)

Michael Conant, Antimonopoly Tradition under the Ninth and Fourteenth Amendments: Slaughter-House Cases Re-Examined, 31 Emory L. J. 785 (1982)

Congressional Budget Office, Should the Federal Government Sell Electricity? (1997)

Tench Coxe, View of the United States (1793)

Daniel A. Crane, Lochnerian Antitrust, 1 NYU J.L & Liberty 496 (2005)

Michel Guillaume Jean de Crevecoeur, Lettres d'un Cultivateur Americain

James A. Dalton and Louis Esposito, Predatory Price Cutting and Standard Oil: A Re-Examination of the Trial Record, 22 Res. L. & Econ. 155 (2007)

Nathan Dane, A General Abridgement and Digest of American Law, with Occasional Notes and Comments (1823)

Joseph Davis, Essays in the Earlier History of American Corporations (1917)

Davis Rich Dewey, Financial History of the United States (1922)

Oliver Morton Dickerson, American Colonial Government 1696–1765 (1912)

Joseph Dorfman, 1 The Economic Mind in American Civilization: 1606–1865 (1966)

Irah Donner, The Copyright Clause of the U.S. Constitution: Why Did the Framers Include It With Unanimous Approval?, 36 Am. J. Legal Hist. 361 (1992)

Joseph J. Ellis, The Cause: The American Revolution and Its Discontents 1773–1783 (2021)

Yassine Essid, A Critique of the Origins of Islamic Economic Thought (1995)

James W. Ely, Jr., Patterns of Statutory Enactment in South Carolina, 1720–1770, (1980)

Daniel A. Farber & Suzanna Sherry, A History of The American Constitution 141 (1990)

Harold Faulkner, American Economic History (1924)

Harry First & Spencer Weber Waller, Antitrust's Democracy Deficit, 81 Fordham L. Rev. 2543 (2013)

Harold G. Fox, Monopolies and Patents: A Study of the History and Future of the Patent Monopoly (1947)

E. James Ferguson, The Power of the Purse (1961)

Daniel Francis, Making Sense of Monopolization: Antitrust and the Digital Economy 84 Antitrust Law J. 22 (2022)

Lawrence Friedman, A History of American Law (1973)

Dan Friedman, The Maryland State Constitution: A Reference Guide (G. Alan Tarr ed. 2006)

Gallatin Papers, New York Historical Society

Jada F. Garofalo, An Electricity Regulation Primer—The History of Electricity Regulation in the United States (2021)

Paul A. Gilje, Rioting in America (1999)

Douglas H. Ginsburg & Joshua D. Wright, Philadelphia National Bank: Bad Economics, Bad Law, Good Riddance, 80 Antitrust L.J. 377 (2015)

Nicola Giocoli, Predatory Pricing in Antitrust Law and Economics: A Historical Perspective (2014)

Julius Goebel, Jr., King's Law and Local Custom in Seventeenth-Century New England, 31 Columbia L. Rev. 416 (1931)

David A.J. Goldfine & Kenneth M. Vorrasi, The Fall of the *Kodak* Aftermath Doctrine: Dying a Slow Death in the Lower Courts, 72 Antitrust L.J. 209 (2004)

Carter Goodrich, ed. The Government and the Economy, 1783–1861 (1967)

Thomas P. Govan, Nicholas Biddle: Nationalist and Public Banker, 1786–1844 (1959)

George Gunton, The Economic and Social Aspects of Trusts, 3 Pol. Sci. Q. 385 (1888).

Muslim Ibn al-Hajjaj, Sahih Muslim (Abdul Hamid Siddiqui 2011)

Alexander Hamilton, Report on the Subject of Manufactures (1791)

Milton Handler, The Current Attack on the *Parker v. Brown* State Action Doctrine, 76 Colum. L. Rev. 1 (1976)

Oscar and Mary Handlin, Commonwealth - A Study of the Role of Government in the American Economy: Massachusetts, 1774-1871 (1947)

Ron Harris, The Formation of the East India Company as a Cooperation-Enhancing Institution, SSRN eLibrary Draft (Dec. 2005)

George Haskins, Codification of the Law in Colonial Massachusetts: A Study in Comparative Law, 30 Ind. L. J. 1 (1954)

Albert Hart, Commonwealth History of Massachusetts (1927)

Louis Hartz, Economic Policy and Democratic Thought: Pennsylvania, 1776–1860 (1948)

Zulkifli Hasan, Islamic Perspective on Competition Law and Policy, International Conference on Law and Commerce, International Islamic University Malaysia and Victoria University (2005)

Barry Hawk, Antitrust and Competition Laws (2020)

Barry Hawk, Law and Commerce in Pre-Industrial Societies (2016)

Eli Heckscher, Mercantilism (1935)

Christopher Hill, The Century of Revolution (1982)

Historical Manuscripts Commission, Report

Richard Hofstadter, The Age of Reform: From Bryan to F.D.R. (1955)

Richard Hofstadter, What Happened to the Antitrust Movement? Notes on the Evolution of an American Creed, in The Business Establishment (Earl F. Cheit ed. 1964)

Richard Hofstadter, The Paranoid Style in American Politics, and Other Essays (1964)

William Searle Holdsworth, History of English Law (1924)

Morton Horwitz, The Transformation of American Law, 1780–1860 (1979)

Herbert Hovenkamp, Technology, Politics, and Regulated Monopoly: An American Historical Perspective, 62 Tex. L. Rev. 1263 (1984)

Herbert Hovenkamp, Enterprise and American Law 1836–1937 (1991)

A.E. Dick Howard, The Road from Runnymede: Magna Carta and Constitutionalism in America (1968)

Alexandra K. Howell, Enforcing a Wall of Separation Between Big Business and State: Protection from Monopolies in State Constitutions, 96 Notre Dame L. Rev. 859 (2020)

J.R.T. Hughes, Social Control in the Colonial Economy (1976)

James Hurst, The Legitimacy of the Business Corporation in the Law of the United States: 1780–1970 (1970)

Jonathan I. Israel, Dutch Primacy in World Trade, 1585–1740 (1989)

Thomas Jefferson, Writings (Washington ed.)

The Papers of Thomas Jefferson (Julian P. Boyd ed.)

E.A. J. Johnson, The Foundations of American Economic Freedom: Government and Enterprise in the Age of Washington (1973)

Herbert A. Johnson, ed., South Carolina Legal History (1980)

Charles Jones, The History of Georgia (1883)

S.R.H. Jones and Simon P. Ville, Efficient Transactors or Rent-Seeking Monopolists? The Rationale for Early Chartered Trading Companies, 56 The J. Econ. Hist. 898 (1996)

Franklin D. Jones, Historical Development of the Law of Business Competition, 36 Yale L. J. 43 (1927)

Paul Kahan, The Bank War (2015)

Daniel Kahneman, Jack L. Knetsch & Richard Thaler, Fairness as a Constraint on Profit Seeking: Entitlements in the Market, 76 Am. Econ. Rev. 728 (1986)

Daniel Kahneman, Thinking, Fast and Slow (2011)

Steven L. Kaplan, Bread, Politics and Political Economy in the Reign of Louis XV (1976)

Carl Kaysen & Donald F. Turner, Antitrust Policy: An Economic and Legal Analysis (1959)

James Keyte, Frederic Jenny & Eleanor Fox, Buckle up: The Global Future of Antitrust Enforcement and Regulation, 35 Antitrust 32 (2021)

Lina M. Khan, The Ideological Roots of America's Market Power Problem, 127 Yale L.J.F. 960 (2018)

Alexandra B. Klass & Jim Rossi, Revitalizing Dormant Commerce Clause Review for Interstate Coordination, 100 Minn. L. Rev. 129 (2015)

Amy Klobuchar, Anti-Trust: Taking on Monopoly Power from the Gilded Age to the Digital Age (2022)

Thomas G. Krattenmaker & Steven C. Salop, Anticompetitive Exclusion: Raising Rivals' Costs to Achieve Power over Price, 96 Yale L.J. 209 (1986)

Allan Kulikoff, From British Peasants to Colonial American Farmers (2000)

Phillip B. Kurland & Ralph Lerner (eds.), 1 The Founders' Constitution: Major Themes (1987)

Stanley I. Kutler, Privilege and Creative Destruction: The Charles River Bridge Case (1978)

Ronald M. Labbé & Jonathan Lurie, The Slaughterhouse Cases (2003)

Robert Lande, The No-Fault Approach to Monopolization: Terrific, Terrible, or Textualism?, Antitrust Magazine (Aug. 2021)

Marina Lao, Ideology Matters in the Antitrust Debate, 79 Antitrust L.J. 649 (2014)

Lawrence Lessig, Copyright's First Amendment, 48 UCLA L. Rev. 1057 (2001)

William L. Letwin, Congress and The Sherman Antitrust Law, 23 Chicago L. Rev. 221 (1956)

Carol Lloyd, Henry Demarest Llyod, 1847-1903, A Biography (1912)

Donald S. Lutz, The States and the U.S. Bill of Rights, 16 S. ILL. U. L.J. 251 (1992)

Christine Macleod, Inventing the Industrial Revolution: The English Patent System, 1660–1800 (1988)

James Madison, Property (1792)

George Mason, Objections to the Constitution of Government Formed by the Convention (1787)

James May, Antitrust Practice and Procedure in the Formative Era: The Constitutional and Conceptual Reach of State Antitrust Law, 1880-1918, 135 U.Pa. L. Rev. 495 (1987)

Cathy Matson, The Revolution, The Constitution, and the Early National Economy in 1 The Cambridge Economic History of the United States (Stanley Engerman & Robert Gallman eds. 1996)

Robert G. McCloskey, The American Supreme Court (1960)

John S. McGee, Predatory Price Cutting: The Standard Oil (N.J.) Case, 1 J. L. & Econ. 137 (1958)

John J. McCusker & Russell R. Menard, The Economy of British America, 1607–1789 (1985)

W.S. McKechnie, Magna Carta (2d ed. 1914)

Douglas Melamed, Antitrust Law and Its Critics, 83 Antitrust L. J. 269 (2020)

Alan J. Meese, Federalism, Free Competition and Sherman Act Preemption of State Restraints, 16 Va. L. & Bus. Rev. 115 (2021)

Newton Mereness, Maryland as a Proprietary Province (1901)

Simon Middleton, How It Came that the Bakers Bake No Bread: A Struggle for Trade Privileges in Seventeenth-Century New Amsterdam, 58 William & Mary Q. 347 (2001)

John Stuart Mill, The Principles of Political Economy (1848)

Joel Munsell, The Annals of Albany (1850)

Thomas B. Nachbar, Intellectual Property and Constitutional Norms, 104 Columbia L. Rev. 272 (2004)

National Commission for the Review of Antitrust Laws and Procedures, Report to the President and the Attorney General (1979)

New York State Bar Association, Report of the Special Committee to Study the New York Antitrust Laws (1957)

Douglass C. North, The Economic Growth of the United States 1790–1860 (1961)

Mary Beth Norton, 1774: The Long Year of Revolution (2020)

Tyler T. Ochoa & Mark Rose, The Anti-Monopoly Origins of the Patent and Copyright Clause, 84 J. Pat & Trademark Off. Soc'y 909 (2002)

Sheilagh Ogilvie, Institutions and European Trade: Merchant Guilds, 1000–1800 (2011)

Sheilagh Ogilvie, The European Guilds: An Economic Analysis (2019)

Dotan Oliar, Making Sense of the Intellectual Property Clause: Promotion of Progress as a Limitation on Congress's Intellectual Property Power, 94 Georgetown L. J. 1771 (2006)

Herbert Osgood, The American Colonies in the Seventeenth Century (1904)

William H. Page, Antitrust, Federalism, and the Regulatory Process: A Reconstruction and Critique of the State Action Exemption, 61 B.U.L. Rev. 1099 (1981)

Thomas Paine, The Rights of Man (1791)

William Penn, The Excellent Priviledge of Liberty and Property Being the Birthright of the Free-born Subjects of England (1687)

Pennsylvania Senate Journal, 1833–1834 (1834)

Edward J. Perkins, Lost Opportunities for Compromise in the Bank War: A Reassessment of Jackson's Veto Message, 61 Bus. Hist. Rev. 531 (1987)

Selig Perlman, The Concept of Class in the Development of the American Labor Program, Meeting of the American Historical Association, New York City, Dec. 27, 1940

James P. Philbin, The Political Economy of the Antifederalists, 11 J. Libertarian Stud. 79 (1994)

Almarin Phillips, Market Concentration and Performance: A Survey of the Evidence, 61 Notre Dame L. Rev. 1099 (1986)

Gifford Pinchot, The Power Monopoly: Its Make-Up and Its Menace (1928)

Steven Piott, The Anti-Monopoly Persuasion: Popular Resistance to the Rise of Big Business in the Midwest (1985)

Lawrence Potamkin, Public Power and the Federal Government, 30 Neb. L. Rev. 375 (1951)

Ratification of the New Constitution by the Convention of the State of New York, 4 American Museum 153 (1789)

Sidney Ratner, James H. Soltow & Richard Sylla, The Evolution of the American Economy: Growth, Welfare and Decision Making (1979)

Paul Samuel Reinsch, The English Common Law in the Early American Colonies, in 1 Robert Remini, Andrew Jackson and the Bank War (1967)

Mariana Griswold Van Rensselaer, History of the City of New York in the Seventeenth Century (1909)

Raymond de Roover, The Concept of Just Price: Theory and Economic Policy, 18 J. Econ. Hist. 418 (1958)

Elmer Beecher Russell, The Review of American Colonial Legislation by the King in Council (1915)

Steven C. Salop, What Consensus: Why Ideology and Elections Still Matter to Antitrust, 79 Antitrust L.J. 601 (2014)

Arthur M. Schlesinger Jr., The Age of Jackson (1946)

Paul M. Schwartz & William Michael Treanor, Eldred and Lochner: Copyright Term Extension and Intellectual Property as Constitutional Property, 112 Yale L. J. 2378 (2003)

S.C. Commons Journal (1703)

Select Essays in Anglo-American Legal History (1907)

William W. Sharkey, The Theory of Natural Monopoly (1982)

Morris Silver, Economic Structures in Antiquity (1985)

Martin J. Sklar, The Corporate Reconstruction of American Capitalism, 1890–1916: The Market, the Law, and Politics (1988)

Barbara Clark Smith, Food Rioters and the American Revolution, 51 William and Mary Q. 3d 1 (1994)

Adam Smith, The Wealth of Nations (1776)

Stokes, Iconography

Harold C. Syrett, Private Enterprise in New Amsterdam, 11 William and Mary Q. 536 (1954)

George R. Taylor, The Transportation Revolution, 1815–60 (2015)

Zephyr Teachout, Break 'Em Up (2020)

The Complete Anti-Federalist (Herbert J. Storing ed. 1981)

Hans B. Thorelli, The Federal Antitrust Policy (1954)

Joseph P. Tomain, The Persistence of Natural Monopoly, 16 Nat. Res. & Env't 242 (2002)

Kenneth E. Train, Optimal Regulation: The Economic Theory of Natural Monopoly (1991)

William Trimble, The Social Philosophy of the Loco-Foco Democracy, 26 Am. J. Sociology 705 (1921)

Frederick Jackson Turner, The Frontier in American History (1893)

Akinori Uesugi, Transfer of Technology and Joint Ventures in Japan, in 1982 Fordham Corp. L. Inst. 347 (Barry Hawk ed. 1983)

Adriaan Verhulst, The Carolingian Economy (2002)

Daniel Vickers, The Northern Colonies: Economy and Society, in 1 The Cambridge Economic History of the United States (Stanley Engerman & Robert Gallman eds. 1996)

Virginia Company Records, I

Virginia Council, Circular Letter (1610)

Virginia Magazine

Donald O. Wagner, Coke and the Rise of Economic Liberalism, 6 Econ. Hist. Rev. 30 (1935)

Edward C. Walterscheid, To Promote the Progress of Science and Useful Arts: the Background and Origin of the Intellectual Property Clause of the United States Constitution, 2 J. of Intell. Prop 1 (1994)

Edward C. Walterscheid, The Use and Abuse of History: The Supreme Court's Interpretation of Thomas Jefferson's Influence on the Patent Law, 39 IDEA 195 (1999)

Gary M. Walton and James F. Sheperd, The Economic Rise of Early America (1979)

George Washington, Works (1787)

Michael Waterson, Recent Developments in the Theory of Natural Monopoly, 1 J. of Econ. Survs. 59 (1987)

Pelatiah Webster, Political Essays (1791)

Leonard W. Weiss, The Concentration-Profits Relationship and Antitrust, in Industrial Concentration: The New Learning 184, 184–272 (H. J. Goldschmid, H. M. Mann, & J. F. Weston eds. 1974)

William B. Weeden, Economic and Social History of New England 1620–1789 (1891)

Chester Whitney Wright, Economic History of the United States 311 (2d ed. 1949)

Stephen Williams, Diary (1776)

Thorp L. Wolford, The Laws and Liberties of 1648, 28 B.U. Law Rev. 426 (1948)

Gordon Wood, The Radicalism of the American Revolution (1991)

Tim Wu, The Curse of Bigness: Antitrust in the New Gilded Age 106 (2018)

TABLE OF AUTHORITIES

(References are to pages)

Cases

Barry v. Merch. Exch. Co., 1 Sand. Ch. 280, 7 N.Y. Ch. Ann. 329 (1844), 128
Bartlett v. Crozier, 17 Johns. 439 (1820), 136
Blanchard v. Ivers, 24 So. 66 (Fla. 1898), 161
Brooke Grp. v. Brown & Williamson Tobacco Corp., 509 U.S. 209 (1993), 179, 181–183
Brown v. Cheney, 350 S.W.2d 184 (Ark. 1961), 156
Brown v. Jacobs Pharmacy Co., 41 S.E. 553 (Ga. 1936), 161
Brown Shoe Co. v. United States, 370 U.S. 294 (1962), 181
Butchers' Union Slaughter-House & Live-Stock Landing Co. v. Crescent City Live-Stock Landing & Slaughter-House Co., 111 U.S. 746 (1884), 147

California Retail Liquor Dealers Ass'n v. Midcal Aluminum, Inc., 445 U.S. 97 (1980), 154
Cancilla v. Gehlar, 27 P.2d 179 (Or. 1933), 161
Cap F. Bourland Ice Co. v. Franklin Utils. Co., 22 S.W.2d 993 (Ark. 1929), 158
Chambers v. City of Roanoke, 78 S.E. 407 (Va. 1913), 161
Cent. Mkt. Co. v. City of Erie, 44 Pa. Super. 191 (1910), 162
Chicago Bd. of Trade v. United States, 246 U.S. 231 (1918), 184
City of Columbia v. Omni Outdoor Advert., Inc., 499 U.S. 365 (1991), 154
City of Havre De Grace v. Johnson, 123 A. 65 (Md. 1923), 157
City of Jackson v. Bowman, 10 George 671, 1861 WL 1993 (1861), 133
City of Louisville v. Roupe, 45 Ky. 591, 1846 WL 3192 (1846), 126
City of New Orleans v. Dukes, 427 U.S. 297 (1976), 153
City of York v. Hatterer, 48 Pa. Super. 216 (1911), 161
Commonwealth v. The Canal Comm'rs., 1843 WL 5057 (1843), 133
Cmty. Commc'n Co., Inc. v. City of Boulder, 455 U.S. 40 (1982), 154

Darcantel v. People's Slaughterhouse & Refrigerating Co., 44 La. Ann. 632 (1892), 148
Darcy v. Allen, 77 Eng. Rep. 1260 (Q.B. 1602), 22

Davis v. A. Booth & Co., 131 F. 31 (6th Cir. 1904), 160
Dutton v. City of Knoxville, 113 S.W. 381 (Tenn. 1908), 161

Eastman Kodak Co. v. Image Tech. Servs., Inc., 504 U.S. 451 (1992), 181
Easton v. Messinger, 13 Just. 289 (Pa. Ct. Com. Pl. 1915), 161
Eldred v. Ashcroft, 537 U.S. 186 (2003), 110–11
Ex parte Levy, 43 Ark. 42 (1884), 132

Fishburn v. City of Chicago, 49 N.E. 532 (Ill. 1898), 158

Gales v. Anderson, 13 Ill. 413, 1851 WL 4368 (1851), 133
Georgia Pac. Co. v. Cook Timber Co., Inc., 194 So. 2d 118 (Miss. 2016), 160
Gibbons v. Ogden, 22 U.S. 1 (1824), 138, 152–153
Graham v. John Deere Co., 383 U.S. 1 (1966), 105
Great Atl. & Pac. Tea Co. v. Supermarket Equip. Corp., 40 U.S. 147 (1950), 105
Guthrie Daily Leader v. Cameron, 41 P. 635 (Okla. 1895), 157

Hager's Town Turnpike Road Co. v Creeger, 5 H. & J. 122, 1820 WL 929, 9 Am. Dec. 495 (1820), 128
Harris v. Tyson, 24 Pa. 347, 1855 WL 7110, 64 Am. Dec. 661 (1855), 128, 188
Hayes et al. v. Harding, Hardres 53 (1656), 24
Henry Vandine, Petitioner 6 Pickering 187 (1828), 136

In re Arcadia Dairy Farms, 259 S.E.2d 368 (N.C. 1979), 158

Klingel's Pharmacy v. Sharp & Dohme, 64 A. 1029 (Md. 1906), 160

Lambell v. The Corp. of Washington, 1 Hay &. Haz. 25 (1841), 136
Landman v. Kizer, 255 S.W.2d 6 (Tenn. 1953), 156
Lens Exp., Inc. v. Ewald, 907 S.W.2d 64 (Tex. 1992), 158
Mays v. Cincinnati, 1 Ohio St 268, 1853 WL 27 (1853), 126

McCullough v. Maryland, 17 U.S. 316 (1819), 119
McRee v. Wilmington R. R., 47 N. C. 186 (1855), 131
Meadville v. Miller, 14 Pa. D. 27 (Ct. Com. Pl. 1904), 161
Mohawk Bridge Co. v. Utica & Schenectady R.R. Co., 6 Paige Ch. 554 (N.Y. Ch. 1837), 141
Munn v. Illinois, 94 U.S. 113 (1876), 149

N. Sec. Co. v. United States, 193 U.S. 197 (1904), 171
N.Y. Trust Co. v. Eisner, 256 U.S. 345 (1921), 102
The Norwich Gas Light Co. v. The Norwich City Gas Co., 25 Conn 19 (1856), 132

Orleans Navigation Co. v. Schooner Amelia, 7 Mart. (o.s.) 632 (1820), 141

Pac. Bell Tel. Co. v LinkLine Commc'ns, Inc., 555 U.S. 438 (2009), 183
Pacific St. Box & Basket Co. v. White, 296 U.S. 176 (1935), 153
Parker v. Brown, 317 U.S. 341 (1943), 154
People v. Weller, 143 N.E. 205 (N.Y. 1924), 161–162
Pike v. Bruce Church, Inc., 397 U.S. 137 (1970), 153
The Proprietors of the Charles River Bridge v. The Proprietors of the Warren Bridge, 36 U.S. 420 (1837), 139–142

Raney v. Montgomery Cnty Com'rs, 183 A. 548 (Md. 1936), 157
Richmond R.R. Co. v. Louisa R.R. Co., 54 U.S. 71 (1851), 141
Roach v. Ephren, 90 So. 609 (Fla. 1921), 162

Sandford v. The Catawissa, W. & E.R. Co., 24 Pa. 378 (1855), 133
Scott v. State., 185 S.E. 131 (Ga. Ct. App. 1936), 161
Slaughter-House Cases, 83 U.S. 36 (1872), 144–148, 152–153
Standard Oil Co. v. United States, 221 U.S 1 (1911), 160, 165, 171, 179
Standard Oil Co. of N.J. v. State, 61 So. 981 (Miss. 1913), 160
State v. Call, 28 S.E. 517 (N.C. 1897), 156
State v. Duluth Bd. of Trade, 121 N.W. 395 (Minn. 1909), 160
State v. Nashville Ry. & Light Co., 268 S.W. 120 (Tenn. 1925), 160
State v. Stovall, 8 S.E. 900 (N.C. 1889), 156
State of Minnesota v. N. Sec. Co., 123 F. 692 (D. Minn. 1903), 160
Stribbling v. Bank of the Valley, 5 Rand. 132, 26 Va. 132, 1827 WL 1194 (1827), 128

Thacher v. Dartmouth Bridge Company, 35 Mass. 501, 18 Pick. 501 (1836), 135
Thomas v. Dakin, 22 Wend. 9 (1839), 125
Thrift v. Bd. of Comm'rs, 30 S.E. 349 (N.C. 1898), 96
Trans Sport, Inc. v. Starter Sportswear, Inc., 964 F.2d 186 (2d Cir. 1992), 189
Tuckahoe Canal Co. v. Tuckahoe & J.R.R. Co., 11 Leigh 42 38 Va. 42 (1840), 141

U.S. Football League v. Nat'l Football League, 842 F.2d 1335 (2d Cir. 1988), 189
United States v. Aluminum Co. of Am., 148 F.2d 416 (2d Cir. 1945), 12, 164, 172, 189
United States v. AT&T Co., [1970–1979 Transfer Binder] Trade Reg. Rep. (CCH) 45,074 (D.D.C. filed Nov. 20, 1974); 1982-2 Trade Cas. (CCH) 64,900 (D.D.C. 1982), 12, 173–174, 179
United States v. Am. Tobacco Co., 221 U.S. 106 (1911), 171, 179
United States v. E.I. duPont de Nemours & Co., 251 U.S. 377 (1956), 172
United States v. Grinnell Corp., 384 U.S. 563 (1966), 172
United States v. IBM Corp., [1961–1970 Transfer Binder] Trade Reg. Rep. (CCH) 45,069 (S.D.N.Y. filed Jan 17, 1969), 173
United States v. Microsoft Corp., 87 F. Supp. 2d 30 (D.D.C. 2000), 12, 175
United States v. Microsoft Corp., 253 F.3d 34 (D.C. Cir. 2001), 12, 175, 182
United States v. Patten, 226 U.S. 525 (1913), 66, 127
United States v. Trans-Missouri Freight Ass'n, 166 U.S. 290 (1897), 184
United States v. United Shoe Mach. Corp., 110 F. Supp. 295 (D. Mass. 1953), 172
United States v. U.S. Steel Corp., 251 U.S. 417 (1920), 11, 171

Verizon Communications Inc., v. Law Offices of Curtis V. Trinko, 540 U.S. 398 (2004), 189
Volvo Trucks v. Reeder-Simco, 546 U.S. 164 (2006), 181

Weyerhaeuser Co. v. Ross-Simmons Hardwood Lumber Co., 549 U.S. 312 (2007), 183

Statutes

Ak. CONST. art. VIII, §3, 155
Ak. CONST. art. VIII, §15, 155
Ak. CONST. art. VIII, §17, 155
Ark. CONST., art. 2, §19, 131

Fla. CONST. art. 1, §24, 132

Ga. CONST. art. 1, § 23, 131

Id. CONST. art. I, §2, 155

Kan. CONST. art. 15, §17, 132

La. CONST. of 1879, art. 248, 147

Md. CONST. art. 41, 95
Md. Laws (Kilty), May 1788, ch. 17, 126
Md. Laws (Kilty), 1793, ch. 59, 126

N.C. CONST. art. 1, §34, 96

Penal Code 1910, §707, 161
Penal Code 1933, §26-7404, 161

The Sherman Antitrust Act of 1890 15 U.S.C. §§1–38, 66, 127
The Statute of Monopolies 1623 21 Jac 1 c 3, 22, 24-25, 52
The Tariff Act of 1789 1 Stat. 24, 113
Tex. CONST. art. 1, §19, 132

U.S. CONST. amend. VI, 133

Va. CONST. art. IV, §14, 155

INDEX

(References are to pages)

AMERICAN REVOLUTIONARY WAR. *See* **REVOLUTION AND FOUNDING OF AMERICA (1763 TO 1800)**

ANTEBELLUM AMERICA (1800 TO 1861)
Generally, 113–116
Banks, 116–125
Corporations, 116–125, 134–135
Engrossing ("cornering the market"), 125–127
Forestalling ("monopolization" practice), 125–127
Government grants of monopoly privileges
  Generally, 129–130
  Local monopoly grants, *this heading*
  State monopoly grants, *this heading*
Local monopoly grants
  Federal constitutional limits on, 137–142
  State constitutional limits on, 130–134
Overview, 8–9
Private firm monopolies, 127–129
State monopoly grants
  Generally, 135–137
  Federal constitutional limits on, 137–142
  State constitutional limits on, 130–134
U.S. Constitution
  Local monopoly grants, limits on, 137–142
  State monopoly grants, limits on, 137–142

ANTITRUST LAWS (FEDERAL)
Cyclical enforcement of
  Generally, 170
  Expansion period (1937 to 1970s), 172–174
  Hibernation period (1920 to 1937), 171–172
  Reasons for cyclical enforcement, *this heading*
  Retrenchment period (1970s to 2020), 174–175
  Trustbusting period (1890 to 1920), 171

Early antitrust movement, 162–170
Enforcement
  Generally, 170
  Cyclical enforcement of, *this heading*
Expansion period (1937 to 1970s), 172–174
Hibernation period (1920 to 1937), 171–172
Overview, 9–15
Private monopoly under
  Generally, 170
  Cyclical enforcement of, *this heading*
  Fundamental conundrum concerning, 186–190
Reasons for cyclical enforcement
  Generally, 175
  Changes in economic theory, 179–183
  Changes in facts (economic conditions), 178–179
  Consumer welfare analysis, predominance of, 184–186
  Legal process concerns, 183–184
  Political support, 176
  Popular demand for action, 176–178
Retrenchment period (1970s to 2020), 174–175
Trustbusting period (1890 to 1920), 171

AUTHOR WORKS. *See* **COPYRIGHTS**

BANKS
Antebellum America, 116–125

BIBLIOGRAPHY
List of sources, 191–203

BOSTON TEA PARTY
Generally, 80–85

CARTELS
Colonial America, 74–78

CLOSED MARKETS
Colonial America, 58–63

COLONIAL AMERICA (1600 TO 1763)
Generally, 17–18
Antimonopoly revolution in England, 21–24
Antimonopoly tradition in the colonies
  Generally, 24–25
  Colonial monopoly grants/privileges, *this heading*
  English trading monopolies and mercantilism, 34–37
  Settlement trading companies, 26–33
Author works (copyrights), 50, 52–53
Cartels, 74–78
Closed markets ("monopolization" practice), 58–63
Colonial monopoly grants/privileges
  Generally, 37–39
  Author works (copyrights), 50, 52–53
  Import-substitution policies, 46–50
  Infrastructure projects, 39–40
  Inventions (patents), 50–52
  Settlement trading companies, 26–33
  Staples and resources, 40–46
English trading monopolies and mercantilism, 34–37
Engrossing ("cornering the market"), 55–58
Exclusive trading privileges. Monopoly grants/privileges, *this heading*
Foodstuffs and resources, 40–46
Forestalling ("monopolization" practice), 63–66
Guilds, 74–78
Import-substitution policies, 46–50
Infrastructure projects, 39–40
Inventions (patents), 50–52
Law(s) in, 18–20
"Monopolization" practices
  Generally, 53–54
  Closed markets, 58–63
  Engrossing ("cornering the market"), 55–58
  Forestalling, 63–66
  Pricing practices, *this heading*
Monopoly grants/privileges
  Antimonopoly revolution in England, 21–24
  Antimonopoly tradition in the colonies, *this heading*

Colonial monopoly grants/privileges, *this heading*
Opposition to, 20–53
Overview, 4–6
Pricing practices
Just prices, 66–70
Price controls (fixing official prices), 70–74
Price fixing (cartels and guilds), 74–78
Settlement trading companies and their monopoly privileges, 26–33
Staples and resources, 40–46
Trading companies/monopolies
English trading monopolies and mercantilism, 34–37
Settlement trading companies, 26–33

COMMERCE AND SUPREMACY CLAUSES
U.S. Constitution, 137–138

CONSTITUTIONS
Federal constitution. *See* **U.S. CONSTITUTION**
Revolution and founding of America
Federal constitution. *See* **U.S. CONSTITUTION**
State constitutions, 95–96
State constitutional constraints on monopolies
Antebellum America, in, 130–134
Modern era, in the, 155–159
Revolution and founding of America, during the, 95–96

COPYRIGHTS
Colonial America, 50, 52–53
U.S. Constitution, 102, 108–112

CORPORATIONS IN ANTEBELLUM AMERICA
Generally, 116–125, 134–135

ENGLISH TRADING PRACTICES
1600 to 1763, 34–37
1763 to 1800, 80–85

ENGROSSING ("CORNERING THE MARKET")
Antebellum America, 125–127
Colonial America, 55–58

Modern era (1870 to today), 159–162
Revolution and founding of America, 85–95

EXPANSION OF ANTITRUST LAWS
1937 to 1970s, 172–174

FEDERAL CONSTITUTION. *See* **U.S. CONSTITUTION**

FORESTALLING
Antebellum America, 125–127
Colonial America, 63–66
Modern era (1870 to today), 159–162
Revolution and founding of America, 85–95

FOUNDING OF AMERICA. *See* **REVOLUTION AND FOUNDING OF AMERICA (1763 TO 1800)**

GOVERNMENT GRANTS OF MONOPOLY PRIVILEGES
Antebellum America. *See* **ANTEBELLUM AMERICA (1800 TO 1861)**
Colonial monopoly grants/privileges. *See* **COLONIAL AMERICA (1600 TO 1763)**
Copyrights. *See* **COPYRIGHTS**
Federal grants, 159. *See also* **COPYRIGHTS; PATENTS**
Modern era. *See* **MODERN ERA (1870 TO TODAY)**
Patents. *See* **PATENTS**
State and local grants
  Antebellum America. *See* **ANTEBELLUM AMERICA (1800 TO 1861)**
  Revolution and founding of America, 95–96

GUILDS
Colonial America, 74–78

HIBERNATION PERIOD OF ANTITRUST LAW ENFORCEMENT
1920 to 1937, 171–172

IMPAIRMENT OF CONTRACTS CLAUSE
U.S. Constitution, 139–142

INVENTIONS. *See* **PATENTS**

LOCAL GRANTS OF MONOPOLY PRIVILEGES
Antebellum America. *See* **ANTEBELLUM AMERICA (1800 TO 1861)**
Revolution and founding of America, 95–96

MODERN ERA (1870 TO TODAY). *See also* **ANTITRUST LAWS (FEDERAL)**
Generally, 143–144
Engrossing ("cornering the market"), 159–162
Federal grants of monopoly privileges, 159. *See also* **COPYRIGHTS; PATENTS**
Forestalling ("monopolization" practice), 159–162
Government grants of monopoly privileges
  Federal constitutional constraints, 152–155
  Federal grants of, 159. *See also* **COPYRIGHTS; PATENTS**
  Public utilities, 149–152
  Slaughter-House Cases, 144–148
  State constitutional constraints, 155–159
Overview, 9–15
Public utilities, 149–152
Slaughter-House Cases, 144–148

NATURAL MONOPOLY
Theory of public utilities and, 149–152

OVERVIEW, 1–4

PATENTS
Colonial America, 50–52
U.S. Constitution, 102–108

PRIVATE MONOPOLY
Antebellum America, private firm monopolies in, 127–129
Antitrust laws (federal), under the. *See* **ANTITRUST LAWS (FEDERAL)**

PUBLIC UTILITIES
Natural monopoly and the theory of, 149–152

RETRENCHMENT PERIOD OF ANTITRUST LAW ENFORCEMENT
1970s to 2020, 174–175

REVOLUTION AND FOUNDING OF AMERICA (1763 TO 1800)
Generally, 79
Boston Tea Party, 80–85
Constitutions
  Federal. U.S. Constitution, *this heading*
  State, 95–96
English trading monopolies and, 80–85
Engrossing ("cornering the market"), 85–95
Forestalling ("monopolization" practice), 85–95
Local monopoly grants, 95–96
Overview, 6–8
Price controls, 85–95
State monopoly grants, 95–96
U.S. Constitution
  Copyrights, 102, 108–112
  No ban on monopoly, 97–102
  Patents, 102–108

SLAUGHTER-HOUSE CASES
Overview, 144–148

STATE CONSTITUTIONAL CONSTRAINTS
Antebellum America, in, 130–134
Modern era, in the, 155–159
Revolution and founding of America, during the, 95–96

STATE GRANTS OF MONOPOLY PRIVILEGES
Antebellum America. *See* **ANTEBELLUM AMERICA (1800 TO 1861)**
Revolution and founding of America, 95–96

SUPREMACY AND COMMERCE CLAUSES
U.S. Constitution, 137–138

TRADING COMPANIES/MONOPOLIES IN COLONIAL AMERICA
English trading monopolies and mercantilism, 34–37
Settlement trading companies, 26–33

TRUSTBUSTING
Antitrust laws, enforcement of (1890 to 1920), 171

U.S. CONSTITUTION
Antebellum America
  Local monopoly grants, limits on, 137–142
  State monopoly grants, limits on, 137–142
Commerce and Supremacy Clauses, 137–138
Constraints on monopolies
  Antebellum America, 137–142
  Modern era (1870 to today), 152–155
Copyrights, 102, 108–112
Impairment of Contracts Clause, 139–142
No ban on monopoly, 97–102
Patents, 102–108